Praise for

A COUNTRY BETWEEN

"If an angel were to write a book, this would be it. Stephanie Saldaña's memoir of her years as a young bride and new mother on Jerusalem's Nablus Road is infused with grace, rich in wisdom. With her French husband, a former novice monk, she makes a home on one of the fault lines where the lives of Israelis and Palestinians, Jews, Muslims, and Christians sometimes mesh, but often collide. *A Country Between* reminds us that grief is as indispensable to joy as light is to shadow. Beautifully written, ardent, and wise."

—Geraldine Brooks, Pulitzer Prize–winning author of
The Secret Chord, *People of the Book*, and *March*

"[A] candid, tenderly rendered love story… Saldaña describes in wonderful detail how, as their family expands, they stay in a place where so little makes sense, guided solely by their hope in the future."

—*Publishers Weekly*

A COUNTRY BETWEEN

Making a Home where Both Sides of Jerusalem Collide

A COUNTRY BETWEEN

Making a Home where Both
Sides of Jerusalem Collide

STEPHANIE SALDAÑA

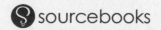

Published by Sourcebooks, Inc.
P.O. Box 4410, Naperville, Illinois 60567-4410
(630) 961-3900
Fax: (630) 961-2168
www.sourcebooks.com

Names: Saldana, Stephanie, author.
Title: A country between : making a home where both sides of Jerusalem
    collide / Stephanie Saldana.
Description: Naperville, Illinois : Sourcebooks, Inc., 2017.
Identifiers: LCCN 2016021329 | (pbk. : alk. paper)
Subjects: LCSH: Saldana, Stephanie. | Americans--Jerusalem--Biography. |
    Jerusalem--Biography. | Jerusalem--Description and travel.

Classification: LCC DS109.86.S235 A3 2017 | DDC 956.94/42054092 [B] --dc23 LC
record available at https://lccn.loc.gov/2016021329

Printed and bound in the United States of America.
UGI 10 9 8 7 6 5 4 3 2 1

In loving memory of my father.
And for Joseph, my first-born son.

"Tanks are perishable. Pears are eternal."

—*Milan Kundera*

Author's Note

This is the actual story of the seven years I spent living in a neighborhood just outside of the walls of the old city of Jerusalem. I have chosen to change many of the names of individuals in order to protect their privacy, but all of the characters are real people.

Jerusalem is complex, and I make no claim of providing a comprehensive view of the entire city, nor even of the entire neighborhood. I have only attempted to write about a single street that took hold of my life and of all of the worlds contained within it.

Part One

In Which an Angel Appears on a Train

"Gabriel garde l'anonyme."

—*Radio Londres*

Dear Joseph,

It's morning. Outside, helicopters are circling over the city. Every now and then, we hear shots of tear gas or stun grenades. Last night, you looked up from the small, square frame of your bed and asked: "Mom, is someone popping balloons?"

I will not be able to hide this from you much longer.

Someday, you will want to know why your father and I brought you into a world of such violence. You will wonder why you have memories—and perhaps even nightmares—of cities that have disappeared and people who you will not meet again. You will want to know about the world that is now gone, but that is part of you.

This book is my attempt to answer those questions.

If I tell you of the time leading up to your birth, it is because I believe that all of us contain what happened before us, that this is our burden and our gift. You are formed of disappeared places and disappeared men. Your heart is composed of the beauty that survived them and was endowed to you when you were born. You are part of what remains: a miracle, with arms and legs.

This, then, is the story of how you were born. I could begin it seven years ago, when I gave birth to you in a hospital in Bethlehem. But I should begin it much earlier, on a morning in India, when an angel appeared to your father on a train.

The Angel

THE MAN WAS SITTING IN A WINDOW SEAT OF THE TRAIN parked in Mumbai Central Station, dressed in his civilian clothes: linen trousers and a tan button-down shirt that seemed designed intentionally to make him disappear into any object behind him. Outside, the remnants of a morning monsoon were saturating the earth, weighing the leaves down on their branches. On his way to the station that morning, he had watched children crawling beneath plastic sheets to shield their bodies from the onslaught, an entire family taking shelter beneath a parked car. But now the rain had stopped, just as he had boarded the train, surprising him the same way it had every day since he had arrived—a flood that came suddenly and seemed to never end, then halted just as suddenly, making way for a space of light to filter through the clouds.

Resting on his lap was a notebook he had brought with him on his journey from Syria. And on the first page, the words he had written that morning:

POUR UN MOINE, QUITTER À JAMAIS SON MONASTÈRE NE PEUT ÊTRE QU'UN ACTE DE FOI, OU UNE DE FUITE.

FOR A MONK, TO LEAVE HIS MONASTERY FOREVER
CAN ONLY BE AN ACT OF FAITH, OR OF RUNNING AWAY.

His name was Frédéric, and he was thirty-two years old, a fact that had not escaped him two weeks before, when he had awakened in his spare, monastic room in the desert and packed his single bag to leave it.

He did not know if he was leaving for two months or for the rest of his life, so he was uncertain of what to bring with him. There was a kind of discipline to what he piled into his bag that morning: two wooden icons, one of Jesus and one of Mary; his journal; his prayer beads; and an envelope full of love letters written in my hand. Linen shirts and trousers, then his monastic robe, which he folded and placed at the very bottom of the pile. And that was all. Into the emptiness of that room—converted from a goat's pen and overlooking the valley below—he had abandoned all the rest: several flutes, Arabic dictionaries, boxes of tea, candles, card-sized pictures of the saints, a French bible, a Quran in Arabic, and the spaces of air that contained the sleep and prayers of the previous three years of his life.

Then he descended the flight of 350 stairs that connected the monastery to the valley, to meet a car that was waiting to take him to Damascus, where he would catch his flight to India. The following morning, in the cheap hotel in Mumbai, he would pass the hours carefully recording in his notebook the names and dates of the monasteries that would receive him in the coming weeks, places where he had introduced himself, in the letters he had sent in advance, as a novice monk traveling on pilgrimage, though he did not feel like much of a novice monk any longer, and this was some strange pilgrimage.

It had been six months since he had stood across from me, in a Syrian desert valley north of Damascus, and said, "I do not love you in that way," as a man only does when he loves you, in that way.

At the time I had been a graduate student in Damascus, twenty-eight years old, taking up no more space in the world than a small rented room in a house in the Christian Quarter, where I passed my afternoons studying Arabic verbs and the Quran. But on the weekends, I often traveled to Frédéric's monastery in the middle of the desert, climbing the 350 stairs up the side of the mountain to pray. The monastery, suspended on a cliff over the desert, with a chapel adorned with medieval frescoes of the saints, was the most mysterious place I had ever seen, and it was easy enough to understand why monks had been coming to pray in the caves around it since not long after the dawn of Christianity. For someone like me, an American who had grown up Catholic but found myself swept into the Islamic world, into a country overrun with refugees from a war in Iraq that my own country had started, the monastery was also an escape, a place where I could be invisible: a piece of home.

The monastery, Deir Mar Musa, is a Syrian Catholic monastery, in ruins for centuries but finally restored in the 1980s, now standing like an unexpected pearl in the middle of the desert. As an Eastern Catholic Church, it marries the traditions of the Catholic and Orthodox rites. The Catholic liturgy was held every night in Syriac and Arabic, with prayers sung out by a community of monks and nuns whose families had likely lived in the region since the dawn of Christianity. Throughout any given year, thousands of pilgrims—both Syrian and foreign—trudged up those stairs in search of something even they could not quite pinpoint. They stayed for an hour, a night, a week, or sometimes months at a time. They were joined by thousands of Muslim visitors, who came after their Friday afternoon picnics to visit with the monks and nuns, take in the scenery, and pay tribute to a shared cultural heritage that dated back centuries. It is like no other monastery in the world—the ideal place for a spiritual, wandering man who spoke every language with the marks of other languages, and had not ever quite found a home.

It was there that I first met Frédéric, standing in the courtyard in his gray monastic cassock, imposing at over six feet tall, his hair a mess of curls, waiting to pour arriving visitors a glass of tea. He introduced himself in a European accent I couldn't place. It was not often that I came upon men from Europe dressed in monastic robes in the midst of the Middle Eastern desert, and there was something about him that piqued my interest. From then on, he was always there when I arrived at the monastery, waiting for me at the top of the mountain with a pot of tea.

I sensed something both wild and self-assured in Frédéric; he carried himself apart from everyone, yet at the same time drew everyone to him. In Syria, where he should have been the most familiar person to me, I had no idea where to place him. He was extremely thin without being frail, his hands bore the marks of working in vineyards and harvesting honey from bees, and he spoke English with what I finally discovered was a French accent— English that I couldn't place as either American or British because he had picked it up during his years traveling alone in India. He spoke Arabic peppered with English and French for the words he didn't know; in fact, every language he spoke seemed to carry a trace of some other language, so that he seemed to be from every-where and nowhere all at once. He had a particular way of speaking so that you were never quite sure if he was teasing or serious, and he was never quick to clarify.

His was a working monastery, and as my visits continued we

often found ourselves sweeping floors or hanging laundry together, two strangers speaking among dirty dishes and ghostly sheets draped above the pale white stones. He had spent his years before the monastery traveling around the world, and he told me stories of India and Pakistan and Iran—travels he spent searching, not in the way of one who is lost, but with the intensity I later recognized in scholars who would go to the ends of the world to find a missing fragment of a text or a buried inscription that might shed light on a story partially told. One day, when he was twenty-nine years old, he arrived in that monastery in the clouds, in the middle of the Syrian desert, and sensed that it contained the something he had been searching for. And so he had, rather simply, remained.

Frédéric entered the community as a novice monk and kept bees, milked goats, and learned to tell the story of the ancient frescoes that decorated the Byzantine chapel. He arose with the morning sun to pray in Arabic and Syriac, took long walks in the desert, and learned the monastic art of patience, waiting at the top of those stairs for whoever might come—for in the desert tradition of the Middle East, any stranger who arrives might be an angel, just as, in a story kept by Islam, Christianity, and Judaism, the angels of God arrived at the tent of Abraham one day, disguised as men, bringing news of what was to come.

"Be not forgetful to entertain strangers," the Letter to the Hebrews warns, "for thereby some have entertained angels unawares."

So he remained for three years, passing arid summers and snowy winters, building a hermitage where he could pray in solitude near the caves beyond the monastery, fasting once a week, memorizing the goat trails through the surrounding mountains in his sandaled feet, until he felt himself becoming part of them. On one occasion, a journalist came from Italy and, finding Frédéric in the desert, took his photograph. He then proclaimed that he had found the last of the real desert monks.

That was around the same time I first met him. I didn't think that I had found the last of the real desert monks. I felt that I had, in the oddest of places, come upon a friend.

We were an unlikely pair—two strangers in an unknown place, his arrival by way of the French Alps, mine from Texas. Yet there was something familiar in him. I had also spent much of the last ten years traveling from place to place, as a writer and a journalist threading through dozens of countries: walking across Spain, living for a year in China, another in Beirut. I knew what it was to contain an entire life in a suitcase. I too had been drawn again and again to that monastery in the desert, a kind of anchor in a world in which so much seemed in motion. There was comfort in a monastery that had lasted more than a thousand years, that was made of stone. Though I spoke of it to almost no one, save for the monastery's abbot, I was struggling to make sense of my place in a Middle East that was tumbling into war, and I also thought that I might have had a calling to become a nun. My weekend trips to the monastery were far from idle: I was considering whether or not, when my graduate fellowship finished at the end of the year, I might climb to the top of those stairs one last time and stay.

That spring, as we sat across from each other in the candlelit chapel, I confessed to Frédéric that I might spend my life there. He had already guessed.

"I have never thought that you have a calling to be a nun," he told me bluntly. "You don't believe in resurrection. You don't love your life."

He accused me of using a monastic vocation to run away from the world. His words stung with the bitterness of being true.

I had long struggled with depression, through a string of failed relationships, and my many years of living abroad had been as much about learning as they had been about grounding myself in realities more chaotic than my own fractured life. There was comfort in contrasting my own brokenness against problems much more severe than any hardship I had suffered. But there was a grace in my life that I refused to see. That spring, I took Frédéric's words to heart, and I set out to discover resurrection. In Damascus, life became lighter somehow. I searched for the hope I had been missing—not in a monastery in the clouds, but on street corners, among strangers, in shafts of light that fell around the Umayyad Mosque. It came slowly: beauty I had never recognized before.

I continued traveling to the monastery, and Frédéric and I spent many afternoons together, speaking about nothing much at all. Then one day, when we were doing the dishes together in the cramped monastic kitchen, I looked up at him and thought that perhaps I could continue this, doing dishes with this man, for the rest of my life—and not because I would be a nun at a monk's side.

That was when he said it: *I do not love you in that way.* As a man only does when he loves you, in that way.

We wrote letters to each other, he from his monastery, I from my room in Damascus. For his thirty-third birthday, I brought him a bag of the season's first peaches and the gift of a single pale blue, hand-blown glass. I kept one exactly like it in my room in Damascus. And as the days passed, we filled our glasses with water in the morning, and again in the evening. And I waited.

It was late spring when Frédéric finally told Father Paolo, the abbot of the monastery, that he had fallen in love with me. Paolo had the distinct weakness of believing that everyone he cared for was called to be a monk or a nun, and he was as set on my becoming a nun one day as he was on Frédéric's taking his final vows the following year. But he let us go. He had no choice. Since he was not at all certain that Frédéric was really in love with me, he suggested that he travel to India on pilgrimage. I would return to America and wait for Frédéric to contact me.

"These decisions must not come quickly," Paolo warned. He thought it better to send Frédéric across the world to decide.

Paolo might have left it at that. But he couldn't hide his disappointment. "But don't you love the monastic life?" he protested.

"It isn't that," Frédéric responded. "Now I have to choose between love and love."

So Frédéric left, an act of obedience, boarding the Syrian Air flight from Damascus to Mumbai, remembering as he flew across the continent the promise he had made to himself, a monastic promise. He had given his life to God. Of this he was certain. The only event that could undo that offering was if God decided to send him a miracle, telling him that he was free to spend his life with me.

He landed in the monsoon. He wore his civilian clothes. And for two days he walked, lost in Mumbai, among millions, thinking, *This I did not even find in a monastery in the desert—to be entirely invisible to the world.*

─────

Now he was sitting next to the window, and the train was departing Mumbai and moving toward Kerala, the landscape becoming increasingly remote as the train left the outskirts of the city. The hills, coated with water, took on an unearthly sheen, and for a while

Frédéric watched each successive hill approach the train, the trees shimmering as the pocket of light in the sky grew wider. He opened the notebook on his lap and began writing:

C'EST COMME SI UN MIRACLE ALLAIT BIENTÔT SE PRODUIRE...

IT IS AS THOUGH A MIRACLE IS ABOUT TO HAPPEN...

Then he turned again to the window.

Three hours later, the train slowed down for the station at Pune, the wheels grinding against the rails and then softening to silence. Through the window he could see the waiting passengers pushing toward the train doors impatiently. The door to his compartment slid open, and two Indian nuns climbed inside, followed by a young Indian woman looking at her feet.

How strange to see them here, he thought, for it was as though his life in Syria had burst in, unexpectedly, from a remote train station in India. Then he remembered his civilian clothes, the simple tan shirt and linen trousers, and his monastic robe folded and concealed at the bottom of his bag. *They won't recognize me now.*

But, somehow, they did. The nun in the front kept looking at the ticket in her hands and walking up and down the aisle. Then she stopped next to Frédéric.

"Are you traveling toward Cochin?" she asked.

He nodded.

She gestured toward the girl. "Will you take care of her? She's never traveled alone."

He nodded again, glancing at the girl long enough to let them know he understood, though he had no idea why they should trust him. It occurred to him that he might tell them who he really was, that he was a novice monk traveling in civilian clothes, to reassure them, but he thought it would be too complicated to explain and so said nothing. The girl took her seat across from him. She folded her hands neatly in her lap. The nuns waved, solemnly, it seemed, before departing from the train and disappearing into the crowded platform below.

Frédéric turned again toward the window, watching the trees pass. The wheels slowly found their rhythm, moving beneath them with a sound that resembled a man trying hard to breathe.

Several minutes passed before he turned to the girl.

"Where are you going?"

She hesitated. "I'm going back home. I was a novice to become a nun for three years in a Carmelite monastery. And now I am leaving, to return and live with my family."

Beneath them, the train wheels continued to strike against the rails. He considered what he should say, what anyone should say in response to such a moment.

"Me too," he finally answered, only understanding as he spoke the words out loud that it was true. "I'm leaving the monastery too."

———◆———

So it was that my life—and your life too, my Joseph—was determined by an angel who appeared on a train. As the carriage passed through the countryside, your father told her about his life: about a childhood in rural France, years traveling through India, a strange calling that had carried him all the way to the deserts of Syria, to a monastery in the clouds. And then he told her about me. They prayed together, in seats forty-one and forty-two of a moving train between Mumbai and Cochin. The next morning, he descended two stops before hers, leaving her with his wooden icon of the Virgin Mary, a rosary, and five hundred rupees that he quietly pressed into her hand, for she was an angel who appeared on a train, but a poor angel. Two weeks later, he entered a small store with just enough money to purchase a simple ring of green stones. He sent me a message in America:

My choice is deeply here. And I've chosen you.

He traveled for eight weeks. Your father carried that ring with him until he flew back to Damascus, where I was waiting for him at the airport, and he asked me to marry him.

A Monastery in November

EVERY MONTH IN THE DESERT HOLDS ITS OWN QUALITY, as though an entirely new world begins at its onset and disappears when the month is done. The monastery of Deir Mar Musa in October still contained the last heat of the summer; in December it was already freezing and alive with snow. But the monastery in November was neither summer nor winter, but a month of transition, of leaving behind one season and approaching another, with the air just cold enough so that the wildlife retreated and the stones were left in silence. Hardly anyone visited, so the sound of every falling branch interrupted a valley asleep.

It was into November that Frédéric and I returned for our first week back in Syria, looking out the windows of the minibus as it turned down a remote road and toward the monastery. We had left our bags in Damascus, carrying with us only enough clothing to hold us over until we could say good-bye to the monastic community, not enough for the force of habit to tempt us to stay longer. The driver deposited us at the bottom of the stairs. We began to climb. The world was so untouched that it felt as though we were disturbing it, simply by parting the air.

I had not wanted to return to Frédéric's former monastery. It seemed like tempting fate, as in a film in which everything is heading in one direction until the final, unlucky scene. I was worried that once Frédéric walked into the chapel, he would lose the nerve to leave it again. But he insisted. He was not the first novice who had left the monastery, and he knew full well the tendency of locals to gossip that such leavings were the result of fear, of running away, or even of tensions with Father Paolo, who was famously temperamental. No, Frédéric would not let it be said that he was escaping. He wanted to say a proper good-bye.

So we climbed, and the silence between us was made noticeable by our breath, increasingly visible in the cold desert air as we ascended. At the top of the stairs, we turned to the front of the stone monastery, each of us ducking in succession through the door of humility, entering the monastic courtyard, where Father Paolo was waiting for us, all six feet four of him. Frédéric had informed him of his decision to leave the novitiate by post from India, along with the date of our arrival to say our last good-byes. He embraced us both at the same time, sighing with disappointment, and I thought that even though he had lived in the Middle East for decades, when he decided to be dramatic, he was still very much an Italian.

Then he looked us up and down: a father, sizing up his children who had come home after being too long away.

It might seem strange that I speak of Father Paolo as my father—particularly as my real father was larger than life and needed no replacement. But Father Paolo is just as essential to this story in his own way. Over the years he had become my spiritual father, guiding me through decisions that had shaped my life.

Though it had been many centuries since Christians had regularly spoken of spiritual fathers and mothers in the desert—referring to those early monks and nuns who had lived as hermits in the remote landscapes of Egypt and Syria—Paolo seemed to belong to another time. He was a Roman and a Jesuit with a giant frame, always clothed in a long, gray, belted robe and ill-fitting sandals, and he could be found at any given moment calling out in French and English and Italian and Arabic, all the while gesturing with his hands, adapting his language and manners to whomever happened to walk through the undersized Byzantine door. The thousands of people, both Muslims and Christians, who walked through that door every year, did so as much to see Paolo as for the medieval frescoes that graced the church's walls. They called him, simply, Abouna. In Arabic, "Our father."

Father Paolo was a complicated figure, towering, proud, and with a terrible temper, yet unexpectedly fragile, like those beasts of fairy tales who turn out, by the final pages, to be the most sensitive creatures of all. He appeared to experience every emotion more intensely than other people, so that each instance of joy or anger possessed him entirely and threatened to overwhelm him. He was also prone to adopting those he met as his own, and it was a sight to witness him calling so many of the monastery's thousands of visitors by name. Like many Jesuits, he was dedicated to helping others decipher their vocation in life, believing in what they call the *magis*, "more," or "greater" in Latin—the idea that there is always something more each one of us can do in the world to serve God. His *magis* had led him to restore the ruined monastery in the desert more than two decades before, transforming the abandoned church in the desert to a sanctuary famous for its dedication to Christian dialogue with Islam, and founding a community of Arabic-speaking monks and nuns. And he was always ready to help others discover their calling. My early meetings with him, as a twenty-three-year-old traveler, had inspired me to return to America to study Arabic and Islam in graduate school, to travel to Syria years later to research the Prophet Jesus in Islam, and to find my way again to him and to Deir Mar Musa. He had seen me through prayer and heartbreak and a month of silent retreat, through discernment and disenchantment, and now he was seeing me as I set off with the man who had been his novice, and would be my husband.

I imagine that he was not entirely thrilled that this was what it all had come to.

Frédéric and I parted ways in the courtyard, and I found my old monastic cell and unpacked my bag, aware that I might not return to the monastery again for a very long time.

As night fell, the bell for the evening meditation rang out in the courtyard, and I could hear the footsteps of guests and nuns and monks scampering on stairs, down from mountaintops, across the courtyard. I traversed the bridge that separated the women's section of the monastery from the chapel. The night came early in winter, and the moon was already visible above the courtyard. Father Paolo was waiting for me, but instead of leading me into the chapel, he motioned me up to his office.

We climbed up the stone stairs together, the railing a long wooden branch worn down by a thousand hands, cracked and full of knots and held in place by rope, so that I barely trusted it to hold us. At the top, we continued on to the office situated above the chapel. Through a window, we could see those gathering for prayer below. We sat down across from each other, separated by a gasoline heater, and warmed our hands over the blue flame. I took a moment to look at him: his beard almost fully gray now, his monastic cassock thinning with age and held together with a leather belt, the black scarf of the Syriac order draped across his shoulders. His hands were massive, and I noticed the ring from his final vows, like a wedding band.

He removed his glasses, rubbed his eyes wearily, and then pinched the frames between his thumb and forefinger, twisting them back and forth.

"Do you remember when we spoke about crucifixion?" he finally asked.

I smiled. He remained the same Paolo, after all.

By virtue of the fact that he lived in the middle of the desert, Father Paolo had developed a remarkable ability to carry on a single conversation, interrupted frequently, over the course of months or even years. It was this ability that allowed him to stay faithful to friends spread across languages and countries, most of whom could rarely make it to the monastery. I had seen him carry a letter in the pocket of his cassock, pull it out, read a few sentences, and then return it to be finished later. He would repeat this over days, and compose an entire response in his head before he ever wrote it down.

We had initiated the conversation he was referring to now, about the nature of crucifixion, ten months before, a few days after I had told him that I had changed my mind about becoming a nun. I had decided that I wanted to get married. I wanted a family. I wanted to write. I wanted to try to make my way in the messy, inhabited world, and could no longer imagine growing old in a monastery in the middle of the desert.

Paolo had been immediately suspicious. In his mind, it made little sense that God would send an American Catholic scholar of Islam all the way across the world, to his specific monastery, so that she could decide to get married and become a writer somewhere else. No, he suspected that I was merely afraid of the rigors of the monastic life—of what he called crucifixion. I remembered his look of disappointment when I disagreed.

Now, ten months later, I reminded him of our previous conversation. "You quoted Simone Weil," I said. "'Every time that I think of the crucifixion of Christ,' she'd written, 'I commit the sin of envy.'"

Paolo laughed. Even he could recognize when he'd crossed the borders of melodrama. "At the time you were angry with me," he added. "You said that I had made an idol out of unhappiness."

I nodded. "I told you that God does not want us to suffer."

"Perhaps you were right," he said quietly. "But I told you that you shouldn't make an idol of this *happiness* either, that you shouldn't run away from unhappiness."

He looked at me with tenderness.

"I know that you always thought that the monastic life would be hard. But *marriage* will also be hard, Stephanie," he cautioned. "You and Frédéric have so many differences between the two of you: cultural, spiritual, even personal. Do not think that this will be easy."

I studied him. "I know, Paolo," I told him, though I did not know at all.

Later, I would remember that conversation, on afternoons when I thought that the monastic life and family life were not unlike each other after all—very different people attempting to live together, with all of their quirks and habits, in the middle of the desert, and despite the romantic ideal, it was often dishes and laundry and silence, not to mention weeks where it felt like the same food over and over again.

He embraced me. We descended the stairs together, into the dim light of the courtyard, beneath a sky full of thousands of stars. He bent down in order to enter the low entrance to the chapel, and I followed behind him, watching as he donned the green robes of a

Syrian Catholic priest. Then he made his way behind the altar, and the room filled up with incense in a ritual that had been carried out in that same desert for some fifteen hundred years. The monks and nuns lined up in front of the iconostasis and began their prostrations. Frédéric, who was not a novice monk any longer, seemed not to know where to stand.

The mass finished an hour later. Paolo blew out the candles, removed his liturgical vestments, and walked toward the door. He had such an immense presence that it often seemed to me that rooms emptied out the moment he left them, even if he was the only person who had departed.

Frédéric called out his name. "Abouna," he said. "My father." I could hear his voice tremble.

Paolo turned.

"I need you to bless us."

There it was: Jacob wrestling with the angel until the break of dawn. The sun rises, and the angel struggles to break free. But Jacob insists: *I will not let you go unless you bless me.*

There it was: a son kneeling in front of his spiritual father.

For a moment, there was only silence in the chapel. Father Paolo took a deep breath. "Of course."

He was so tall that he covered the space between us in three long strides. We followed him to the ancient baptismal font in the corner, where we could stand. On the wall nearby, a fresco of an angel was holding a towel, as if to bless us. Paolo held the hand of his almost monk, and his almost nun, and he watched as Frédéric took the engagement ring and placed it once again on my finger, and then he whispered the words of the blessing ceremony in the ancient Syriac tradition.

He blessed us.

If I had known then what I know now, I would have locked the door to the church, and remained in that corner until morning—Frédéric holding my hand beneath the worn frescoes, Paolo blessing us.

That moment would enter into eternity. It would print itself into everything that happened afterward, for better and for worse.

———————

The next morning, we awakened early to leave. Father Paolo quietly slipped Frédéric five one-hundred-euro notes—enough money to see us home. Then he embraced him and kissed me on the forehead, and he said good-bye to him in French and to me in English, and then finally to both of us in Arabic, as though he couldn't tell into which world to place this parting, and we began the long journey down hundreds of stairs and toward a new life. I looked back once, to see the monastery hanging over us in the distance.

A few days later, we caught a bus from Damascus to Aleppo, and from there we boarded a train to Istanbul that stretched on for some thirty hours, snaking through ancient Antioch and along the coast, past olive groves and rocky hills and finally the coastline. From Istanbul we would purchase tickets to fly to France, though I had no idea where in France we were going. That had been my promise: that if Frédéric left the monastery, then I would follow him anywhere in the world.

We slept. When we awakened, the sea was visible out the windows of the train, a strange comfort after the desert, blue and alive. Frédéric unfastened a fountain pen from his notebook and wrote out in neat handwriting:

My First French Lesson

Epouvantail	Scarecrow
Ami	Friend
Douleur	Pain
Chanson	Song
Jardin	Garden

It seemed an odd assortment of words from which to start, when I spoke no French at all. I tried, softly, to pronounce them in turn: the *eur* and *on* strange on my tongue.

Douleur. Chanson.

I looked up at the man who would be my husband, and who I had only really known as a novice monk in a monastery. I asked him, hesitantly, if he could tell me his middle name.

France

IF LIFE COULD FOLLOW A PERFECT NARRATIVE, THE STORY would end there: with your father and me together, spending the rest of our lives happily married in France. But life does not follow a perfect narrative, and at times it does not seem to follow any arc at all. For me, meeting your father was a complete rupture from the past. The rest was less moving forward than starting over.

It would be six long months before our wedding. Father Paolo had wanted us to get married immediately, while we were still in his monastery in the desert, but in a rare act of defiance against my spiritual father, I had flatly refused. One of the complications of falling in love with a novice monk was that, until he'd made his final decision to leave the monastery, I couldn't tell anyone about him. I was now marrying a man that almost no one in my life even knew existed. I at least had to introduce him to my family first.

And, in truth, I wanted the fairy tale: the white gown, the flowers, the chapel in the French countryside, the perfect ending to the story of a monk who left his monastery for love. And we all live happily ever after.

So we scheduled a wedding for May, the soonest that we could realistically assemble friends and family from across the world in Europe. In the meantime, we arrived in France, where we would spend the first months of our life together. Not having spent much time in France, I was under the mistaken impression that the country was composed largely of museums and castles, some postcard version of a Juliette Binoche film in which every street was cobbled and there was little to do but pass the afternoons strolling between bookstores, eating croissants. I was not the first American to make this mistake, and I will not be the last. I would later realize that my error had been watching American films about France instead of French films about France (one of the most famous French love films, *Jules et Jim*, ends with two of the characters driving themselves off of a cliff). It was far harder to appreciate in person the war-scarred villages, the farm-hardened old men, the cafés with their terrible coffee, and the complexity of a single country bordered by eight others, each region distinctly its own. It would take me years to find all of that complaining endearing rather than frustrating.

We disembarked from our train in the French countryside of Drôme Provençale to find a ruggedly elegant woman, with a shock of gray hair and fierce blue eyes, approaching us and turning her cheeks to be kissed. I had been expecting a mother-in-law who would either be Coco Chanel or a French version of Julia Child, but Frédéric's mother was something else. She possessed the hardened assurance of a woman who had raised three children mostly alone, hiked the Himalayas every year for pleasure, made her own alcohol, and had nearly lost her fingers as a teenager from frostbite. She was a force.

"*Bonjour, mon grand*," she sang out to Frédéric.

She turned to me, kissed me, and then inspected me from what seemed to be the soles of my shoes up to my hastily brushed hair.

"I bought her Coca-Cola," she remarked to Frédéric dryly, her way of acknowledging the unfortunate fact that he had brought home an American.

To be honest, it's a miracle that we lasted the first week.

We began our new life in the house of my *belle-mère*, as she was called in French, in a hamlet in a region I had not known existed until that morning: a cluster of red-roofed cottages surrounded by open fields, with a few horses grazing. It was colder even than the monastery, and with seemingly fewer people living nearby, with a single, small wood stove to heat the house, like I had only seen, I believe, in episodes of *Little House on the Prairie*. I spent the first day huddled beside the stove, busily rubbing my hands together.

There was a single clock in the house, hanging in the kitchen, which I soon understood to be intentional. That evening, we sat down to dinner at exactly seven o'clock, for French meals happened on a schedule that was rigidly monastic (the afternoon snack, for instance, is called *le quatre-heures*—the four o'clock.) I attempted to begin a conversation, but after a few moments, Frédéric's mother gave up trying to respond in her limited English, and she turned to her son and began speaking French. I had met him in a world where Arabic and English and the occasional Syriac were spoken, and I had rarely heard him speak in his own language. His whole body became animated, and he gestured with his hands, agitated about some subject I could not comprehend.

For the next hour I sat, understanding nothing of what he said, not wanting to stop him to ask. I had the sense that he was a different person in his own language, a person who I did not yet know. And yet he was the man I was about to marry.

In vain I thought of the five words he had made me memorize on the train.

Douleur. Chanson.

We had no home of our own, and almost no money. I had not once considered that, in all of the months I had waited to learn if he would leave the monastery, but now it terrified me. Most of all, we had no idea of what we were doing next. I was beginning to suspect that we had set out on a long-distance journey for which we were woefully unprepared. He had spent three years trying to rid himself of everything that belonged to the world: giving away his guitar to a friend, making gifts of his collection of books, even losing his French identity card (which I thought was unnecessarily dramatic), methodically shedding his material possessions so that he could fulfill the monastic vow of poverty.

For three years he had lived in a world where he did not handle his own money, where the toll of the bell in the monastery courtyard determined breakfast and lunch and dinnertime. He tried to lose his attachments to everything he could, no matter how small. On days when he fasted, if a guest offered him food, he always accepted it, hoping to overcome even his own desire to hold a fast rather than observe the highest virtue in monasticism—accepting hospitality. His goal, he once told me, was to be invisible to the world, and visible only to God.

But the inhabited world had no patience for such ideas, and the very qualities that had made him a successful monk in his monastery in the clouds—poverty, obedience, and humility—were handicaps in the world below. I did not dare broach this subject with him, but there was no need, for he understood it intuitively, in the same way that he could watch the sky for patterns to see what storms were approaching.

Two days after we arrived at his mother's house, we drove to the nearest village, and I waited outside as he reluctantly walked through the revolving doors of the bank and opened an account under both of our names, into which he deposited what little remained of the money Father Paolo had given us. I had never seen him look so despondent—as though after so many years of his trying to fight it, the world had managed to win after all.

The next day, a neighbor who remembered a favor that Frédéric had done for him a decade before decided to give us his old car for free, a white Citroën BX with tires that inflated and lifted the body into the air before we could start the ignition, straight out of some children's science fiction book. It was so old that Frédéric would whisper to it each time he started it, coaxing it to move: "*Allez allez, on y va.*"

Only a week had passed, but he had managed to become weighted down to the earth.

I called my father and announced that I was getting married. In a few weeks we would be coming home. Immediately, he asked me to put Frédéric on the phone.

"Don't you have something to ask me, young man?" he demanded.

Frédéric stumbled. "Yes, of course. But I'm just waiting to ask you when I meet you in person." He then hung up the phone and turned to me in shock. "Is there something I'm supposed to ask your father?"

I sighed. While I had clearly watched far too many Hollywood movies, he had not watched nearly enough.

———

I spent the first two months of our life together watching Frédéric stumble through the inhabited world. We took ambling walks through the forest in the afternoons, and he told me tales about his years wandering the earth. There was a wistful quality to his voice as he recounted them. He had stopped attending school when he was sixteen, working in vineyards and as a musician between voyages, amassing an immense and bizarre amount of knowledge on his own: how to play the Iranian lute and the Armenian *duduk*, the philosophy behind certain Hindu and Buddhist texts, traditional French folk songs, beekeeping, forestry, a strong opinion of the virtues of Schubert over Chopin, and the Islamic ninety-nine names of God. He had never desired a formal education and had not needed one in the monastery, but he sensed that he would need one in this new life with me. Now, intent on completing his high-school degree before our wedding, he spent his early mornings and late evenings at the dim light of the kitchen table, hunched over books, studying for exams. I did not ask him what he wanted to do with his life, because I suspected that I knew the answer: he wanted to be a desert monk. The fact that he wanted to marry me did not negate the desires of the past, as I had somehow, quite foolishly, imagined it would. It simply made them impossible to fulfill.

It was a few days before I first discovered rosary beads in the pockets of his jacket when I was gathering clothes for the laundry. They clinked in the way coins or keys might break against one another in the pockets of another man. The second week, on Thursday, I noticed that he was not eating his usual bread and honey for breakfast. When he did not eat lunch either, I understood that he was discreetly continuing his monastic habit of fasting once a week. I awakened in the morning to find him warming himself near the woodstove, wearing his gray monastic cassock, drinking a cup of tea. It had been tailored exactly for his size, and so he had kept it with him. He was the exact vision of the novice monk I had met in the monastery, only without the glow.

As they might say in Texas: "You can take the man out of the monastery, but you can't take the monastery out of the man."

I had promised Frédéric that I would follow him anywhere in the world, mistakenly thinking that this would ensure us a home together. The problem was that he no longer belonged to the world. The monastery had demanded that he take a vow of poverty, which for other men might have proven difficult. But for a man like Frédéric, the poverty of the desert had been almost effortless. It was no great sacrifice to give up everything he owned in order to spend his life in prayer, among the rockscape and clouds. No, for him this new life was the real poverty, when he was asked to give up his past and become tied once again to the earth.

I watched him: surveying the sky for incoming rain, motioning to wild rose bushes and edible berries in the forest paths around the house, awakening early to salvage some semblance of solitude. The monastery had concealed both humor and grit, and I came to recognize them slowly. He was hesitant to trust the earth. His great-grandfather on his mother's side had died from gas in the First World War, and his great-grandfather on his father's had died of tuberculosis. His grandparents had lived in the high mountains, teaching in a one-room schoolhouse. He took it for granted that the world was harsh and one had to be prepared to navigate it. This skill, it turned out, would be of great use in our life to come.

I could not keep up, but tried not to get lost entirely. Before dinner, in an effort to be helpful, I began to peel potatoes for soup. I moved quickly, a thick pile of shavings amassing on the countertop. He surveyed me from across the room, then approached wordlessly, placed his hand on top of my right hand, curved the fingers, and showed me how to peel the potato closer to the skin, so as not to lose a single, unnecessary inch.

I wrote. I read. I tried to memorize sentences in French. I planned our wedding.

"You're not happy," he whispered, finding me reading in the corner at night.

"I'm happy," I whispered through my tears.

None of it was as I had imagined. I had not fully comprehended, when I had asked him to leave the monastery, how completely he would have to start over. How lost we both would be.

He printed a kiss softly on my forehead. I knew that he loved me, but was less certain that it was a love worth starting over for. There were two possibilities: that leaving the monastery to marry me was the most romantic gesture that anyone could hope for, or that one day he would wake up and blame me for what I had asked him to do.

Time did not seem to pass. I thought that we had arrived in the midst of winter, but in fact it had only been its onset, so that each day seemed to slip more deeply into the dark. The only neighbor was a horse who occasionally approached a nearby fence and looked over at us wearily, and a postman who some days came in for tea. Even the sky retreated into itself.

A few weeks in, Frédéric's mother caught me, unguarded, staring out the window toward the open fields. The grass outside was glazed with ice, a world in mourning.

She poured me a cup of tea. There are those moments between women that defy differences. An American marrying her son was unfamiliar to her. A young woman, alone and worried about the future was not.

She bided her time, sipping out of her mug. She looked out at the field with me, but as though to see through it, to another time.

"You know, Frédéric—when he was a child, he was always friends with that one boy in his class who no one else would play with. He was always drawn to—what do you call them in English? The ones who do not belong."

"To outcasts?"

"*Oui*, to outcasts. Since as long as I could remember, that boy followed his own path."

I smiled at the amount of English she could speak when she put her mind to it.

"Don't worry," she continued. "I can understand why you're worried, but you don't need to be. I was worried about him all the time. When he was nineteen years old, and he came back from traveling in India, I told him that he needed to immediately go out and look for a job." She smiled. "He told me not to worry. But we fought. I thought that he was living in a dream world." She shook her head. "But then someone called him the very same day and offered him work." She placed her hand on my shoulder, in the brief solidarity of two women who both loved the same mysterious and somewhat impossible man.

"He always finds a way, that boy," she concluded, her voice both wistful and defiant. "*Il est né sous une bonne étoile.*" He was born beneath a lucky star.

A Game of Chess

THAT DECEMBER, WE TRAVELED TO TEXAS SO THAT MY FATHER could meet Frédéric at last. In typical fashion, my father was waiting for us at the airport, wearing a red-striped shirt, and it struck me that in France the shirts were not nearly as colorful and the cars were not nearly as big, that merely landing in Texas amplified the world so much that it almost induced a headache.

When we walked into his house, the living room was decked out in what seemed to be a testimony to American excess: two Christmas trees fully decorated, an almost life-sized Santa Claus figure standing beside the front door that bobbed up and down and rang a bell, the Three Tenors singing Christmas carols on a recording in the background. My stepmother had set out a platter brimming with French cheeses: Camembert and Brie and Bleu d'Auvergne, as if cheese were the only thing French people knew how to eat.

"So you come from France?" she asked him. "Do you know Tony Parker?"

Tony Parker was the French point guard for the San Antonio Spurs. He admitted that he did not.

I could see my father standing in the corner of the room, watching Frédéric squirm. He seemed to be enjoying himself. He sauntered over and put his arm around my shoulder.

"You *do* realize, Stephanie, that your ancestors were sent by the king of Spain to San Antonio to found the city, don't you?" He shot Frédéric a look of distaste. "And do you know *why* he sent them? He sent them in order to defend Spanish territory from the French. And now, after all of these years, you invite one of them into our home?"

For a moment I was not certain if he was kidding. Then he grabbed Frédéric by the arm and whisked him outside to a table beside the pool in the backyard.

I could see the two of them through the clear panes of the glass door. My father was pouring him a beer. Frédéric had been dreading this meeting for weeks, worried that my father would think it strange that his future son-in-law had spent three years living in a monastery. But that didn't worry me at all—contemplating the religious life was practically a rite of passage in my Catholic family, and my father had wanted to be a priest, as had most of his brothers, who had attended a Catholic seminary in high school. I was more worried about what my father would say when he realized that we were nearly penniless.

Besides, my father never liked *anyone* who I brought home. Not the millionaire I had dated for years, who he thought was a snob. Not the brilliant scholar who spoke ten languages, who he thought was a bully. I was particularly haunted by the memory of a high school boyfriend whom my father had ordered out of the house until he removed his earring.

But, through the window at least, the two of them appeared at ease with each other. For a while, they just drank their beer, my father seeming to study this curious creature who had dropped into his home, a strange combination of compassion and Alpine toughness. I was his third of four children, but the first to be engaged. He had not quite expected it to happen like this.

But I suspect that he also recognized something in Frédéric: a generous stubbornness that might make him able to handle his youngest daughter. Frédéric was the sort of man who, if he saw me in deep water, would both want to save me and know how to build a boat.

Later, I would learn that their conversation outside went something like this:

"Son," my father told Frédéric, "I have four children, and I love all of them. But Stephanie is different from the others. She's... You'll see. She's special. She's not easy, but she's special. I love her very, very much. So I know that you'll take good care of her."

Then he paused. "And if you do anything to hurt her, know that I have a shotgun, and I will kill you."

Frédéric didn't flinch. My father challenged him to a chess game for my hand. Frédéric had been playing chess since he was a boy and won handily, much to my father's surprise.

———————

There was one other place we needed to go before we could return to France. My father had managed to procure for us two tickets to a San Antonio Spurs basketball game. Just as I had only known Frédéric as a monk in the desert, he had also only known me as a student and a traveler—certainly not as a girl who shouts at seven-foot-tall men and drinks bad beer out of Styrofoam cups. It was only fair that he know what he was getting into.

We found our seats in a stadium-sized sardine can of spectacle and noise, amid the deafening pounding of the sound system. More people were packed into that stadium than Frédéric must have come upon in a year in the monastery. He had been expecting cowboy outposts when we landed in Texas and so was not quite ready for this. I pointed out a man in a coyote suit dancing with the Spurs Silver Dancers.

"Is it always like this?" he asked. I didn't even ask if he was referring to the dancing coyote, the hundreds of foam hands waving in the air, the towering players, or the cheerleaders.

"It's always like this."

The buzzer sounded. Frédéric tried to focus on Tony Parker, the French point guard, his only point of reference, particularly since he had been asked about him three times since his arrival. He, like other Europeans, was mostly accustomed to soccer, and could not believe how often the basketball teams were scoring. He found it rather exhausting.

We were well into the second quarter when the Jumbotron announced that the kiss cam was starting.

"The kiss cam?" Frédéric repeated.

"You don't know what the kiss cam is?" I teased him. "The camera focuses on a couple, and one of them has to kiss the other."

"*C'est pas vrai.*"

"*Oui, c'est vrai.*" The camera moved across the crowd, stopped. Frédéric glanced up, to see the two of us projected above thousands of screaming fans.

He panicked. "What do I do?"

"You kiss me."

He seemed to hesitate for a moment. Then he turned and kissed me. When he pulled away, his cheeks were flushed red. The crowd roared in approval.

When the cheering died down, I turned to the man who would be my husband.

"Your secret is out. There's no going back to the monastery now."

That night, my father stopped me at the base of the staircase as I headed up toward my childhood bedroom.

"I like him," he whispered. "He's solid. He'll take good care of you."

I grinned.

"Really," he said. "I told him about my shotgun. I hope that I didn't scare him too much."

"You should have seen him with the kiss cam."

He embraced me, and we held each other on the last step of a long flight of stairs, my father and his youngest daughter.

"You're my beautiful little girl," he whispered.

Joseph, if I had known then what was to come, I would have held him longer too.

Passing Storms

WHEN I WAS FIVE YEARS OLD, I AWAKENED ONE NIGHT from a nightmare. In the dream, my mother was falling from the top of a cliff. I watched her fall, a sliver disappearing over the edge of the rocks, and heard the impact of her body in the valley below. I woke up screaming.

"Dad! Dad!"

I could hear my father scrambling to get out of bed. Then he was beside me, holding my hand, whispering, "It's okay. It was only a dream."

He waited until I stopped shaking. Then he whispered, "Close your eyes. Now picture a field full of green grass. Do you see it? There are trees growing, and a piece of shade perfect for sitting, and yellow daffodils. And there are so many butterflies. Do you see the butterflies?"

I closed my eyes until all I could see was a field of yellow flowers, waving in the breeze with butterflies hovering over the petals.

"Now keep your eyes closed," my father whispered. "Go to that place."

I fell asleep. Those words were stitched into my heart. I did not know that they would guide me through what would come after: wars, marriage, death, birth. Behind every dark moment, there is hidden another world. The trick is to hold out long enough to make it there.

———————

Frédéric and I returned to France, and I somehow managed to survive the following months. I memorized a dozen words—*myrtille*, *noisette*, *sauvage*; blueberry, hazelnut, wild—and the simple art of singing *bonjour!* while entering village cafés. On my birthday, Frédéric coaxed his beat-up car all the way to the city of Avignon, a fortified city of cobbled streets surrounding a palace. It rained the whole afternoon, and he held my hand as I tried to keep my balance. As the sun set, I peered into a shop window and saw a pair of pink ballet flats with bows. We had no money at all, but he saw my expression and rushed into the shop to buy them nonetheless.

It stopped raining. I slipped them on. For a moment, it was the fairy tale.

The days passed. Impossibly, I received news of my first book deal, so we were no longer forced to confront the prospect of living in dire poverty, at least for the immediate future. I could allow myself to dream, again, that we might have a home of our own. And as our wedding approached, I became more adept at reading the language that was Frédéric, the moods that I at first read as distance revealing themselves as his own worry that he might have given up an entire world, only for the new world he had chosen to collapse beneath him. Such were the terrors of being attached to the world: they brought with them the possibility of loss. But there was no other way forward.

One morning, he looked out at the fields with alarm.

"Look, the *hirondelles* are flying low. That means a storm is coming," he called out.

But then he looked again at the swallows and corrected himself.

"No, I was wrong. They're not flying low enough."

And indeed, the storm passed us over.

For as long as I could remember, I had longed for a home of my own. I had left my home in Texas when I was eighteen, moving to Vermont and then to Boston and England, traveling through the Middle East and walking across Spain, passing a year in China, another in Lebanon, a third in Syria. There were details I came to long for that others took for granted: a postal address, books to fill up my bookcases, my piano. Phone calls within the same time zone. I sometimes feared that I would spend my entire life living in other people's rooms.

Now, after so much wandering, it was not so much that I longed for home, but that I could no longer imagine what home might look like. If Frédéric no longer belonged to the world at all, I no longer belonged to a country. On a recent trip to New York, I had spent an afternoon walking through the rooms of the Metropolitan Museum of Art before I finally sat on a bench in the center, overwhelmed. There, reflected against paintings and stone sarcophagi, were hundreds of moments from my past: my childhood with my father in the American wing among the quilts and Tiffany glass; my hours with Father Paolo in the monastery among the Byzantine art; my time studying the Quran with a Syrian *sheykha* (a female sheikh) among the Islamic pottery; my year stumbling and overwhelmed in Beijing among the Ming vases. Here, months walking through Rome; there, the cathedrals of England. If only home could somehow also contain all of these rooms of the past, a dozen countries side by side beneath a roof of the present.

This was too much to ask. But it felt more and more like France was not a compromise but a complete annihilation of my own past, and that every day spent in it was a life inhabiting someone else's rooms. I had promised Frédéric that I would follow him anywhere. Now I was only hoping that he wouldn't hold me to it.

———————

That May, Frédéric and I were married in a small, blue-and-rose-frescoed church near his mother's village. Father Paolo traveled from Syria to celebrate the mass in his characteristic blend of Arabic, Syriac, French, and English. My father, wearing a tuxedo, walked me down the aisle, and he wept as he lifted my veil to give me a kiss. In the audience sat a nun from the monastery, friends from America and Syria and Iraq and Israel and India, from a lifetime of travels that had finally landed us in that place. Frédéric's sisters, who were anarchists, refused to wear the same blue dress as the bridesmaids, and somehow that made sense too. We forgot to bring our written vows. One friend, an Iraqi war photographer I had met in Syria, kept running up to the altar to snap close-ups, as though we might explode at any moment.

In one photo of the event, my father stands beside me lifting my veil, and Paolo stands in front of us with his hands clasped in blessing, his eyes aglow with reluctant joy, so that it is hard to tell which one of them is giving me away. Frédéric stands across from me in a linen suit with his shirt untucked, wearing a tie for the first time in his life.

And I loved him. God, how I loved that man. I loved all of

them, Joseph: my Texan father; my spiritual father; and your father, a man who had climbed down from his monastery in the clouds to marry me.

I whispered the vows that I knew, and he said them back, in the beautiful mess that was everything that we set out to do:

In richer and poorer.

In sickness and in health.

Till death do us part.

I do. I do. Somehow.

Dear Joseph,

By now you must be wondering when your part of the story will begin. We are almost there. The problem is that so many threads led to your arrival that it is hard to remove any of them, lest the entire story fall apart. If this were fiction, then I could decide what moment led to your birth. But I have so much less confidence in piecing together our own history. I have told you that your story began when an angel appeared to your father on a train. But now I am beginning to doubt myself. Is that really when it began? Perhaps it was only when Paolo blessed us in the corner of the church. Or when your father won my hand in a game of chess.

I suspect that all of them are beginnings, in their own way, that we carried the places and the people of our past in our bodies as we traveled forward. I was once told of Armenian priests who, in the violent upheavals of 1915, were given orders to flee their monastery. And so they tied their holy books to their backs and carried them as they escaped.

It was something like that. We carried men and countries and languages with us, until we were bound up somewhere between the countries we were in and the places we left behind. Only your father and I had very different books tied to our backs.

Jerusalem

IN JULY OF 2006, TWO MONTHS AFTER OUR WEDDING, I summoned up the courage to ask your father if we could live somewhere other than France.

We thought, at first, we would move to Beirut. We bought our tickets and packed our bags, deciding to spend a few weeks in Istanbul en route. We were about to depart when the news came that bombs had started falling in Lebanon, and that refugees were packing their bags and fleeing the city where we were supposed to be arriving. Israel and Lebanon had gone to war.

I glanced toward Frédéric.

"Maybe it will pass?" he suggested.

I reminded him that the Lebanese Civil War had lasted fifteen years.

We decided to set out anyway. We arrived in Istanbul, and during our first night in the hotel, I turned on the television and saw footage of a family in Lebanon piling their bags on the top of their car quickly but calmly, with a manner of finesse, as though packing their belongings and fleeing bombs was something that they did all the time.

We settled into uneasy sleep.

We spent the next week waiting for the war to pass, and it didn't. Finally, as we strolled in Sultanahmet in downtown Istanbul, I spotted a man working for a travel agency unfolding a sign on the sidewalk.

> ## CHEAP TICKETS:
> ## ISTANBUL—TEL AVIV.

Frédéric and I looked at each other. I suppose there is a danger when two monastically trained individuals are given, literally, a sign.

"Could we move to Jerusalem?" I asked.

It was a legitimate question. For the last several years, both of us had been forbidden to travel to Jerusalem; we would have been unable to reenter Syria with an Israeli stamp on our passports. Israel, which had occupied the Golan Heights region of Syria in the Six-Day War of 1967 and held onto it ever since, was permanently at war with Syria. Travelers in Syria did not even dare say the name of Israel out loud.

But now that we had decided to leave Syria, we were free to travel to Jerusalem for the first time in years, without the fear of that stamp in our passports.

For a moment I forgot the rather obvious complication: since Lebanon and Israel were now at war, by moving to Jerusalem instead of Beirut, we were simply foregoing one side of the fighting in exchange for the other.

"No one will bomb Jerusalem," Frédéric offered. "That's the good thing about moving to a city holy to everyone."

I nodded, deciding in a stroke of magical thinking to ignore the fact that many bombs had gone off and wars had been fought in the city holy to everyone.

"Why don't we just try it?" he suggested. "If it doesn't work, we can just move somewhere else."

He made it sound so easy, like stopping into a shoe store to slip on a pair of ballet flats that might or might not fit.

———————

Three days later, we arrived at the airport in Tel Aviv. At passport control, we were quietly escorted away by security for interrogation. Frédéric still had a Syrian residency in his passport.

"Why didn't you get a new passport?" I whispered to him.

"I didn't know we were moving to Jerusalem until three days ago," he whispered back.

The woman who questioned us was composed of creases and sharp corners, her shirt perfectly ironed and her hair pulled back—some combination of an army general and a flight attendant. When she spoke, it was with a Hebrew accent and the false casual tone that I recognized from interrogations in Syria as meant to inspire trust.

"Frédéric?" she called. He stood up, and she opened his passport and looked at the photo, then looked at him, and then looked at the photo again.

"So you were living in Syria?" she asked.

"Yes."

"For how long?"

"For three years."

"And what were you doing there?"

"I was a novice monk."

"A what?" She seemed honestly confused, and I wondered if she truly did not know what a monk was, or if she was simply exceptionally good at her job.

"A novice monk."

"And what is a monk?"

"A monk is a religious person. Who prays."

"I see. And you were praying in Syria."

"Yes."

"And where were you living?"

"In a monastery."

"Where was this monastery?"

"In the desert."

"Okay." She seemed to lean forward on one foot, and pursed her lips as though it was not okay at all. "And they do not have any of these places for you to pray in France?"

"They do. But I wanted to live in the one in Syria."

"I see." She clearly did not see at all. "And you spent three years in this place."

"Yes."

"Praying."

"Yes."

"But now you say that this is your wife?"

"Yes."

"So you are done with this praying now?"

"Yes."

I had to smile at that.

He was questioned for the next six hours. Other officers arrived and posed the same questions as the woman with the crisp uniform and perfect hair, before she returned and asked them again. I did not know what story they were waiting for that was more ridiculous than that of a man who had lived in the desert for three years, only to show up now in an airport with his wife.

We had arrived at night, but by now the sun was coming up outside. I nodded off on Frédéric's shoulder. I opened my eyes, and the woman was standing there again. She ran through the same list of questions, and I wondered if she tired of them. When she finished, she moved to walk away, but then hesitated. She turned.

"Is it nice, Syria?" she asked, her voice now almost vulnerable. "Because you know we cannot go there. I always wondered if it was nice."

"It's beautiful," Frédéric said quietly.

She disappeared. I was sleeping on Frédéric's shoulder again when she returned and handed us our passports, with two entry stamps inside.

———◆———

I should have known then that we would be strangers in this new country—strangers to whom everything would feel oddly familiar, strangers who carried the memories of neighboring countries that were not supposed to coexist with this place, but that resembled it all the same. But that would take much longer to understand. As it was, as our taxi made its way to Jerusalem, the sun was rising over the mountains of the desert, endowing them with color.

Frédéric looked out. "It looks just like Syria," he whispered. "I think the mountains of the monastery run all the way through the desert to here."

I peered out at the landscape, stark and bare, and remembered that Paolo and the monastery and the world we left behind were only two or three impossible hours away, across borders that could not be traversed.

It was late morning when we arrived in the city, so we retired to rest. In the early afternoon we pulled ourselves from sleep, and Frédéric took my hand as we walked across West Jerusalem. I tried to absorb the magnitude of what we had just done. For the first few streets, it was not so different from an American or European city: modern hotels with their evenly spaced rows of windows and balconies, tourists speaking English, signs in Hebrew, coffee shops with tables outside, and signs for King of Falafel. But the August air was on fire. Then the Old City came into view, a walled city so compact that it resembled a fortress on top of a hill, the roofs within it alive with crosses and minarets and balconies and the satellite dishes of its inhabitants. After living in the isolated French countryside, I was relieved at the sheer presence of so much life. We followed the line of gravity, descending along the Old City walls and down a hill and into a valley, and I was conscious that the largest city in the country felt both like a village and a wilderness. A gust of wind hit us, a tunnel of air that swept us into it. We stopped at the lowest point and stood at the entrance to Nablus Road.

Invisibly, in the space between a few city streets, we had crossed into another country entirely. Now the vendors shouted not in Hebrew but in Arabic. Veiled women walked by in ankle-length coats, and a row of men grilled lamb kabobs on skewers over roasting coals, the smoke clouding a section of the pavement. A vendor wearing a maroon fez wandered back and forth, pouring glasses of prune juice from an immense copper pitcher strapped to his back. Buses honked, but they were different buses from those crossing the other side of the city. Tomatoes were ten shekels for three kilograms. A voice shouted, "*Tenzilat, ya banat!*" Sales, girls! Sales!

In front of us stood the Damascus Gate, carrying the name of the city we had left behind.

Frédéric pressed my hand. I looked up at him.

"What do you think?" he asked.

I did not tell him what I was thinking: that it was the first time since I had met him in Syria that we were both strangers together, bound by our strangeness.

"It feels like home," I said.

Part Two

Nablus Road

———————————•———————————

"It began in mystery, and it will end in mystery, but what a savage and beautiful country lies in between."

—Diane Ackerman

The Valley

So it was, my dear Joseph, that your father and I came to live in Jerusalem.

The first house of our married life lay in a country between, near the beginning of Nablus Road, close to the invisible line dividing Jerusalem into East and West, Palestinian and Israeli. Our house stood just outside of the Old City gates and fell on the eastern side of the border, the only house like it on that part of the street, an enormous Arab stone edifice of red roof tiles and a facade of Jerusalem stones, surrounded by grocery stores and convents and shoe stores and butcher shops. Later, even old Jerusalemites would tell me that they had passed the house thousands of times without noticing its presence, because it was so out of place there that it refused to be seen. Most of the other houses in the neighborhood had ended up on the Israeli side of the Green Line after the 1948 Arab-Israeli War left the city divided. Ours was one of the few in the neighborhood remaining on the Palestinian side, a remnant of a country now gone.

The house seemed to have been purposefully built as an observation point and was set high enough above the street so that it was possible to navigate Jerusalem below—with all of its complexities and contradictions—by looking out the windows. On one side of the house, stretching from Nablus Road all the way out toward the Mount of Olives, lay Arabic-speaking East Jerusalem, which from the end of the British Mandate in 1948 until the 1967 war had been part of Jordan. In many ways, it did not feel markedly different from the surrounding Arab countries I had lived in for years, and so it was easy to imagine how visitors had once climbed into taxis from Damascus Gate and continued on to Amman and Damascus, transferring for even farther journeys to Baghdad or the *hajj* to Mecca. Visible from the windows on the opposite side of the house, from the parking lot and up toward Jaffa Road, was Hebrew-speaking, largely Jewish West Jerusalem. Our house was in the middle, just barely on the Palestinian side. The sun rose in the east speaking Arabic and set in the west speaking Hebrew, and we tried to find our way in between. In the sky above, thousands of migratory birds flew over the narrow strip of land between Europe and Africa that we lived on, a riot of woodpeckers and sunbirds, warblers and starlings and hoopoes. In the earth below, the bodies of the dead dating back centuries kept to their sleep, and Byzantine houses lay long abandoned and buried beneath the pavement stones.

Jerusalem was a city in time, and as the days passed, the streets' noises came to rule our lives, imprinting our bodies with the movement and habits of the city's inhabitants. At dawn, the call to prayer would filter into our sleep from the corner mosque, finding its place among our dreams. An hour later, at five thirty, the faint chiming of bells would sound from the garden beneath us, awakening us and summoning nuns to their prayers. The sound of their feet scampering across the courtyard resembled that of cats moving among rose bushes. By seven o'clock, more insistent bells would toll, this time from the chapel at the Notre Dame of Jerusalem Center at the top of the hill in West Jerusalem. At seven thirty, the opposite side of the house would swell with the excited cries of the uniformed girls from Schmidt-Schule, the German school across the street, chasing one another and jumping rope. The doorbell of the doctor's office in the building beside us would play a song like an ice-cream truck every time a patient would ring it. A few streets away, a dog belonging to the taxi drivers who headed to the Jordanian border would yelp and bark. At the neighboring bus station, drivers would shout out the names of destinations in Arabic: Ramallah! Ramallah! Beit Hanina! Shuafat! Al-Issawiya! So the world would rise to us every morning, long before we descended into it. I would make my way from the bedroom to the kitchen, parting the air of different sounds as I passed through each room.

Then there was Frédéric, your father and now my husband of three months, which was still a much shorter time than the three years he had spent as a novice monk in a monastery. Even now he had not lost the habit of awakening early in the morning for monastic matins, so he would always be waiting for me at the kitchen table, already awake for hours, standing in his gray ankle-length monk's cassock, which he had not given up wearing, and offering me a glass of tea.

"Must you continue to wear that?" I asked him one morning. He smiled.

"It was tailored for me," he answered. "You know it fits perfectly."

Then we sat down and drank our morning tea together on the seam between two countries, in our first home.

———————

Later, Frédéric would say that we did not move to a country; we simply moved to a house. And it was not only a house, but a house in time, situated at a moment in history. For centuries, Damascus Gate had been the main entrance into Jerusalem's Old City, the thoroughfare to some of the most important sites of Christianity, Judaism, and Islam in the world, and the largest gate of the Ottoman Empire. Pilgrims would pass by our house on their way to see the Church of the Holy Sepulchre, which stands on the site where many Christians believe that Jesus was crucified and raised from his tomb; the Western Wall, sacred to Jews as the last remnant of the Second Temple, which they believe had housed God's Divine presence; and the Al-Aqsa Mosque, called al-Haram al-Sharif—"the Noble Sanctuary"—by Muslims, where, according to their tradition, the Prophet Muhammad mounted a winged horse and ascended through the seven heavens. A single road into a single gate led to all three of these holy sites, like an artery into the city's beating heart, the earth beneath it bearing the memory of thousands of years of footprints.

When life within the Old City walls became too cramped during the late nineteenth century, wealthy Christian Arabs moved just outside the walls and formed the neighborhood where our house would stand: Musrara, an elegant patchwork of large stone houses interrupted by narrow, cobbled lanes; staircases of Jerusalem stone; colorful tiles; and gardens. Situated directly beside the Old City walls, it was as if Musrara was always standing at attention, finding its meaning in its proximity. As Jerusalem expanded under the British Mandate to include more neighborhoods beyond the confines of the Old City, Musrara also found itself at a crossroads—as one of crossing points between the Old City and the New.

This is not a history book, and many others have already written about the tragic events that passed along the old city walls over the past century. So I will be as brief as I can be—for as much as I don't want to dwell on those wars, their effect on this story cannot be denied. Musrara was once a continuous neighborhood, and it was only in 1948 that it was divided, a casualty of what would be referred to as the Nakba, or disaster, by the Palestinians and the War of Independence by the Israelis. When the British abandoned their Mandate and war broke out between Israel and the surrounding Arab countries, the neighborhood found itself trapped in the middle of the fighting. When the war was finished, most of the original inhabitants were gone—some having fled, some having been pushed out and not allowed to return—and the neighborhood was split, unevenly, in two. Now, in the middle of what had been a single city, a hostile border separated two countries. Most of the houses of Musrara ended up on the western side of the line, in the newly declared State of Israel, precariously close to what was now the new border of an enemy country on the eastern side of the wall: Jordan. The houses that had been emptied of their Palestinian inhabitants on the Israeli side now filled up with new Jewish immigrants, many of them Mizrahi Jews fleeing Arabic-speaking countries in the Middle East. Dozens of other houses were bulldozed to the ground to create a no-man's-land, and only a few houses—including ours—ended up on the eastern side, in Jordan. The neighborhood found itself gouged out and then divided, one part exiled from the other.

In 1967, Israel captured the Old City and East Jerusalem during the Six-Day War, and our street—still inhabited by Palestinians—came under Israeli control. The dividing wall in the middle of the neighborhood came down, and the Israeli government would say that the city was finally reunited. On a map, our neighborhood appeared whole again, but that was not the reality: three quarters of it remained up the hill, inhabited by Israelis who spoke Hebrew; the no-man's-land was now a parking lot and a highway; and in East Jerusalem, only two small, Arabic-speaking streets of Musrara remained—one of which was ours. In time, the municipality changed the name of the Israeli section of the neighborhood from Musrara to Morasha, which was meant to sound Hebrew. But no one ever called it that—not even the Israelis—so Musrara it remained, despite what the street signs said. Whatever it was called, it stood wounded and confused, in its same place beside the Old City walls, containing all of the contradictions of a city now claimed by two countries as their capital. As for the United Nations, it deemed Jerusalem neither Israeli nor Palestinian, but instead as *corpus separatum*, a separate body, not belonging to anyone, whose identity would be decided in the future.

We arrived in a divided city still bearing its scars. But somehow, the identity of our street—Nablus Road—had long been in flux. For now, our house stood in Palestinian East Jerusalem, on a street claimed by both Israelis and Palestinians. A street that, in the previous century, stood under the control of the Ottoman Empire, the British Mandate, and Jordan—always the same street, the same houses, the same people, but the country through which it ran named something else.

House Hunting

THE QUESTION OF HOW WE ENDED UP LIVING IN OUR house is as complicated as anything belonging to life with a man like Frédéric. I was learning that he was the kind of man who could easily start a fire in the wilderness and fix broken windows with a pocket-knife, but who couldn't type into a cell phone and was convinced that people became sick when exposed to air-conditioning. He had very strong opinions about sleeping with the window open and the healing properties of various herbal teas when sick, much like other people's Mediterranean grandmothers.

So it should not have surprised me that his ideas for how to find a house were more appropriate for the thirteenth century. My immediate impulse upon arriving in Jerusalem had been to log onto the Internet so that we could see what apartments were available to rent. As I scribbled down neighborhoods, Frédéric kissed me on the cheek.

"I'm going to Mass," he said. "You can stay here and rest."

I had no idea that by saying, "I'm going to Mass," Frédéric was actually saying, "I'm going to look for a house."

Like any good novice monk, particularly one from Europe,

Frédéric understood that the Roman Catholic Church functioned as a mini-empire, with its own schools and honey and printing presses, its own vineyards and soapmakers, its own postal stamps. In a city like Jerusalem, in which each community tended to take care of its own, it would not be a bad place to start if one were searching for a place to live. So while I slept, Frédéric walked to the Church of St. Thomas, hidden in a drab, concrete alley in East Jerusalem, across from a ceramic street sign that read "Nablus Road" in English, Arabic, and Hebrew and was pocked with bullet holes from the wars and uprisings that had passed since its installation. The church itself, looming like a fortress, was squeezed between a parking lot and a mom-and-pop grocery store named Che Guevara, and it had been built only two decades before, to replace a much older church that was destroyed in the fighting of 1948. It had very little to distinguish it in a city with some of the most famous churches on earth. Compared to Gethsemane, where Jesus spent his last hours before his arrest, and the Church of the Holy Sepulchre, where Jesus was crucified and raised from the dead, this church barely warranted mention.

Yet hidden within this modern building was one of the oldest spoken languages in the region—if not the world—and a remnant of Frédéric's former life. The Church of St. Thomas was the sole Syrian Catholic church in Jerusalem in which Christians still prayed in Syriac—a dialect of Aramaic, the language of Jesus. It was in this liturgy that Frédéric had worshipped during his three years in the Syrian desert, in one of a handful of communities—scattered throughout the Middle East and now almost extinct—that passed on, from generation to generation, the traditions deemed closest to those practiced by the earliest Christians and Jesus himself. And if there was one thing that Frédéric believed, it was that prophecy was bound up in the tiniest details of our lives, and that if we remained faithful to the events of the past, then they would always lead us, in some mysterious way, to what would happen to us in the future. In other words—Frédéric could only hope to move forward in his life by remaining faithful to his past.

As he entered the sanctuary, he took in a familiar vision: a church wafting with smoke and incense and the light from lines of candles burning in front of icons.

The congregation sang out in Syriac:

> *Qadishat aloho*
> *Qadishat qadishat*
> *Qadishat hayilthono*
> *Qadishat, qadishat*
> *Qadishat lo mo you tho*
> *Qadish, Qadish, Qadishat*
> *Ithiraham ilein*

Holy, holy, holy. As the mass finished, Frédéric, recognizing the bishop from his distinctive liturgical clothing, waited at the door for him to pass. He leaned down and kissed the ring on his hand and spoke to him in Arabic. The bishop, originally from northeastern Syria but having recently arrived in Jerusalem after years of living in Montréal, answered him in French. It was a promising start.

Frédéric carefully set out his case. He told the story of how he had arrived in a Syrian Catholic monastery in the deserts of Syria, where he had remained for three years, intent on becoming a monk. And there he would have stayed, for the rest of his life, had he not fallen in love. He spoke of the community he had left behind, of the abbot who had married us, and of the life he now hoped to live in

Jerusalem. He no doubt spoke as a man who had prayed in a monastery for three years and had been married for less than three months, so that it was not quite clear where he belonged.

The bishop listened.

At last, Frédéric posed his question:, "I was wondering if the church might know of some place where we could live?"

The bishop thought. He was a serious man, but he allowed himself to betray the barest hint of a smile. "There is a place, just down the road at the beginning of Nablus Road," he said. "It is an enormous old Arab house, owned by the Franciscans, but lived in by a group of religious brothers for twenty-three years." He paused. "I believe that they turned in their key yesterday."

The Bishop Sent Us

THE FOLLOWING MORNING, AN ELDERLY FRENCH NUN named Sister Pascal was waiting for us in front of the Franciscan convent to show us the house. Frédéric was perfectly at ease, but I had been married to a former novice monk for such a short period of time that I still felt nervous in the presence of clergy, as though they were store clerks looking at me like I might steal the merchandise. Sister Pascal was not helping matters. She was of that generation of nuns who still played the part with almost cinematic perfection, with her white hair closely cropped behind her ears and her face set in a mask of stern disapproval, so that she reminded me instantly of a particularly difficult fifth-grade math teacher named Sister Candice, who always tapped our desks with her ruler. Sister Pascal had placed the key to the house in the front pocket of her nun's smock, and every few seconds she removed it and weighed it heavily in her palm, to remind us that it was hers, before placing it back into her pocket again.

Frédéric took her frail hand. "*Bonjour, ma sœur,*" he greeted her.

"*Bonjour,*" she answered curtly.

"Shall we go?"

She turned and reluctantly led us down the street, steadfastly ignoring everyone we passed. "Normally the house is reserved for religious communities," she reminded us.

"The bishop sent us," Frédéric answered cheerfully.

"I heard." It was clear that this was the only reason she had consented to show us the house.

The three of us reached a gray metal door just a few meters down from the convent, hidden behind a man selling piles of sesame bread and balls of falafel. He looked up at us and nodded.

She turned the key and pushed open the door. Then we were inside, in an inner courtyard with a staircase ascending to the second story. Sister Pascal climbed the stairs carefully, pausing so as not to stumble on the Jerusalem stone that had worn away from more than a century of footsteps, shaded beneath a bougainvillea tree that littered the steps with bold, pink petals. Looking down from the top of the stairs, we could see a larger courtyard below, revealing a secret garden belonging to a community of Mexican nuns, with rows of lemon and orange trees and two long lines of pink rosebushes ringed in white stones, all hidden in the midst of one of the busiest streets of the city. On the garden's edge, a pomegranate tree was alive with red bulbs pressing up against the windowpanes. I had imagined encountering a house, but not an entire ecosystem.

We passed along the balcony until Sister Pascal led us through yet another set of doors. Then we were inside. I must have gasped at the size of it. At its heart stood a cavernous salon with an arch in the center and stone-rimmed windows on the sides, looking down at the street below. The ceilings were two stories high.

There are those moments in life when you allow yourself to hope for what is impossible: for an angel to appear on a train or a garden to reveal itself in the midst of a city street. For a house of light and space to arrive just when you need it most, with nothing more than a very stern French nun keeping you from grabbing hold of it.

We strolled from room to room. There were two ways of life molded into a single structure: the bygone ways of the old Palestinian Christian world with its grand stone houses, and the monastic life of the nuns who had been gifted the house and inhabited it earlier in the twentieth century. One grand receiving room led into another, only slightly smaller public room, which then led to a long and narrow hallway. On the sides of the hall, a series of tiny bedrooms sat clustered like boxes in a beehive, each one barely large enough to fit a bed and a dresser inside, cloisters for the nuns who had slept there long before. I felt their presence, still. At the end of the hall, a slight room of exposed stone must have once been a chapel. Next to it, a bedroom had been left entirely vacant, save for a mural still painted onto the wall of a turquoise sky, a sea of waves beneath it, and a boat set to sail.

"This room belonged to a Brazilian," Sister Pascal explained, clearly not amused by the spectacle of a sailboat set adrift on the walls of her property. For a moment, I could see the Brazilian too, in that house on a busy street, painting his dream of somewhere else.

The previous tenants had been six male members of the Focolare, a Roman Catholic movement, and though they had not officially been monks, they had nonetheless taken lifelong vows to serve the church. Their austerity was admirable but had done the house no favors. Rarely had I seen a house so badly in need of what my grandmother would call a "woman's touch." The doors had all been painted a utilitarian shade of gray, and the door handles would have been right at home in prison cells. When the front doorbell was pushed, a loud, echoing buzz rattled the entire house. The men had taken everything with them when they moved out, even the light sockets and the hooks in the walls, so that each wall was bruised with the evidence of what had recently been there.

Even still, it was not so much a house as a monastery in the world, complete with two salons, six bedrooms, a narrow kitchen with an attached breakfast room, and a single bathroom with two sinks, two toilets, and two showers. From the edge of the kitchen, a door led out to an immense roof terrace. I stood there with Frédéric and the disapproving Sister Pascal, and I could see the walls of the Old City just ahead and the majestic Damascus Gate, the houses of West Jerusalem in the near distance, the gardens of nuns below us on two sides, and finally, Nablus Road. The sky was studded with red roofs and laundry hung out to dry, tanks full of gasoline for the winter, folding chairs left out on terraces, and windows—an entire level of habitation existing just over the earth.

"It's much too big for two people," Sister Pascal remarked.

"I think we can manage," Frédéric assured her, and I smiled.

She was right, though—not so much that the house was too big, but that there was something unwieldy about it, too much for a couple to handle. There was a sense that the house would possess its owners, and not the other way around. When we returned to the salon, she pointed to a series of long, jagged cracks in the walls, to a dozen tiles lifting from the floor. Paint was peeling from two of the bedrooms, and long tubes of fluorescent lighting were hanging, exposed, from the ceiling. I would later suspect that the cracks dated back to the great Jerusalem earthquake of 1927 and had never been fixed.

"We were planning on renovating this year while it was empty," she lamented. "Now what will we do?"

"Why don't I help to renovate the house?" Frédéric suggested. I shot him a look. I had never known him to fix anything. He shrugged.

"We'll have to ask the Mother Superior in Jordan before we

know anything," she said. "It's her decision. Until then you'll just have to wait."

And then we left.

If I had learned anything from my years in the Middle East, it was that hope is a dangerous and fragile thing, something to be handled carefully. But that night, I allowed myself to hope for passing a few years in an impossible city, in rooms suspended over the earth. We gathered our bags from where we had been staying across town and moved into the guesthouse of the Franciscan Sisters, the nuns who owned the house, where we would stay until they gave us a response. We had decided that the best way to encourage them to give in was to force them to confront our poor, homeless faces every day at breakfast. Our room in the convent had two single beds with a desk and a crucifix between them, and I quietly removed the desk and pushed the beds together.

From the window of our room we could peer out at the house we hoped to rent next door: its rows of windows, the terrace overlooking gardens on each side, the thick stone walls that I knew concealed its many rooms.

That evening, an elderly Spanish nun named Sister Flores knocked on our door. She spoke French gently, with a thick Spanish accent, and had the air of an elderly grandmother who was coming to tuck us in.

She poised herself at the edge of the bed. "I hear that you want to live in the house next door," she began.

"It's a beautiful house," Frédéric answered.

She nodded. She was the kindest nun we had met so far, and yet she still seemed to be measuring us up. I was bewildered as to why these nuns were so suspicious of us. I did not yet know that we were moving into a neighborhood in which dozens of houses had been lost in wartime and never returned to their original owners, in which the act of allowing strangers to move into your home would be fraught with fear and historical memory.

She managed a look of encouragement and gently touched my shoulder.

"When will you know?" she asked.

"They need to ask the Mother Superior for permission," Frédéric said.

She sighed. Something in our conversation seemed to have drained her of her initial enthusiasm. "I see."

She wished us luck. When she reached the door, she turned around abruptly.

"Do you believe in the Holy Spirit?" she asked.

I was momentarily taken aback. It was Frédéric who answered. "Yes."

"Good," she snapped. "Then you'd better start praying now. That Mother Superior isn't easy."

———✦———

We waited for three days. In the same way that landlords ask potential new tenants for references, the nuns looked to the last house where Frédéric had lived for any length of time, which happened to be an ancient monastery in the Syrian desert. Unable to phone Syria directly from Jerusalem, they phoned instead a convent in Jordan, whose nuns phoned in turn Frédéric's former monastery to speak to Father Paolo. They informed him that his former novice had turned up in Jerusalem. He seemed pleased to hear this.

"Frédéric is a fine man," Paolo insisted. "No, he didn't leave in scandal. He met a nice girl, and I even married them myself. You can trust him... What? He said he'd fix the walls? No, as far as I know, he doesn't know how to fix anything."

The nuns in Jordan passed this news on to the Mother Superior.

That night, Sister Pascal knocked on our door. When we opened it, she was trying her best to conceal a mischievous smile.

"The Mother Superior called," she announced. "It seems that four years ago, when she was on pilgrimage in Syria, she decided to visit a desert monastery. She had to climb hundreds of steps in order to reach the monastery, and when she finally arrived, she was exhausted and thirsty."

She stopped for a moment and examined Frédéric. "She said that a young Frenchman who had just become a novice monk approached her. She still remembers him. He very kindly offered her a glass of tea."

The Opening and Closing of Windows

WE MOVED IN THE FOLLOWING DAY.

Since Frédéric had given most of his belongings to the poor and I had spent the last year living out of a suitcase, we were hardly prepared for the task of furnishing an entire house of many rooms. We possessed two highly sentimental bags between us: Frédéric's old traveler's backpack swelling with flutes and diaries and icons, mine with short dresses I had purchased in France but could never wear on Nablus Road, scraps of paper inscribed by friends I had left behind in Syria, and a carpet I thought I could not live without. There was not a pot or a cookbook between us.

Luckily, the Franciscan convent had been an orphanage earlier in the century, so the nuns were well prepared to take care of us. Sister Pascal led us to a storage room full of pea-green curtains, an ancient stove with a door that closed only with twine, several 1970s art deco tables in orange and lime green, egg cups for poaching eggs *à la coque*, forks and knives with plastic blue and white handles, two desks, threadbare sheets that had covered the bodies of hundreds of sleeping pilgrims, and several twin-sized beds with metal frames and old, sturdy mattresses designed to conjure in the brain nothing but discipline and prayer. Most of the items had clearly not seen the light of day since before the 1967 war.

"Whatever you want, it's yours," she announced.

So far, the only thing we had discovered in the house from its previous inhabitants was a bag full of wooden rosaries in one of the dresser drawers.

"We'll take everything," I responded.

We spent the rest of the afternoon dragging mattresses and old tables out the side entrance of their convent, through the rose garden and up the stairs to our front door. Soon the house was furnished with an assortment of mismatched green and orange tables and plastic-backed chairs that even the nuns knew were outdated. I hurried out in search of a bedouin woman I had seen sitting at the entrance to Damascus Gate, surrounded by desert plants, and came back laden with potted mint and thyme and a small bougainvillea tree, determined that, even if the house felt spare, at least it would be alive.

"How is it possible?" I asked Frédéric, heaving from lugging the mattresses up the stairs. "The more we fill it, the emptier the house becomes." We had somehow managed to obtain the clown car of ancient Jerusalem houses. "And there's no way we'll keep it clean."

Frédéric, accustomed by now to my anxiety, took my hand by way of answering.

I chose one of the six bedrooms and sat on the floor. A pigeon with a red breast stopped in the window frame and looked in. I dragged two mattresses from the salon onto the floor in front of her. The bird came and went and came again, until we closed the arched metal shutters and collapsed onto the floor in sleep: the first night we'd ever slept together in a home of our own.

Frédéric initiated the next morning—and every morning there-after—by walking the length of the house on the western side and opening the windows, one by one, to let the cool air in. For the first half of our day, we lived in that country facing west, sealed off from the noise of Nablus Road and the oppressive sun. On the western side, birds moved among the branches of an enormous tree that stood at the center of the Mexican convent's garden beneath us, every now and then breaking free and fluttering down onto our windowsills, and a Syrian woodpecker with his red tuft of feathers assumed his place high upon its trunk and began hammering. Beneath the tree, the nuns walked back and forth in their Alice-blue habits, the sound of their brooms *wshsh*, *wshsh*, *wshsh*ing against the courtyard floors.

Beyond the courtyard, a row of shops sold dried goods, pomegranates and dates, and whatever fruit was in season, and lambs hanging by their ankles in glass windows. In front of them, a parking lot had replaced the vacancy that used to be no-man's-land—the space dividing the city in half after dozens of houses had been razed following the 1948 war. Then the earth moved uphill, and we could see the first Israeli houses and the outer wall of the Old City lifting toward the New Gate.

In the late afternoon, the sun began to set, and Frédéric closed the windows on the western side to keep the heat out as the sun passed over. To let the house breathe new air, he opened all the windows on the eastern half, facing Nablus road, which by now had grown cooler. Up came the wind of our street, the smell of mint and *za'atar* spice, and with it voices—of our neighbors calling out greetings to one another in Arabic, of merchants singing out prices of hats and herbs and hot tea for sale, of shoppers in the grocery store beneath us, which also, somehow, occupied our house, as though a single building could be broken up into infinite compartments—and the noises of a truck emptying trash bins, of a car speeding past with its radio blaring Arabic *dabke* music, of a street that had been tread upon for more than two thousand years.

In time, I would come to think of Nablus Road as not entirely East or West but a country of its own, so weighed down with history that it seemed insincere to limit it to whatever nation it happened to find itself in during a particular moment. Even to call it a "road" seemed to limit it in time, for in the longer view it was not a road but a valley disguised as a road, still called *wadi* in Arabic, a paved-over gorge running through the center of a city built on hills. It was a natural barrier, with two different worlds rising on either side. Though the sides tried to keep separated, as the lowest point of gravity in the city, everything from both sides fell onto our street. When it rained, the water flooded down, both Hebrew and Arabic, and when it stormed, the wind formed a tunnel of air that howled through the night. Any direction in which we headed required us to climb, so that the smallest tasks of daily life required effort, and coming home was a kind of falling to the lowest possible place in the city and remaining there, both for the sake of being home and for the sake of not having to climb out again. So it was with people, with voices, and with birds, that they lived in all directions, and yet gravity urged them, at certain moments, to land at our front door.

———————

For days I kept awakening in the middle of the night, uncertain of what exactly had roused me. It had not escaped me that my husband had left the monastery only to move us into a convent, and during that first night, I felt uneasy with our proximity to the nuns below, as though they were part of a past he could not yet release. We dragged the mattresses to another room, where still, I slept fitfully. The shouting from the street below, on Nablus Road, reminded me of Damascus, so that I woke up disoriented. The following night, we moved again. We tried the rooms against the garden, the rooms against the street, the rooms abutting the ice-cream-truck doorbell. For a week, every night, we moved from room to room. Each room was different, so that it was too warm or too cold, too bright or too full of shadows—in a city where the ecosystem shifted not by street, but by centimeter. The rooms on the eastern side of the house were too loud, while the western rooms were burdened by their uneasy proximity to no-man's-land, that eerily silent scar, which even now carried the ghosts of those who had fled or died. Finally, after a week of moving from room to room, we dragged the mattresses to the room where we had started, with the bird at the window, facing the garden of orange and lemon trees, and settled there to stay.

At night, when Frédéric fell asleep, I looked at him, trying to recognize him. And, in his sleep, I could remember the man I first knew, tall and full of grace in a monastery in the clouds. The way he raced after children in the monastery courtyard, his robe lifting as he ran. His face catching the light. The way he disappeared into the paths of the desert as though he belonged to them. Leaning over to talk to birds. The way he could, so very quickly, break into laughter. And the way he always told me, gently: "Why would God give a man stones who asked for bread?"

POUR UN MOINE, QUITTER À JAMAIS SON MONASTÈRE NE PEUT ÊTRE QU'UN ACTE DE FOI, OU UNE FUITE.

FOR A MONK, TO LEAVE HIS MONASTERY FOREVER
CAN ONLY BE AN ACT OF FAITH, OR OF RUNNING AWAY.

Until then, it had only been waiting, an entire year of waiting. First I had thought that he would never leave the monastery, and there had been months of waiting to see if he would. Then there had been months of waiting to be married. Then the months of waiting to see where we would move next.

And now we had finally landed—not in his country, not in mine, but in a precarious landscape scarred by war. It was not, perhaps, what he had imagined.

I watched him, his sleeping body almost aglow in the faint light coming in through the window. Here was a man who had expected to spend the rest of his life sleeping in a small, stone cell in his monastery. A man who had convinced himself that leaving to marry me was his final, and greatest, act of obedience. I allowed a thought to surface that I had been carrying within me all of those months.

What if he had made a mistake?

It was early morning. I sensed a quiet trembling in the house: the call to prayer from the nearby Al-Aqsa Mosque inside of the Old City. It was the first time I'd heard it; though it would have called out five times every day, it must have been muffled by the noise of cars and feet and voices. Only now did it come—a whispering, a quiet singing beneath the floorboards of the house. It continued for a long, long time, so faint and so distant that it seemed to occupy the space between sleep and waking.

I left Frédéric's side and went to sit alone in the salon. Outside I could hear faint footsteps, answering the ritual of calling and being drawn into the half-light. The lantern outside turned on automatically each time someone passed by.

I sat in the dark. The prayers trembled beneath me. I watched as the room filled up with the flicker, flicker, flicker of passing men.

Borders

I HAD WILLED MYSELF NOT TO THINK TOO MUCH ABOUT the war between Israel and Lebanon still raging on the northern border. But a week after we arrived, it was still raging, and by now nearly a thousand people had died—many of them Lebanese women and children. Though the fighting would not come to Jerusalem, it was present in other, less visible ways, playing out on the border that was our street. The tension in the air was palpable. The Green Line, which now ran invisibly through our neighborhood, seemed to function in some way as a microcosm of the front lines of other distant battles, so that every struggle that happened to the Palestinians anywhere in the country would simultaneously find its way to our front door, as if our street were wired to react in resonance with the surrounding region's tensions. Young men would gather to protest or throw stones, or to pray if they were banned from entering the gates of the Old City.

The image of Damascus Gate became a fixture on the international news, and even when conflicts happened in other places, journalists would gather and interview the men passing on our street, near our front door, as though it were the same as traveling to the war itself. And there was something to their logic. From the bus stations on either side of our house emptied out passengers from separate corners of the region, from Ramallah and Bethlehem and Hebron, as they arrived in the city and headed to Al-Aqsa Mosque to pray, all of them funneling past our house, carrying their lost hopes and battles with them. Yes, our street was still a battlefield, in ways it would take me years to understand.

In time, I would determine that this was a city of tens of thousands of borders, where every inch of earth was accounted for, battled over, and protected fiercely. Our home was not exempt, and its border was marked precisely at the line of the door onto Nablus Road. Though the two steps in front of our door on Nablus Road technically belonged to us, the world had decided long before we arrived that they in fact belonged to Abu Hossam, the falafel seller who worked on the sidewalk in front of our house. He in turn had decided that they belonged to everyone else on the street, and he invited them to sit on the steps with the same hospitality that one usually uses to invite guests into the home. Abu Hossam had the full authority to make such grand decisions, because he was not just a falafel seller—in reality he was also a neighborhood leader who had taken hold of half the block, running with his eight children a sidewalk empire that included hawking hats, women's headscarves, baby socks, Coca-Cola, syrupy drinks, and walls and walls of stacked sesame bread in long, pale ovals, referred to in the local parlance as *kaak*. In the morning, after Frédéric served our tea, I would walk down the outside stairs that connected our second-story house to the lower courtyard and open the door to find Abu Hossam already in front of it, assembling rows of sesame bread.

"*Ahlan!*" he would announce, welcoming me to his steps.

"*Ahlan.*"

I would then attempt to hand him money for sesame bread, which he would refuse.

"*Khaliha a'lay,*" he'd insist, "Take it as an offering from us."

We would argue back and forth until I gave up and let him give me the bread for free. Local custom dictated that I should let this continue for three days, but three days turned into four and then six and then a week, and I was still helpless to stop it, held hostage by the hospitality of this falafel vendor, who seemed to take particular delight each morning in welcoming me to my own front steps.

"*Selem,*" he would call as I closed the door, imploring me to send his greetings to my husband and anyone else who might need to be blessed.

The front steps to our house were rarely the same any two days in a row, or even any two hours in a row, and I had to build up courage just to open the front door and discover what might be waiting for me there. In the very early morning, the bakery would make deliveries of sesame bread before anyone arrived on the street, so that if I tried to go outside before Abu Hossam took his post, I would be confronted with a tall wall of bread rings on old wooden trays, stacked several layers high and blocking my exit. Since there was no way to move them, I was stuck inside until someone came to my rescue. A few hours later, if I descended again, the bread would be gone, but instead I would often find two or three old, whiskered men sitting on the step, leaning up against the front door, drinking coffee—perturbed by the fact that by opening the door, I effectively removed the back of their chairs. The first few times I interrupted them, they apologized profusely and made way for me, and Abu Hossam at least pretended to admonish them for being in my way. But after a few days, there were no more apologies, and it became clear enough that the step, by some unspoken consensus, had become the neighborhood front porch, like those of old southern houses in America, where neighbors sit and greet all who pass by. In fact, as far as the street was concerned, it wasn't that those two steps were in the way of our house, but that our house was in the way of those two steps. In the afternoons, women out shopping would pile their heavy bags up against the door to retrieve later. On the left-hand corner of the top step, Abu Hossam kept a steady flame from a small yellow gas tank going, on which he made rotating cups of coffee for workers on the street, as well as an afternoon meal shared by other vendors, who huddled shoulder to shoulder on those same steps, passing sesame bread among themselves.

A few days into our stay, I descended the stairs to find a tough young boy with thick, gelled black hair standing beside the falafel stand, talking nonchalantly to one of Abu Hossam's sons while a giant snake made itself comfortable around his neck. Like the steps, the snake also belonged to the entire neighborhood; later that afternoon it appeared on a different teenage neck farther down the street, and then wrapped around a man waiting to receive a haircut in the corner barbershop. The snake was later replaced by a neighborhood parrot that was so popular that they hung a white sheet from the entrance to Schmidt-Schule across the street, where brave pedestrians could have their photo taken, for a few coins, with the parrot on their shoulder.

The outside world was not so much hostile as it was unpredictable, an amalgam of bread walls, circus animals, curious neighbors, war, and other people's groceries. Abu Hossam, the falafel seller who was unknown to us save for our daily exchange of bread, nonetheless assumed the role of our official spokesman, taking it upon himself to explain our presence to the neighborhood. As I descended and ascended the stairs, I would hear him lecturing to crowds of local shoppers assembled around the front porch, as though describing a rare species of bird to a hiking group in the Amazon:

"She and her husband are from the Catholic church. They speak Arabic. They are from somewhere in Europe." And for the moment, at least, that seemed enough to satisfy them.

Once I could get past how unfamiliar it all was, I came to appreciate the beautiful messiness that was our street. One could find blenders and tea sets, cheap carpets with pictures of Mickey Mouse or tigers on them, dancing dolls, year-old chocolate coins left unsold from Hanukkah on the other side of town sold at a deep discount, Islamic cookbooks, and long rows of old, cast-off, second-hand shoes. Bedouin women sold mint and wild spinach from mesh bags, and a blind man held out his hand and begged for coins, shouting out:

"May God bless your daughter."

"May God bless your son."

"May God bless you."

Over and over, in summoning and in gratitude.

Spies

THOSE FIRST DAYS, AS TWO SOLITARY PEOPLE UNACCUStomed to living in the world, we often arrived at the end of the afternoon to discover that we had no food in the house. After a few days of this, I became determined to at least accomplish one task each day: to simply venture a few streets over to buy vegetables. It might seem like buying vegetables should not warrant mention, but a great many of the dramas that happen in the Middle East begin with the simple intention of leaving the house to buy vegetables. Anyone who has lived in the region for any amount of time has become so scarred by these stories that they approach even the simplest tasks with odd, existential dread. The stories are all the same: a woman leaves her house to buy vegetables and is killed by a bomb or hit by a car, or she tries to return and discovers that there is a checkpoint that she can no longer cross between the vegetable stand and her house, or that in her absence the vegetable stand has been declared to be in another country, or that her brothers have been arrested, or that some other unimaginable horror has occurred that could have been avoided entirely had she had the foresight to simply not go outside and buy vegetables that day. I could imagine a fitting tombstone epitaph: "She was full of promise, and then she went to buy vegetables."

Nevertheless, I was off to buy vegetables. It was a hot September afternoon as I parted the crowd on the front step and made my way to a vegetable stand two blocks to the east, where two very conservative Muslim men with long beards and clothing in the Salafi style were busy arranging mangoes in heaping piles. On a radio, they were listening to Hassan Nasrallah, the leader of Hezbollah, speaking in Lebanon about the ongoing war, so that his voice cried out over lemons and apples, dates and pomegranates.

I selected cucumbers, tomatoes, avocados. I approached one of the men and asked in Arabic how much it cost. He jumped back in surprise.

"Are you Syrian?" he asked me.

I had been aware that my accent might betray that I had lived in Syria and learned most of my Arabic there, but I wasn't expecting it to happen with two words.

"No, but I lived in Syria."

"I swear by God, you speak just like a Syrian," he said, laughing.

"*Likan!*" I answered, "Yes, of course!"

He thought for a moment and then asked, "Which is more beautiful, Jerusalem or Syria?"

I looked at him blankly, briefly stunned. It was an innocent question, but something about it had caught me off guard. I tried to regain my composure. "They're different," I lied. "There are beautiful things here and beautiful things in Syria."

He sadly shook his head and looked at the ground. "*Suria ahle*," he pronounced, his voice lingering on the second word. "Syria's more beautiful."

And he was right.

It was 2006, and Syria was more beautiful. There were no soldiers in the pedestrian streets holding guns, and the shops stayed open late into the night, when warm half-moons of chocolate croissants would emerge from ovens. Strangers constantly asked visitors to tea, and to dinner, and to stay in their homes. The custom of the local dialect was to be overly kind—so that beat-up old cars were compared to princesses, women compared to stars. I remembered the evening call to prayer from the Umayyad Mosque, down the street from my old home: three voices threaded together, descending the stone stairs and walking across the roofs, whispering through the windows.

We had barely arrived in Jerusalem, but already it seemed that Damascus Gate held little in common with the city it was named after. Nablus Road, which had once been the departure point for journeys from my house here, all the way to my former home in Syria, was now tied up with walls and barriers and checkpoints, UN soldiers, and countries at war with one another. Something had been lost in the interim, and little of the lightness I had come to expect from the rest of the Arab world was on display here. East Jerusalem, and Damascus Gate in particular, wore its toughness aggressively on its sleeve. Everything was charged. Here was a city that could make you tired just from walking through it.

The man told me the price of my vegetables, giving me a discount because I spoke Arabic like a Syrian, and I walked the two blocks home. Two young boys passed me and taunted me in the street—calling *"Shalom! Shalom!"*—mistaking me for an Israeli who they clearly felt had no business walking in their neighborhood. It seemed that I was always reminding people of somewhere else.

I missed Syria then. I wondered if I had made a mistake by so quickly dismissing Frédéric's suggestion that we return. It was hardly perfect—a land where citizens and visitors alike lived under the constant surveillance of the secret police, where all of the movies at the cinema were censored, where I was judged as a member of an enemy state. But that wasn't really why I had been reluctant to go back. It was more that I could not summon up the courage to return to a place where people used to run across the street to kiss my husband's hand because he had once been a novice monk. If I were more honest with myself, I would admit that I could not return to a place where the beauty of his past would always be measured against what I could offer him in the present.

Yet in saying no to Damascus, I had also said no to the bazaars—Ottoman houses converted into cafés, pistachio ice cream, boxes made of inlaid wood—to Father Paolo, and to easy access to Lebanon and Jordan. When we decided to move to Jerusalem, I had thought only of whether, after living in Syria, they would let us in. Only now did I understand that they had let us in, but as a result we could never easily go back.

In Lebanon and Syria, Jerusalem had always been described as paradise, a city longed for by the millions who could not access it. It had not occurred to me that for those in Jerusalem, paradise might be imagined to be on the other side. There was an Arabic expression for this: *everything that is forbidden is desired*. I did not yet understand much about Jerusalem. But I did know that being here meant severing ourselves from entire worlds we had previously inhabited—cutting ourselves off from belonging to the rest of the Middle East. The border to Syria was closed. The northern border to Lebanon was at war. Forty years ago, we could have hopped in a car and driven to Damascus that very afternoon. Depending on traffic, it may have taken three hours, the same as it used to take someone from Jerusalem to drive to Beirut or to enjoy dinner beside the sea in Byblos.

I had been waiting in vain for the neighbors on Nablus Road to invite us to tea, but so far it had not happened. There were other small details from life in Damascus that I missed already: there, when you asked a stranger for directions, he almost always left his work and walked you himself. It seemed that no task was so important that it could not be dropped in favor of human contact.

But here, my mere presence on the street seemed to be met with suspicion, and I had the sense that we were not wanted. No one was talking to us. Everyone was watching us.

"I think the neighbors might think that we're spies," I finally told Frédéric.

"They don't think that we're spies."

"Why not? I would. We look like Europeans, we speak Arabic like Syrians, and we moved into their neighborhood in the middle of a war."

"You're making movies in your head. Where did you come up with this idea?"

This was a typical Frédéric expression. Other people imagine things. But we Americans make movies in our heads.

"Why don't they ever invite us for dinner?" I challenged him. "Or for tea? No one is inviting us to anything."

"It's going to be different here," Frédéric answered. "You can't be in conflict for this long without becoming closed in on yourself. People are more suspicious. And they have reason to be."

There are few more frustrating moments in a first year of marriage than when one's husband is perfectly reasonable and absolutely correct.

I remembered Hassan Nasrallah's speech drifting over the mangoes. "I thought that the whole point of coming here was to move to a place that would feel more familiar than France. But this doesn't feel familiar at all. I mean, do you see how many children are playing with plastic guns? And they're not even normal plastic guns. They're some kind of Russian-made machine guns. I didn't even know that toys like that existed."

He held me, in a room on the seam of two countries. "These kids have lived with war their whole lives. We'll just have to be patient."

"I know. I guess I just didn't realize how hard it would be."

The next day, exhausted from Nablus Road, I climbed the long hill from our street to Jaffa Road in West Jerusalem. I just wanted to travel to a landscape where no one would notice me. Because the city was essentially two countries, I wore modest clothes for the space of a few blocks passing through conservative East Jerusalem. When I reached the top of the hill, I took off my scarf and cardigan and put them in my bag, allowing my bare arms to be exposed to the sun of what was effectively another country. Now I ambled through a country of coffee shops and outdoor cafés, with menus written in Hebrew and English—a country that, at first glance, was more Brooklyn or Berlin than Cairo. A few minutes later, I arrived at the entrance to Mahane Yehuda, the sprawling outdoor market crowded with religious Jews in long black coats with dark hats, Iraqis and Kurds and Yemenis and Moroccans, young Israeli hipsters in cafés, and old men from Baghdad playing backgammon in a hidden courtyard. It was one of those Jerusalem curiosities, a place where you could find Moroccan pickled lemons, real Iranian barberries, Russian pork sausages, and Ethiopian lentils—a testament to the diversity of Jewish people who had immigrated to the city over the course of a century. I bought two baguettes, a log of French chèvre, and Italian gnocchi, and I held them to my chest like some absurd comfort as I made my way home.

I was crossing the threshold into my neighborhood, into the heart of East Jerusalem, when I noticed the Hebrew letters on all of the grocery bags that I carried, advertising that I had slipped into the other side. I tried to fold one bag into another in order to conceal them. I panicked. Perhaps my neighbors would suspect that I was secretly Israeli and living among them, a common concern for them as more and more settlers took over houses in East Jerusalem. I pressed the bags against my body, hastily said hello to Abu Hossam, fussed with my key in the lock until it mercifully caught, and made my way up the long staircase and home again. I was exhausted from living in a place where everything was political, even where you buy your cheese.

That evening, I was boiling water for the gnocchi and found that I had forgotten salt. I ran down to a grocery store not far from the house, passing on the way Abu Hossam, who nodded his greeting in a way that made me feel, for a moment, that he knew everything.

As I browsed the aisle of dried goods, I noticed something peculiar. Much of what was stocked in this Palestinian grocery store, in the most nationalist area of the city, was labeled in Hebrew. A large section of the store was dedicated to Israeli products: Israeli cookies and Israeli juices, Coca-Cola written out in Hebrew letters. Confused, I bought Israeli salt and made my way back home.

I was accustomed to a world where borders marked the lines of wars, but in Jerusalem it appeared that the borders kept moving and changing shape. In cities like Tripoli in Lebanon and Damascus, Israeli products did not exist. Some Arab shops specifically boycotted products that they perceived to be tied to Israel in any way. As a young journalist, I had once covered the story of a Kentucky Fried Chicken in Lebanon that was bombed because it was thought to represent American culture. I tried to make sense of the fact that in parts of the Arab world, people were engaging in protests against

Israel as an act of solidarity with Palestinians, but that in Jerusalem, Palestinian shops stocked Israeli products. Clearly, this was partly because Israel controlled much of what was exported from and imported into the city, leaving shopkeepers with little choice, but that was not the only reason; in several instances, the Arab and Israeli brands of the same product pushed up against each other on the shelves, side by side. I could not make sense of it. These were not enemies as I had come to think of them. The lines were blurred. Many of the Palestinians on my street could speak some Hebrew, and it was not uncommon to hear a Palestinian speaking Hebrew on the phone, or deciphering for a neighbor a bill from the Israeli electric company. Some of these neighbors, during more peaceful times, had worked in Israeli hotels, in two worlds that merged and unmerged like tides, depending on the weather. The city seemed to exist in contradiction: in some respects, the boundary between two worlds was clear, but in others, it was impossible to understand where one world ended and the other began.

And the next day, I did not understand when two Israeli soldiers with their guns, stationed in the middle of my street to monitor potential unrest, took their lunch break in the early afternoon. They headed to the Palestinian falafel stand just around the corner, rifles and all, where they stood at the counter and calmly took their lunch, chatting with each other among the Palestinian patrons, before paying their bill and returning to their posts.

Abu Hossam

IT HAD NOT BEEN IMMEDIATELY APPARENT TO US WHEN we moved to Nablus Road that we were moving to a shady border town, hidden in the guise of a city street. But the neighbors knew this very well, and Abu Hossam, by virtue of his location in front of our house, soon appointed himself our protector. By the laws of the street, we were now an extension of him and his family. Anyone who harmed us harmed him. The endless rings of free sesame bread he offered us every morning were not only a small kindness, but also a reminder that, though he had only a tiny falafel cart on wheels and we had eleven rooms, it was we who were guests in his house.

There was a timeless quality about Abu Hossam that made it impossible to ascertain how old he was—he could have been anywhere from forty-five to sixty-five, and his face was both battle-hardened and kind, with graying hair and a moustache, leathery skin, and eyes that looked in need of sleep but nonetheless crinkled around the corners, almost reluctantly, when he smiled. He did not speak often, but when he did it was in a thick Hebronite accent and with absolute and total authority. When I'd pass his cart on the way into the house, he would relay information. "It's going to rain this afternoon," he would announce, or, "A *khamsin* is on its way," referring to the dust storms that blew into the city several times a year. If I returned in the afternoon, he would inform me, "Your husband just left the house ten minutes ago," or, "A nun from next door just came by to see you. I told her that you would be back around three o'clock."

I would not have told Abu Hossam that I would be back at that time. He just possessed a sixth sense and was able to determine what time it would rain, how the weather was changing, and if children would fall sick. On days when there were skirmishes between locals and the Israeli army on our street, I would descend the stairs to find his falafel stand locked, as though he had predicted that such a thing might happen.

And so, in a city where we had no family, Abu Hossam took on the role of my father, as if I were a child, inspecting me as I left the door, reinspecting me when I came home.

"Your bag is open."

"It's too cold to be outside."

"It's going to be windy."

"*Deer balik.*" Take care of yourself.

———————

Beside Abu Hossam's cart, a slightly chubby man stood in front of his shop, and I regularly noticed him observing me and making mental notes as I entered the street. Finally, I descended the steps one day to find him waiting. He had clearly been anticipating making his grand entrance into my life.

"You're new here?" he asked in perfect English.

"Yes."

"I'm Michel," he said, offering his hand.

"Stephanie," I answered, shaking his hand with a bit of confusion, since no one in this part of the world said hello like that, especially to a woman.

Behind him, I could see a store stocked with an array of objects selected seemingly at random: vegetable peelers and plaques with verses of the Quran, staples and coffee cups, plastic toy trucks and toilets for toilet training, notebooks and Tupperware and Christmas tree decorations.

"What are you doing here?" he asked.

"I moved here with my husband."

"From where?"

"I'm from America."

"You moved into the house of the Focolare?"

"Yes."

He nodded. "I used to go there sometimes and drink tea. They had these chairs that were made out of tree trunks and you could sit on them. Except now, of course, it is too hot to sit outside."

"I see."

"Do you still have the chairs made of tree trunks?"

"No, they took them with them."

He sighed. "Oh, that's too bad. They were really nice chairs."

———❖———

The shops outside were built into the wall of the street itself, so that they curiously became part of the landscape. Our house had been on the street for such a long time that the bottom of it had been incorporated into the wall of the street as well, with the lowest part of it serving as a grocery shop. The effect was that everything felt separate but interconnected, like a honeycomb, and the neighbors slowly worked their way into the intimacy of our lives, much as their noises siphoned into the air of our rooms when we awakened in the morning.

A week after our first meeting, Michel stopped me again. His shop fell at a particular angle so that if he intersected me, I would be trapped between him and Abu Hossam's falafel stand, with no way of accessing the street.

"Are you part of a religious community?" he demanded.

"No. We just rent from nuns."

"So, are you Muslim or Christian?"

"Christian."

"Really?" He sounded suspicious.

"Really."

"Well then, say the Our Father."

I could not believe that I was being interrogated in front of my own house.

"Seriously?"

"You said that you're Christian!"

Dutifully, I stood in the street and chanted the Our Father in Arabic, thankful that I had passed enough time in a monastery in the desert to know it by heart.

"*Abana, alladhi fi as-samawat...*"

"Okay, okay." He looked briefly satisfied, but then appeared to change his mind; perhaps he thought I could have memorized it just to trick him. "Well then, do you know anything about Islam?"

"I studied it."

"Well then, say the Fatiha."

This was absurd. I took a deep breath and began to recite the opening chapter of the Quran:

"*Bismillah al-Rahman al-Rahim…*"

He quickly interrupted me. "I thought you said that you were Christian!"

"I *am* Christian!" I had fallen for his trap.

"What kind of Christian?" Everything here, even Christianity, was broken into families.

"Roman Catholic."

"Well then, say the Nicene Creed." Great. He was asking for the Christian profession of faith adopted at the Council of Nicaea in the year 325.

"Are you kidding me? I can't say that in Arabic."

He sighed. "Okay. Then say it in English."

This time I was thankful for all of those years of Catholic school. "I believe in one God, the Father, the Almighty, maker of heaven and earth…"

He dismissed me with a brush of his hand, as if he couldn't bear the sound of it in English, and then began to recite it in Arabic. "*N'oumin b'illahi wahid…*"

"Now you're just showing off," I accused him, and he laughed. "And you? What are you?" I challenged.

"What do you mean?" he scoffed, apparently offended that I had asked the very same question he had just asked me. Just then a street sweeper came by and leaned on his broom. "Speak to her in Arabic!" he scolded Michel. "I heard her earlier. She speaks Arabic like a parrot!"

I had no idea that the street sweeper knew me well enough to have formed an opinion of me. Michel waved his hand to brush him off and leaned in with a conspiring tone in his voice. "I prefer to speak to you in English so that no one else will understand me. So what was I saying?"

"You were telling me what you are."

"Well, *you know*." He waved his hand dismissively.

I did not know. I had no idea what he was talking about.

"I used to be Greek Orthodox. But then I like going to the other churches. Sometimes I go to the Greek Catholic. Sometimes to the Syrian Catholic church. It depends, you know, on what I feel like. I just don't like to go to the Evangelical church. Have you seen that church down the road? They have all of those Koreans. I've heard strange things about them."

From then on, I had to navigate both Abu Hossam and Michel on my way out the front door. Abu Hossam provided the weather report. Michel was more complicated. He stopped me nearly every morning, as if he had been waiting for years for someone with whom he could speak English to show up. I was writing a book? Well, it didn't sound very interesting. Did I know that there were flies that came into the back of his shop? It was terrible, really, the result of plants from the side of our building climbing up into his shop windows. Could Frédéric and I talk to the nuns about it and make them take those plants down? Where did we go to church? Were we missionaries? You know there had been missionaries on the street. They handed out verses from the Bible, and people threw them on the ground and into the trash. One local woman was so appalled to see the Bible on the sidewalk that every day she walked up and down the street, gathering the pieces. Had I ever seen her?

So I settled into the street, and I slowly became familiar with the logic of a one-street village with thousands of visitors who passed through daily. I could say nothing, wear nothing, or feel nothing without it being noticed by the neighbors and pocketed as potential information, something that might help them make sense of these two strangers who had moved into their territory.

And within the house, Frédéric and I were watching each other, also as two strangers—every day a little less strange—grabbing any scrap of information so that our life together might become a bit less complicated.

———◆———

My dearest Joseph, I have not told you much about those first weeks in Jerusalem with your father. It's hard to know what to say about the beginning of married life. Before I met him, I had lived in relationships much as I had lived in houses, moving between them, from country to country. I was terrified—that compared to all that he had given up to be with me, I would disappoint him, that an ordinary life, among vendors and plants and sesame bread, could never measure up to the holiness in which he had lived in the desert.

Rainer Maria Rilke once said, "Love consists in this, that two solitudes protect and touch and greet each other." Still, I was not prepared for how lonely falling in love would be, for being put in front of the vast fields of foreignness contained in the one you want to be closest to. There was something in how far I felt from him that was parallel with how foreign I felt in the world we now inhabited, a strangeness from both within and without. More than once, the words of Paolo echoed in my head: "Stephanie, do not think that this will be easy."

And I was just as scared that he would discover me, and that I wouldn't be the same woman he'd imagined he'd met in the desert. I may as well tell you this now, because, in my experience, this is the secret of marriage that no one wants to talk about—that you look at another human being and understand that he contains an entire world, full of trees and roads and turning points, languages and birthmarks and doubts, and moments of despair, and that it might take a lifetime for you to even approach that world. I am guessing that perhaps not all men are that mysterious, but I had not married all men, just your father, and he was a country unto himself. I was scared that I would never know him completely. I felt haunted and still somehow touched by the words of the poet Czeslaw Milosz, who wrote of his wife of more than forty years, after she died: "I loved her, without knowing who she really was."

I loved your father, without knowing who he really was.

I was also not entirely sure who I was, either.

Even when two people hold each other, a border passes between them. I watched your father across this border. He seemed to be getting used to the inhabited world—accustomed as he was to living on the top of a mountain, some fallen bird trying to find his bearings. After the desert, he seemed alarmed to be in a world of so many *things*.

And I came to accept that even though it took him only one afternoon to descend from his monastery, in reality it would take much longer to leave it behind—years perhaps, a fact that I remembered whenever I came upon another pair of rosary beads in his pockets when I did the laundry, or discovered him up early in the morning, sitting in a quiet corner of the house in prayer.

That November, your father left for a week on a religious retreat. I found myself living alone again for the first time since our wedding, walking between the empty rooms, trying to fill them.

In the grocery store beneath the house, I placed instant noodles, spaghetti, and jars of tomato sauce into a basket.

"*This* is what you cook for your husband?" the shopkeeper scolded me when I went to pay. Imad manned the store with his father, his younger brother, and assorted youth from the street who moved boxes and measured out blocks of white cheese and ladles of olives, like a mom-and-pop affair from the 1950s.

"Frédéric is out of town," I responded.

He sighed in exaggerated relief. I had spared him the scandal of knowing that I was preparing noodles and canned sauce for my husband's dinner.

"When is he coming back?"

"In a few days."

"Where did he go?"

"On retreat."

"Ahhh." He winked. "On retreat."

I scowled at him. In what world was it okay for my neighbor the grocer to suggest that my husband was having an affair? I was tempted to tell him that if my husband were in love with someone else, then that someone else was God.

Still, I did not easily forget what he had said.

That night, I sat in the empty house, settled on a very crowded space on the earth, to take stock of what had happened to my life in the twelve months since Frédéric had left the monastery and we had boarded that train. I remembered a dream I'd once had in the monastery, when I was contemplating becoming a nun, of my childhood piano, passed on from my grandmother, an enormous grand piano of worn wood and old keys. In the dream, I heard a voice say: "You cannot take the piano with you."

——◆——

Your father had passed through the knowledge of all that he could not take with him into the monastery. And on returning to this world, the hardest thing to give up, in the end, was not things, but his poverty—the freedom of being unbound to anyone but God. Being married had obliged him to be attached, once again, to the world and what was in it. To be attached to me. I sometimes wondered if he could bear being bound to the earth.

Because the shopkeeper was right: he was still in love with the monastery, even if he was also in love with me. And what I had told the neighbors was not true. He was not on retreat. He had traveled to Syria, using his new, clean passport to visit his old monastery in the desert, to see his best friend Rana be ordained a nun—in the ceremony that had been meant to be his own ordination into the monastic life. They had been so close that when he decided to leave the monastery, she had been angry—not that he was leaving, but that he had kept a secret from her.

She had traveled all the way to our wedding in France, and now Frédéric had promised her that he would not miss the equivalent of her wedding day, in spite of the risk of traveling between enemy countries. So he had gone. He was there, visiting his past life, and I had remained here, visiting my past life.

I missed him. Even if I still didn't know entirely who he was.

I had expected marriage to be a leap. Instead, it had turned out to be a total migration—like the story of Abraham, leaving everything for a promise of a blessing still far off, or that of Mary, saying yes to an angel, without having any idea of what that yes meant. I had not known this when we caught that train in Syria—that both of us were leaving our former lives, perhaps forever, for a future that promised something that we could not yet see.

It had taken such courage that I had not allowed myself to think about all that I'd left behind. But now the eleven rooms of the house were empty, and they began to fill with images from my past. I sat by the window and wrote them down.

I had left a language.

I had left my family. Friends.

I had left embracing my father at the bottom of the stairs.

I had left certain blue flowers that came into season in Texas every spring.

I had left skirts that came to the knee, and exposed shoulders.

I had left libraries of books I could choose at random.

I had left the ease of ordering in restaurants, of reading street signs, of not bearing the burden of translating an entire world. I had left a life in which I knew the names of the most intimate and random objects: doorknob, corkscrew, glass shard, light socket, filament, dust mite.

It struck me that, even if I spent the rest of my life in the Arab world, I would never learn to say *grain of sand*, or be able to describe the equivalent of *paint chipping* or *color bleeding*, that the time in my life in which I could absorb such obscurities in another tongue had passed. Now I would inhabit a world far less precise.

I had not become a nun. And yet, still, I could not take the piano with me.

———————

I awakened the next morning to the faint bells in the garden below. There was no reason to hurry out of bed. When I finally roused myself and went to the kitchen, Frédéric was not there with my morning cup of tea. The house was out of balance, and I could not remember which windows to open and which ones to close.

I went to make breakfast, only to discover that the insistent hum of the refrigerator had gone silent. The food would spoil quickly. The mere act of telling the neighboring nuns that the refrigerator had broken would require me to speak French, which I could not do. I picked up the phone and dialed the number, stumbling in my few words of French, then restated the problem in English, and then a final time in Arabic, hoping that they might understand enough from one of the three versions to send a repairman.

Twenty minutes later, he rang downstairs. I descended the staircase and opened the door onto Nablus Road. The meeting of men on the front step of my house looked at the repairman, looked at me, and then shook their collective heads in disapproval. As a woman whose husband was out of town, it was a scandal that I should let in a man who was not a relative.

"He's fixing the refrigerator," I explained desperately. I could hear them clucking as he mounted the stairs.

For a moment, I stood on the stairs, beneath the bougainvillea raining petals, exhausted, before mounting and letting him in. The man fixed the refrigerator as quickly as he could and hurried out the door.

When I heard the door bolt shut, I sat on the stairs with my face in my hands. I had lost a great deal by that small miscalculation. Next time I would know better, and I would let the food spoil. It was only food, after all. It was easier to replace than so many other things I was trying to keep.

The Man
of the House

FRÉDÉRIC RETURNED FROM SYRIA MORE SETTLED TO THE earth. It was as though he had simply needed to make sure that the monastery still existed and had not disappeared while we were away.

I had a sense that Father Paolo had shifted also, that he had finally come to accept that we were married for good and that we wouldn't miraculously find ourselves back in his monastery as a monk and a nun. Soon after Frédéric's return, strangers began stopping by the house on Nablus Road to say hello, to ask for a bed to sleep in, or to deliver a letter.

Each of them would say the same thing: "When Father Paolo heard I was coming to Jerusalem, he said that I should knock and find you here."

I would arrive home at the end of the afternoon to Abu Hossam pointing out letters taped to our front door by strangers passing through—Paolo's way of telling us that he had not forgotten us. In a world of such separation, I held onto these envelopes and scribbled messages as consolation, as hope.

In the meantime, Frédéric took a job at the English-language bookstore of the American Colony Hotel, the iconic Jerusalem hotel

originally built for a pasha and his four wives and later acquired in
the nineteenth century by the Christian family that founded the
American colony of Protestants settling in the Holy Land. Now
perhaps the most luxurious hotel in the city, decorated in colorful
ceramic tiles and adorned with fountains, it was not the type of
place I had anticipated Frédéric would find work. But he was rarely
predictable, and the fact that he did not read in English did not stop
him from confidently striding into the bookstore and asking for a job.
He had a self-assurance about him from his years in the monastery
that seemed to encourage people to take his advice, in matters of life
and in books, and soon he did a brisk business selling travelogues,
fiction, and books of political analysis to diplomats and journalists
who passed through. In the afternoons when he returned home, he
would ask for my suggestions and then push those tomes fervently,
so that he must have sold half the city *Ali and Nino*, an obscure novel
by Kurban Said that takes place in Baku, Azerbaijan. When the heat
kept customers at home, he would sit alone for long spells, interrupted every now and then when a total stranger would come and
asked him for advice. It was not unlike the monastic life.

I would sit in my office and write draft after draft of my first
book, about the year I spent living in Syria, and as I would close
my eyes and remember the men calling out from the streets outside
my home near Straight Street in Damascus, they would converge
with the voices calling out from Damascus Gate, so that I sometimes
had difficulty distinguishing where one world ended and the other
began. In the evenings, we would reconvene at home, just in time to
close the windows on the western side and open up the windows to
the east, to the let the voices in.

Frédéric and I had lived in the house for a month before the
Alice-blue habits that skirted across the garden beneath us finally

properly introduced themselves. The tiny community of Spanish- .
speaking nuns also rented from the French nuns next door, and one
morning Maria, the Mother Superior of the community, invited
us to tour the bottom half of our own house, which happened to
be their convent. The house had taken such hold of us that it felt
like finally being reconciled to the other half of ourselves. Their
rooms circled a garden of roses and fruit trees hedged in by stones.
Maria, at first stern in her habit, led us to their chapel, where she
showed us the Eucharist contained in a compartment behind the
altar. Catholics consider the Eucharist—or Blessed Sacrament—to
be the body of Christ.

"He's the man of the house," she said, pointing and trying to
keep a straight face. It was a very Catholic joke.

We were ambling in the garden among the rose bushes when she
turned serious. "We were relieved when we learned a family would be
moving upstairs," she said. "We were scared to be alone in the house."
Maria lived with two other nuns from Mexico, and none of them
spoke a word of Arabic. I thought of the sound of their brooms, the
faint twinkling of their bells holding us in place. Perhaps, in the end,
we balanced each other.

I mentioned to Maria that I had grown up in San Antonio, and
that Spanish was my mother's first language. From then on, the sisters
greeted me in Spanish every time we crossed one another at the bottom
of the stairs. We had decided that the sisters owned the entrance to the
house, while we owned the stairs. So they dutifully swept the entrance
every morning, and I let the stairs go wild, so that pink bougainvillea
petals marked the border between us.

"¡Buenos días!" Maria would sing out every morning at eight o'clock.

"¡Buenos días!" I would sing back. And for a moment I would be
carried back to childhood afternoons with my mother's family in San

Antonio, and the vision of her pressing the moons of tortillas beneath her palms, speaking in a mysterious language I could barely understand.

And so it was that our street revealed itself to carry traces of distant homes. During the British Mandate, the convent next door, called the Franciscaines de Marie, taught a generation of young Palestinian women to sew, insisting that they only speak in French. Though the sewing machines and pupils were long gone, the nuns, hailing from Malta and Spain, France and Lebanon, still spoke to one another largely in French. When Frédéric would go next door to pay the rent, he would enter into his native country, complete with its former colonies.

"Bonjour, ma sœur. Ça va?"

"Bonjour, Frédéric! Est-ce que vous êtes contents dans votre maison?"

Watching him, I had the impression of glimpsing a man in exile who had spoken in his native language for just an instant—and who, for a moment, was home again.

That is how we found ourselves, in a far-off country, but with the languages of southern Texas and the French Alps—and the daily reminders of a monastery in Syria—mysteriously in the background of each moment, inhabiting the spaces around us, and lingering within our eleven rooms.

It was not the Metropolitan Museum of Art, but it was something.

Palimpsest

As the war slowly faded into the background of our daily lives, I found the courage to venture out more and more in search of the street on which we lived. Nablus Road was not so much a single story as it was a palimpsest, cities and eras written over one another in time, some sections erased, others remaining through a single family, a doorway, an accent, a house. No era was ever truly wiped out; it only became harder to see, among all the clutter and noise, the fish tanks and bread. You had to learn to see *through* the world as it appeared to be into the world as it actually was. And, as I came to know them, the neighbors helped me by telling me the stories of their pasts, over cups of coffee or daily errands of purchasing milk. I began to recognize the fragments of other eras, languages, countries, stories—for ours was a street of stories, if ever there was one.

The surface level of Nablus Road was really four or five streets from different eras collapsed into one, with remnants of the first Arab families from the seventh century, of the Crusades, and of the British Mandate, to name a few. Yet this mishmash of history was unintelligible at first glance, and a visitor to our street looking at a map might be forgiven for believing that the British Mandate had never really ended and that European Christians still owned much of the street, from that period when foreign powers used their churches to stake claim on properties beside the Old City. German nuns still ran the Schmidt-Schule for girls, across the street from us, an enormous, castle-like fortress designed in the nineteenth century. Beside it, British volunteers still ushered groups around the Garden Tomb, where some Protestants argue that Jesus was crucified and buried, and where once I happened upon tourists speaking in tongues. Farther down the street, French Dominican priests in long white habits still lived in the walled complex of the École Biblique, where they translated the Bible into French and occasionally appeared beside the gate, looking out of sorts and angelic beside the Che Guevara grocery store. For a moment, the Empires appeared alive and well.

Yet in reality, the monks, nuns, priests, and pilgrims largely stayed behind their walls, leaving room for the real presence of our street: the Muslim Palestinian vendors who would show up every morning and unpack their juices, bags of candies, winter hats, fish aquariums, used vacuum cleaners, old shoes, and spices and set out to work. They commuted in from the outskirts of town, so that the street had the feeling of a bustling and crowded carnival that appeared only in the mornings and disappeared entirely at night, a city of phantoms. Many of the vendors were originally from Hebron—a city famous as the burial place of Abraham, and named in Arabic Al-Khalil, "the friend of God." Hebronites carried a reputation both for their toughness and their extreme piety—and they spoke their own distinctive dialect of Arabic, so that when you descended onto Nablus Road you were hit by the sound not of Jerusalem but of another city, calling out the price of bread.

Between the vendors and the European buildings, in a narrow seam separating the two, was a third story: a single row of shops that contained the very last remnants of more than a thousand years of old Jerusalem families. The shop beneath us was owned by Greek Orthodox grocers named Freij, who hung a picture of the Virgin Mary over the entrance beside a wall hanging of the Hail Mary in Arabic. The Freij family had been in the Middle East for centuries, and in this century their name had become synonymous with the grocery stores that they owned throughout the region. The one beneath us was run by a man in his sixties named Nadim, along with his two sons.

Nadim was one of eight Freij brothers. When I asked him how long his family had been in Jerusalem, he shrugged. "Four hundred years? A thousand years?"

His oldest son piped up from the dairy aisle. "We've just always been here."

Nadim Freij had the misfortune of being born in 1944, in British Mandate Palestine in a house in the Katamon neighborhood of West Jerusalem, up the hill. When the war of 1948 broke out, he and his family fled their house, believing that they could return in two weeks. "It's been fifty-eight years," he remarked sadly. That year Nadim's father opened their family store on Nablus Road, where he grew up beside the wall that separated Jordan from the just-declared State of Israel—and from his family's longtime home. The wall also cut him off from the other half of the neighborhood of Musrara, which before the war had been inhabited largely by Greek Orthodox Christians. The Freij family now found themselves to be a minority. In the space of a year, his entire world had, in every imaginable way, turned upside down.

"We were Bab al-Amoud boys," he said, giving the Arabic name for Damascus Gate. He had passed most of the last sixty years on Nablus Road, watching as more and more Christians moved away, until they were reduced to only a fragment of the neighborhood—and the city. He had not moved, but the country he was born in had all but disappeared.

Only our front door and Abu Hossam's cart separated the Freij grocery store from Michel and his older brother, Abu Tamer, who together ran their shop of Christmas-tree lights, Chinese dishes, plastic dolls, and Quranic verses. They were also from an old Jerusalem Christian family, but with a far more complicated history, for they descended from the historic Baramkeh family—whose story was so complicated that Abu Tamer told me, simply, to "look it up." To my astonishment, I found it immediately in *Encyclopedia of Islam*, scattered among academic articles. According to scholars, the Baramkeh family had likely been Buddhist priests in Afghanistan before they were called by the Abbasid caliphs to move to the city of Baghdad, where they converted to Islam. Yahya ibn Khalid al-Barmak became the mentor to Harun al-Rashid, who went on to become the caliph during its Golden Age, making the Baramkehs one of the most powerful families in the Empire. Yet theirs was not a story that ended well. In 803, the family fell out of favor for reasons that are still controversial. Djaf'ar, Yahya's son, was executed, his remains left on display in Baghdad for a year. The rest of the family was sent into exile. According to family tradition, Michel and Abu Tamer's ancestors fled to Turkey and then to Greece, where family legend said they converted to Christianity and became icon painters, so famous that they eventually came to Jerusalem to paint the icons at the Church of the Holy Sepulchre.

Beside Michel and Abu Tamer's store, the nondescript grocery store belonging to the Abu-Khalaf family, where I went for essentials like toilet paper and paper towels, concealed the legends of the Crusades and great medieval battles. A portrait on the shop wall of a gloriously dressed man on his horse soon led me to the story that the Abu-Khalaf family had ridden into Jerusalem with the Kurdish tribes that fought along Saladin in the twelfth century, later settling in Jerusalem and Hebron. Now in his late seventies, the eldest Abu-Khalaf still sat behind a desk, with a long white turban around his head tied with a black rope. Though the shop didn't look like much, for decades his family had been in charge of organizing the *hajj*, the pilgrimage from Jerusalem to Mecca. I would never see the simple act of buying paper towels in the same way again.

Beside the Abu-Khalaf's shop was likely the most respected family on the street: Omar and Sheikh Mazen, who ran a small grocery store. Sheikh Mazen only appeared to be a typical grocer—in reality he was a sheikh at Al-Aqsa Mosque and an Islamic scholar who also happened to spend his off hours manning the store counter and selling olives and bread. He was one of the last remnants of the Sufism—Islamic mysticism—that had thrived in Jerusalem during the Ottoman period, when devout Muslims completed their *hajj* to Mecca by blessing the visit at the nearby Dome of the Rock, and when Sufis asked to be buried as close as possible to the place where Mohammed ascended into heaven on his winged horse—known as the place in which the distance between earth and heaven was short-est. According to tradition, Sheikh Mazen's family was descended from the Prophet Mohammad, with some members having come to the city with Umar ibn al-Khattab in the seventh century, when Arab armies first took control of the city from the Byzantine Empire. The Mazens brought the corner grocery store business to an entirely new level.

"How are you doing?" Omar would ask me when I went to pay.

"Alhamdulillah! Thanks be to God!" I would answer.

"Alhamdulillah! Alhamdulillah! Daiman alhamdulillah!" he would answer joyfully. Praise God! Praise God! We must always praise God! And it was worth going there to buy yogurt, just for that.

Finally, the last and most famous vendor on the street was barely visible on the corner. Every morning, Abu Salaam, the seventy-six-year-old newspaper vendor, would set up shop from a blue iron window frame lodged into the wall of the street, from which he sold Israeli and Palestinian and American and Egyptian newspapers, their headlines displayed to the hundreds of pedestrians who passed by on their way to the Old City. Every night, he would magically collapse his shop into the wall of the street, so that it disappeared entirely. The next morning, he would unfold it again, complete with a lip just wide enough to serve as his chair. He had been selling newspapers on that exact corner since he was seven years old, through the British Mandate, the Jordanians, the Israelis, and Palestinians—he had handed out the headlines of wars and horrors and could show the bullets that had lodged in his iron cabinet. I once asked him which of the governments that he had lived under had been the best, but he refused to indulge me with an answer. I had the sense that he'd had his fill of bad news from all of them.

"The Jordanians?" I suggested.

"The Jordanians threw me in prison for being a Communist!" he replied.

———————

Ours was a neighborhood made holy by nearness. Musrara watched the holy city from a quiet corner, content to be next to the ancient walls instead of within them. Sometimes I would walk across the open space that used to be no-man's-land and find myself among those houses a block away on the other half of Musrara, now in Israeli West Jerusalem, houses that looked identical to ours, but which had been broken up into pieces after the war of 1948. A house such as ours was now five apartments, the spacious salons split into twos and fours. Houses built to accommodate large, extended Palestinian families became the refuges of Moroccan, Syrian, and Iraqi Jews, who had fled their own countries and now crowded into the beautiful tenements that had become theirs only because, as second-class Israeli citizens after the war, no one had minded putting them close to the shelling along the newly created border. A different world had moved in, families calling out in Hebrew and hanging their laundry out to dry, tending their olive trees, playing Moroccan music out the window.

Yes, life changed from place to place—not even from street to street, but from shop to shop, from layer to layer. And there was Abu Hossam knowing all of this in advance, one day selling umbrellas, the next day scarves to keep the sand from our eyes, and the very next day icy beverages to keep us cool from the heat, all the while noting our coming and going, and insisting, "*Khaliha, khaliha.*" *Take it as an offering from me.*

Seasons

WE PASSED THROUGH SEASONS. WHEN WE HAD ARRIVED THE AIR
was hot and smelled of mint, but in time the cold came with a
vengeance and the smell of the air turned first to *za'atar*—wild thyme
sold on the sidewalks outside—and finally to sage leaves, bruising
the air. The wind was bitterly cold and, like everything in Jerusalem,
winter came quickly and harshly, settling beneath our bones. The
winds accumulated in the valley that was Nablus Road, amplified,
so that the world took on a force. Rains glazed the windows with
water and breath, swelling the walls, shaking the trees. The entire
world was pulled forward in space. I tried not to venture outside. The
streets flooded. The wind refused to let up. We woke one morning to
find that the entire bougainvillea plant had been lifted from the roof
and then held up over the earth, stripped bare, so that the stairs were
awash in pink petals and wet green leaves. When I went outside and
ascended the hill toward the New City, the sidewalks were littered
with the skeletons of defeated black umbrellas, torn inside out by the
wind and finally abandoned on the roadside.

Then one day I walked outside into a nearly empty street, to men
covering their mouths with scarves. The *khamsin* had come: those

sandstorms of legend, named after the fifty-day period during which they were said to blow through, though here they mercifully lasted only for the space of an afternoon. But for that afternoon, the air was yellow dust, rapping against our eyes, flying into our mouths, some otherworldly, biblical storm. Our scalps crawled with dust. Orange found its way into the winter hats Abu Hossam was still selling outdoors. The wind stripped the leaves from the trees, suddenly and with violence, so that the gutters filled up with blossoms and branches and all of that sand from the deserts outside the city: the earth of another place that had blown into ours.

I would write, and Frédéric would keep his hours in the small bookstore, and in the afternoons we would cross through the streets between us—the streets of memory and the actual ones, the graves and the thieves, the invisible boundaries—to meet.

Frédéric once told me that he fell in love with me the moment he met me. I fell in love with him one afternoon, months later, when we were washing dishes in a desert monastery. We both loved each other first, and knew each other later. I have met those couples who claim to know everything about each other, and I have sometimes envied them, but I mostly look at them like aliens who inhabit a planet different from mine.

Perhaps we did everything backward. We had no other choice.

In those early months on Nablus Road, I called to him. No, we were calling to each other; two strangers who wanted to find their way to each other but did not know, quite yet, how. I loved him then. I did not know how to do so well. This much I am certain of. I had worked hard all of my life to be good at things, but I was not sure that I was any good at being married, and I was still too young to know that almost no one is good at being married—at least not in the beginning—and that for those accustomed to solitude, marriage is like a muscle we have to work on because it has never been used. The romance, in the end, was a walk to meet each other, day after day, a promise, a shy approaching, two people still terrified of the permanence of this long dance we had entered that no one had prepared us for. In time, we walked faster. I left early in order to meet him more than halfway. Earlier still. Then early enough so that I could pretend to browse books in the bookstore where he worked, while I peered from beside the shelves, watching him become animated as he gave advice to customers.

My husband. The way he spoke with his hands, a patch in his beard that never grew, the patterns of his breathing in sleep—a stranger slowly coming into focus. Time stitched us together, the opening of some windows and the closing of others, so that a balance settled into the house. In time, I learned that though leaving the monastery had been the ultimate grand gesture, that was not what came naturally to my husband. Frédéric was a master of the small gesture, and three years in a monastery had prepared him for the art of noticing as prayer. So he did, over and over: the cup of tea he infused each morning, the leaky faucet that needed to be fixed, the glass of water asking for refilling, the creak in the door, the windows patched up so that the wind would not seep in. Hot water prepared for the shower. A constant and quiet repairing of the immediate world. His way of showing affection was rarely by saying anything, but instead in placing my damp shoes beside the heater to dry.

So we danced closer to each other. The neighbors sensed it now, and they were watching us, protecting us. A vegetable vendor on the corner silently slipped in a bunch of mint with my cucumbers, or opened the black plastic bag in front of me so that I could place the carrots inside—an inch of relief, but enough. Abu Hossam wordlessly placed a circle of date bread into my hands along with the sesame bread and nodded, instructing me to take it. The men on the front stoop moved aside in the morning without me asking them to. The same world that had worked to push us away now silently—as though it realized that it had bent us too far——conspired to make an inch of space for us.

I do not know what marriage is like for other people. I only know that for us there was the initial "I do" in the church, and then the one that happened each day after, the "I still do." We had married as strangers, and as we came to know each other we had to say it over and over: *I know you miss the monastery, but I still do; I know you don't like having guests in the house, but I still do; I know you don't wake up early enough, but I still do; I know you don't speak my language, but I still do...* That daily renewal of promise: *I still do, I still do, I still do.*

———◆———

A Sunday morning before church. We disagreed about how we would spend the afternoon. Our argument must have been audible as we descended the stairs. We opened the door. Abu Hossam was waiting for us.

He scolded Frédéric. "You must never disagree with your wife in public. But in fact, you should never argue with her at all."

I was embarrassed. I was the one who had started the disagreement, but Frédéric didn't correct him. I thanked him silently for that. We stood side by side, admonished on the front two steps of our own home.

Abu Hossam removed a silver Arabic coffee pot from a flame burning next to the front door. He poured two strong cups of coffee. It was the traditional Arabic sign for the settling of any dispute. He handed one to each of us.

"Now drink," he ordered.

We drank.

And we continued on through the filthy streets of Nablus Road, absolved.

Invisible

FROM VERY EARLY ON, THERE WERE SIGNS THAT SOMETHING on our street was off. Frédéric and I woke up. We drank our tea. We went to work. We bought our spaghetti from the Freij family, our glasses from the Baramkehs; we spoke French and Spanish and Arabic with the neighbors. But it was now early March, months since the war with Lebanon had finished, and it was increasingly clear that some other, more invisible war was being carried out on the streets where we lived.

At any moment, it could break to the surface. But no one would talk about it or even say its name out loud—as though simply mentioning war would summon it into being.

I began noticing Palestinian men being asked for their papers in the streets around our house. Nearly every day, just at the top of the hill, two or three Israeli soldiers were stationed, dressed in green uniforms, with guns slung casually over their shoulders. Every few minutes they would spot a Palestinian making his way into the New City, call him over, and ask him to show his papers.

The first time I saw it, I thought that it was a coincidence. But every day I saw it happen anew. Usually these brief interactions came to nothing, and yet I often watched young teenage boys from my neighborhood, schooled in toughness, with slicked-back hair and crisp blue jeans, wrestle with how to respond to being asked for their papers within the streets of their own city. Sometimes they shrugged, but just as often they laughed—visibly, defiantly. And so it unfolded again and again, these small encounters and the even smaller laughter: young men pushed against walls, their hands pressed behind their backs, patted down and searched, then hastened along their way.

This drama played out in the very center of the city in plain sight, but the strangest thing was that no one appeared to notice. Cars continued past. Pedestrians waited for the light to turn and then hurried down Jaffa Road, the main thoroughfare in the city center. Even the other Palestinians continued walking, eyes on the concrete. It was not normal, and yet an entire city had decided together, in some bizarre contract, to pretend that it was.

In time I learned that the soldiers were asking those boys for their Jerusalem ID cards, the blue IDs all Palestinians in the city were required to carry at all times, in order to prove that they were allowed to enter into the city of Jerusalem. Most young Palestinians had no passports, unlike the Israelis in the city, who were citizens, and these cards were a painful proof of their liminal and fragile status.

I found myself bound to these invisible people, even when I left the confines of my neighborhood and walked in West Jerusalem. I did not speak Hebrew, but I spoke Arabic, and so my ears perked up every time one spoke. It was like a secret that I never intended to be let in on. They were everywhere. But no one seemed to notice them.

I walked down the streets of downtown, and my head kept turning at the signal. They were beneath the bowels of the earth, wearing fluorescent vests and digging into the ground, placing metal grids for the tramway. This line of men extended throughout the city, singing songs by the legendary Lebanese singer Fairuz, in Arabic, a thread of men lifting out dust in the heart of the metropolis. Sometimes they paused to pray in the middle of the road, the cars seeming to disappear around them.

I heard them working in kitchens in restaurants throughout the mainly Jewish West Jerusalem, under an unwritten rule that an Arab could wash the dishes or chop the vegetables, but could almost never wait a table. I heard them through the barrier between front counter and kitchen, boys slicing tomatoes and calling out to one another—in a language of intimacy that seemed certain that no one else around them could ever understand.

There they were, sweeping streets, cleaning parks, driving taxis. Fixing the electrical wires. Scrubbing the municipal toilets. Hiding in plain sight, collecting cigarette butts, holding the city in place. In the Israeli market of Mahane Yehuda, bag boys maneuvered boxes behind the scenes, hurriedly throwing out garbage, pushing back and forth great carts of fish. If I should chance to brush against one by accident, he would blush and whisper, immediately, "*Slikha*"—"Excuse me" in Hebrew—as though apologizing not so much for the accident as for the very fact of making himself known.

There they were, there they were. Everywhere in West Jerusalem, over the hill, tidying the streets of neighborhoods that had once housed Palestinian aristocrats. Arab taxi drivers memorizing the Hebrew names for places they had long known by Arabic names— Talpiot for Tel Beyout, Shar Yaffo for Bab al-Khalil, the ancient gate named after the Prophet Abraham. Women silently mopping floors, living among streets that had slipped away. Trying to hide as well as they could in plain sight, mindful of the signs out the window: the old Arabic lintel still hanging on a building in the German Colony, the Muslim graves still scattered in Mamilla Cemetery in the center of the city, which contained the bones of the soldiers of Saladin, every moment a reminder of how fragile the earth was, and how quickly it could be lost.

And then those same men and women passed the dividing line back to East Jerusalem, and they walked onto Nablus Road, and they instantly became visible once again. They shouted. Yes, they always shouted greetings at the top of their lungs: *"Ahlan, ahlan ahlan!"* So it was that my street was always loud, as if to compensate for all the silence of so many other places in their split lives.

Even then I knew that it could not be sustained. There was so much despair in the hiding. So much violence in those daily encounters, in plain sight, the asking for papers. I did not know what I was seeing yet. I only knew that the city was split between itself, and that we had placed ourselves on the scar. It was not only the two languages. There were two separate bus systems, separate school systems. Our streets were filthy and our trash was not always taken out, the health clinics in our neighborhood were in shambles, and more than two-thirds of the Palestinians lived below the poverty line. I had to remind myself that my neighbors considered themselves lucky, for at least they were better off than the vast majority of Palestinians who lived on the other side of the separation wall, who had green ID cards and in most cases could not enter Jerusalem at all, unless they applied for a permit. Many had never seen the city in their entire lives.

So Frédéric and I passed the first months of our marriage, entangled in a space that we could not understand but that felt, more and more, like it might erupt at any moment. The most tragic invisibles we knew were those we could not meet: Palestinians who lived in Jerusalem but did not have Jerusalem identification papers, and so could not risk leaving their homes at all. I learned about these by accident, when I asked about the wife of an acquaintance, only to be hushed and told later that she was "at home." This was the secret of East Jerusalem—women from the West Bank who had married Jerusalem men, despite the fact that they were not entitled to assume their husbands' status as residents of Jerusalem. These women had been lucky to enter Jerusalem once, somehow, but now they were imprisoned in their own homes, for fear of policemen asking them for their papers, forcing them to leave the city.

Whenever I saw that acquaintance, out of superstition, I never asked about his wife and did not even say the traditional "*Selem*," give my greetings to her, afraid that by mentioning her name, I might summon her onto the street, from which she might then be gone.

One morning I woke up and opened the front door to a military checkpoint set up directly in front of our house. It had simply appeared, in the early hours of the morning, while we were sleeping. Soldiers outfitted with guns stood watch in their olive-green uniforms, and they had made a metal gate with a small opening in the center where people might pass. They stopped all Palestinians, most of whom were headed to the Old City for Friday prayers, and asked them for their papers. All of the men who were under fifty years old were turned away.

Life continued around it, with Michel still selling his plastic plant holders and stickers and engraved prayer plaques, his plastic animals and training toilets. The girls still went to school and jumped rope in the school courtyard. Yet there it was, in the midst of everything, with the line of men and women growing every second, preparing their papers, then parting quietly in two as half of them were turned away.

On another afternoon, we watched from the balcony as a fight broke out among teenage Palestinian boys, just outside of the gates of the girls' school across the street. One after another, the boys removed their belts from their waists, as though choreographed to do so, and brandished them as weapons.

It was in those days that I began to understand that violence, once it had happened, would remain on Nablus Road, in the same way the wind and the dust settled there. We could feel the residue of it, hovering for hours and sometimes days after the fact, and it would rub into the shoulders and into the bones, so that I would be exhausted when I fell asleep and still exhausted when I woke up in the morning. Enemies walked past one another and often against one another in a strange intimacy. Whatever violence could not be expressed between enemies was expressed among one another instead, like a law of physics that seemed to demand that violence, once triggered within the body, must be set in motion.

To cope, our neighbors sought solace in invisible cities, the cities of the past. Abu Tamer would speak of those days of his childhood when thousands of Christians from Syria and Lebanon and Egypt and Jordan would rush onto Nablus Road during the Easter holidays, and the cafés would stay open late at night as children ate sweets and parents lit candles at the Holy Sepulchre.

Omar and Sheikh Mazen shared the memory of their father's tailor shop, where suits were designed for the aristocracy and fabric was ordered from the Armenian who had a fine shop around the corner. Those stairs in front of Damascus Gate? They only appeared to be stairs. And beneath them lay the memory of the taxi stand, where, according to our neighbors, taxis used to go directly to Damascus in two and a half hours, to Beirut in three, or to Amman, where you would transfer if you wanted to continue on to Baghdad.

Back then you could even travel to Gaza to swim in the sea.

Maybe we all possess cities of memory, but on Nablus Road, people lived in the memory city. They had even kept the memory name for Damascus Gate: Bab al-Amoud, which in Arabic meant "the Gate of the Pillar." For centuries, Arabs called it that, perhaps without even knowing why. It was only when archaeologists unearthed the sixth-century Madaba Map that they discovered that, during the Byzantine period, a giant pillar had stood at that entrance to the Old City of Jerusalem. Locals back then must have called it the Gate of the Pillar.

My neighbors never stopped, long after the pillar was gone.

Bird Country

It was not easy to build a marriage in such a place, where so much weight was leaning toward the past. It was hard to look forward, to resist the temptation to fall into nostalgia for what was irrevocably gone. We learned, together, every day a terrifying act of hope. We lived each day in wait of either grace or violence, knowing that one or the other would break through.

It took time to find a place of solace. I had learned to pray—truly pray—only when I climbed to a monastery 350 steps above the earth in a desert in Syria. That world was lost to me now. On Nablus Road, our stairs were infinitely smaller, only a flight of ten or so steps leading to the second story where we lived. But on difficult days, even that was something, and on those afternoons when the world became too much, I learned to look skyward, where the cramped quarters of our life on earth opened up and bird country appeared.

In all of my years in the Middle East, I had never stayed in one place long enough to notice that the slender expanse of earth between Europe and Africa formed a bottleneck—the only stretch of land over which more than five hundred million birds would pass each year, threading their way from Europe all the way to Africa and back, filling the sky with their riot of wings. It was a narrow space of survival, for if they veered too far west they would arrive over the sea, with no place to land, and if they veered too far east they would be stranded over the desert. So they came to us for sanctuary, millions of them.

In central Jerusalem, where pavement and houses and cars had, in the last century, eaten up the area outside of the less-than-square-mile of the Old City, there were precious few green places left for the birds to find shelter. I could imagine them, on each successive migration, discovering old fields and trees and open spaces covered over. But the Great Tree in our backyard survived one generation to the next, so they arrived to it on pilgrimage, seemingly almost all of them at once, and what had been a simple backyard was transformed into a bird sanctuary.

I had never formed a relationship with a tree before. I came from a city dense with trees, so that I never took much notice of cedars or pines, or felt drawn to one over another. But trees here were different; they contained the roots of other times, some semblance of a world more permanent than the world of men that was constantly shifting. Tradition said that an olive tree on the Mount of Olives had witnessed Jesus weeping at Gethsemane before his crucifixion. A sycamore in Jericho was marked as precisely the one that Zacchaeus climbed to see Jesus on the road. An oak in Hebron was reported to be the place where the three angels visited Abraham at Mamre.

The Great Tree in our courtyard also possessed stories. It was a massive, impressive tree, a presence—like some storybook tree guarding the entire neighborhood, with an immense, rough trunk that featured a hollow in its center, where birds could find shelter. It rose high above our house—indeed, above the entire neighborhood, its branches extending out onto our balcony and then up, so that from the vantage point of our second story, we looked into limbs and twigs and nesting places. All year long, resident birds filled its branches: great tits and woodpeckers, swifts and bulbuls, their voices in conversation. The birds would spill over onto our balcony, a cascade of laughing doves and sparrows, and the Palestine sunbird, with its dark coat of silver blue, would gather among the red flowers of the pomegranate tree and hover near the orange trees.

Then migration season arrived, not so unlike the monastery's busy tourist season, and the birds of Europe circled overhead and descended to meet us—starlings and kestrels and swifts and robins, the air around us alive with wings. They brought news of countries we were exiled from—the Bekaa Valley in Lebanon and the coast of Syria—and of movement in freedom. They graced us, settling among the trees like ornaments, like stars.

One day I left the house door open and was astounded when I returned to find a yellow-vented bulbul quietly flitting about in the kitchen. I expected to see it startled when I entered, but it merely glided, quietly, quietly, from nook to nook, until we cradled it in a handkerchief and released it into the open air outside, its belly flashing like a burst of fire as it disappeared into the trees.

On another afternoon, I left the house and forgot to check if the front door had caught on its hinge when I swung it closed. When I came home, the door was wide open, and there was a pigeon trapped inside. He flew frantically in circles, attempting to escape through the closed window, unable to conceive that what looked like air was a pane of glass. I rushed to rescue him. The house echoed with the desperate flapping of his wings. On the other side of the window, another red-breasted bird waited for him. Was it his mother? His mate? Neither of them could understand the invisible line between them—how they could still be so close to each other, but one of them in a room beyond retrieving. I grabbed the wooden edge of a broom and tried to guide him to the door. I opened all of the windows.

For a terrible moment, he was trapped behind the door. Just on the opposite side of the window, the other bird waited for him to appear.

Then he escaped, finally, into the open air.

———————

I still missed our monastery in the clouds of Syria. I had expected to find holiness in Jerusalem, in the hundreds of churches, but the longer we remained, the more I felt alienated from them, full as they were of postcards and pilgrims flashing cameras. But there was holiness in the sky that March, as birds that had escaped from Europe in the fall slowly, tentatively made their way home again— proof that all storms pass if we give them time. An endangered species of falcon known as the lesser kestrel stopped in the red-tiled roofs of Musrara to make their nests. Swifts nested in the crannies of the Western Wall.

Even at my most exhausted, I could summon up the courage to walk onto the terrace and wait for the birds to appear. The family of pigeons who had greeted us when we arrived never left, and they laid their nests in the windows of the house. Now and then, we'd find a shattered egg on the staircase; now and then, a small, still fragile bird. Sunbirds found their way to the wine-colored, collapsing shells of pomegranates, and at breakfast we could watch the beating of their wings through the windows.

Then there was the afternoon when Frédéric pointed out a ring-necked parakeet squawking in the highest branches of our tree, a strange transplant from a distant, tropical forest. He did not stay—but on rare afternoons we would see him passing through to rest, with his elegant green feathers, red-rimmed eyes, and red beak, cut off from his original homeland and now with nowhere left to go. The hoopoe, known as King Solomon's messenger, appeared with his long black bill and distinct black-and-white wings, as did the robin redbreast, which legend said had stood by the cross of Jesus, its chest pricked red by the thorns on his crown.

Above the birds lay thousands of stars, with names like *akhir alnar*, meaning the end of the river, or *al-ghumaisa*, the bleary-eyed one, from when Arab astronomers first witnessed them more than a thousand years ago. And beneath us another layer: for our house was just beyond the city walls, where the dead were traditionally buried, and so it made sense that they would pile up in layers and centuries around the places of my daily life, where I bought my bread and drank my coffee.

Those first several months, we moved along the gentle crust between the birds and the dead. There is that which is hidden that is terrible, and that which is hidden that is beautiful. They appeared in turn. But when the beautiful came, I tried to turn to it and call it by name. Maybe love was always, in the end, composed of this noticing, the small gesture repeated over and over again until it becomes the country in which we live.

Months passed like this. And then one night, Frédéric and I settled into the room we had finally chosen, with the window looking out to the light of the garden, and we held each other in the spare patch of earth we had been given, between countries, in order to rest. I remembered a dream I once had, of the monastery drifting from its mountaintop and quietly descending to the world below.

"You don't ever leave me, okay?" he whispered. "Because if you leave me, there's no one else in the world for me. I'll have to climb all the way back to that monastery."

We held each other, in that slender place in a country between, perhaps the only thin space in the earth where we belonged. But it was enough.

I married a man who believed in miracles. Who could tell the weather based on the movement of clouds. Who dreamt in a language I could not understand. Who seemed to draw birds to the window, and who saw an angel appear to him on a train. Who loved through the opening and closing of windows, the replacing of lost keys, the finding of houses.

As I lay my head on his chest, I knew that I would never be able to replace the monastery for him. I was never supposed to. He had known what he was giving up all along. I was never meant to take the place his old life. I was supposed to be a new one.

It would take me longer—years even—to understand his silences, voids I first thought of as distance, but later learned was fear—that something might happen to me, that he would lose me too. There is only so much loss a person can take. This is the risk of giving up a life of non-attachment—of attaching oneself to what can be lost. But there is no other way.

It is tempting to tell the story of a marriage by leaving out the difficult parts. It is even more tempting to pretend that there existed some perfect arc, a gradual ease toward harmony after a rocky beginning. And it is true that marriage is an act of migration, of outlasting storms and making a home on the other side of them.

But, if I am honest, I can recognize that love for me was not an arc but a rupture in the natural order of things, a defiance of gravity. There is no getting used to it. It is a permanent interruption. I suspect that most miracles happen that way.

Later, I would read what Simone Weil wrote, that love has its own physics, that the smallest amount of love, of pure good, is enough to outweigh much greater darkness. That is what Frédéric taught me first, in those early months of marriage—that love is in the small, the almost invisible, but that this is enough to save. The number of times, in the midst of sorrow, that he lifted me with a glass of tea. It takes time to recognize such physics: the loaf of bread, the hand held out across the bed, the kiss on the forehead, and the eternity contained within them.

Every single one a vow of its own: *I still do*.

Friday

FOR AN ENTIRE WEEK, FIGHTING BETWEEN PALESTINIANS and Israelis raged in the city. Our front door became the front line. Riots broke out in the surrounding streets, and young boys, their faces covered to conceal their identities and protect them from tear gas, launched stones at Israeli soldiers. On Nablus Road, just beyond our front step where our neighbors congregated, soldiers set up a roaming checkpoint, banning Palestinian men under the age of fifty from entering the Old City for Friday prayers.

The violence became such that we could not leave the house. We lay in wait. Frédéric collapsed in the salon to rest. I walked out to the back terrace, which afforded a view of both gardens, as well as Nablus Road. There they were. The soldiers appeared to be in their late teens. They stood, fully armed, holding steady at the metal barriers, turning back men, one after another.

I watched them until I understood that the men knew they could not pass and had entered the line for the express purpose of being turned away, a strange ritual of resistance. When they were turned away, they did not disappear. Instead, they gradually formed rows extending down the road, until there must have been two hundred men, waiting for something to happen.

The soldiers braced themselves. A man released himself from the rows of men, walked, confidently, to the front of the crowd, and slowly called out the call to prayer.

I watched, holding my breath.

C'est comme si un miracle allait bientôt se produire.

The men all stood at once.

And then.

I waited for riots, for the fight between men that everything in front of me told me would happen next. But instead there was no collision. Hundreds of men prostrated together on the filthy asphalt of Nablus Road, and they prayed.

I watched them for a long time. It was almost as though their bodies were moving against gravity. Their heads approached the asphalt. The street took on stillness. The soldiers seemed unsure of what to do. The street filled up with walls and walls of bodies pressing their foreheads to the ground, and there were no cameras and no microphones and no one watching, not even the men themselves, who appeared focused on redeeming the filthy earth in their gestures.

When it was finished, the men stood. And then they walked away.

I went inside, into the salon where Frédéric was waiting.

He looked up at me.

"What is it?" he asked.

Then I was in his arms, whispering, "I want to have a child."

Part Three

The Child
in Bethlehem

―――――――――――――――◆―――――――――――――――

"Here is the world. Beautiful and terrible things will
happen. Don't be afraid."

—*Frederick Buechner*

Dear Joseph,

If I could have built you myself, I would have written a map of the world inside of your body. There would have been rivers, great open spaces, and very particular trees that you could climb and then swing from; and there would be long, straight roads extending from one country to another, easy to navigate. You would be able to see your destination many miles in advance. The names of cities would be signposted large, always in your language. Resting stations marked. And into yourself I would bury the name of every spring of water, the coordinates, so that all of your life you would be drawn, without understanding why, from source to source.

And I would have written names into your bones, so that you would never have a moment, standing in a shop in a corner, or pointing to a sign at a bus station, when you could not understand the destination, or the name of a flower. If I could have written your body I would have given you a compass, etched into your heart like an extra organ. I would have carved in the instructions to build a fire, or to purify water, to sail a boat, or to make your way out of forests after your tracks have been washed out by rain.

As it was, I gave birth to you across a border, in a place that was not yet a country, and may never be one.

A Test

IN APRIL OF OUR FIRST YEAR IN JERUSALEM, I WALKED into a pharmacy on Sultan Suleiman Street, just along the ancient walls of the Old City, to buy a pregnancy test. I had chosen a pharmacy far enough from the house on Nablus Road that no one would see me entering and ask questions later. If I *were* pregnant, I at least wanted my parents to know before the falafel vendors did.

An elderly man behind the counter, with a graying moustache and dressed in a white pharmacy coat, smiled at me, slightly amused that I was waiting for everyone else to finish their purchases and leave before I approached the counter.

"I need an *imtihan*," I said quietly, using the only Arabic word I knew for "test," though I had originally learned it in the context of "Arabic language test."

"A test?"

"Yes, a test. To see if I'm carrying something." My Arabic was failing me.

He laughed. "Do you want a pregnancy test?" he asked me in English.

I looked around. "Yes, exactly."

"Are you pregnant?"

"I have no idea. That's why I need to take a test."

He smiled, clearly enjoying himself. "We have three models. The expensive test, the cheap test, and the middle one."

"How much is the middle one?"

"Twelve shekels. It should be fifteen shekels, but since you speak Arabic, I'll give it to you for twelve." He winked at me.

"That discount will be good luck for the child," I assured him, though using an unborn child already as leverage in bargaining seemed in poor taste. "Does it have directions in English?"

He opened the package, pulled out the directions, and confirmed that it did. "That's good. One needs to understand these things."

"We have it in Arabic, if you prefer."

"No, no. No Arabic."

He chuckled.

"Can I have a bag, so that the neighbors won't gossip?"

He smiled knowingly, took the pregnancy test, slid it into a black plastic bag, and then folded it over as though he were concealing a secret. He handed it to me.

"This is between us, until I know the answer, okay?" I reminded him. "Don't tell a soul."

He laughed. "Good luck!" he called after me as I went through the door, the small, tingling bell singing behind me as I swung it closed.

Once home, I drank a liter of water, chose one of our two toilets, and then took the test. For a full ten minutes I stared at the white plastic stick, as though time might change the one faint line on the test to two. I emerged from the bathroom to find Frédéric nervously waiting at the kitchen table.

"I'm not pregnant," I announced.

"Are you sure?"

"Of course I'm sure. Look at the test. There's no second blue line. There's not even the shadow of another line."

"Maybe it's too soon."

"It says in the directions that the test can detect a pregnancy in a few days. It's been two weeks."

He took my hand and led me to the salon. "We'll try again. It will be fine."

I felt tears stinging my eyes. I remembered how it had happened: how I had returned from watching the men praying in the street and collapsed into my husband's arms. How we had held each other after making love, both of us so certain that we'd conceived a child that Frédéric had whispered in my ear, "Wahh! Wahh!" like a baby crying.

Outside, I could hear the merchants calling back and forth. Frédéric was oddly quiet.

"Frédéric?"

He looked up at me.

"You didn't tell the neighbors I'm pregnant, did you?"

He blushed. "Just Abu Hossam."

"What?"

"And Abu Walid."

I stared at him. "You told the falafel guys before we told our parents?"

"I was excited," he mumbled. "I didn't say that you were pregnant. I said that you *might* be pregnant."

"Oh God. Now they'll think that something went wrong."

"They won't say a thing, Stephanie. They know how to be discreet about these things."

The child I was not carrying became like some seed of sadness planted in me. Spring passed on. Each time I left the house, the neighbors subtly examined me, trying to measure if I looked more tired than usual, if my clothes were tight, and finally, if I might have lost the baby. Eventually Frédéric told them that he had been mistaken. From then on, I sensed their quiet sympathy as I pushed the door open onto the street, and they were gentler with me. Times had not changed much since the book of Genesis, I guess. There were few things, it seemed, more tragic in the region than a woman who had tried to have a child but did not.

Joyeux Noël

THAT SUMMER WE ESCAPED THE BLISTERING HEAT AND returned to France, traveling to Frédéric's vacant family house in the high Alps. After my months of disappointment, I had rarely been so grateful to see the world disappearing beneath me. I sought solace in loaves of bread and Beaufort cheese, in the din of cowbells moving in the fields. I comforted myself with the names of flowers coming into season: eglantine and alpine aster, coltsfoot, marguerite, dog violet.

The last month had felt like an accumulation of losses. Fatah and Hamas—the two main Palestinian political factions—had gone to war in Gaza, and I'd read about militants being thrown off the roofs of buildings. It was unclear who would take control of the West Bank—another development in an area that was already becoming intolerable, with checkpoints and walls and settlements eating up the landscape. I had recently begun part-time work on a development project in the West Bank, which required traveling regularly through checkpoints, and the week before I left for France, every single partner had quit. I also found myself physically depleted. My feet ached upon touching the ground. I imagined my back a field of blue and green bruises.

Once we arrived in France, I repeatedly collapsed into sleep for hours at a time—a dark and faraway slumber unlike any I had known. Frédéric would tiptoe into the room and kiss my forehead. I told myself that it was war that had been building in my body, a poison that I now needed to extinguish. But days passed, and the pain intensified. I sensed that it might be something else.

We had been in France for a week when I received an urgent email from my friend Julie, who I had known during my year in Syria. She informed me that she had tested positive for exposure to tuberculosis. Since the two of us had been together regularly—at times daily—chances were that I had been exposed too.

I was almost relieved that the news was as terrible as I had anticipated. I had always suspected that I would die some horrible death, like John Keats or the Brontë sisters.

"I have tuberculosis," I announced to Frédéric.

"You do not have tuberculosis."

"I do. I'm probably dying."

"You are not dying. Didn't you get shots?"

"I don't think they give those shots in America, because no one there gets tuberculosis. I made the mistake of traveling to countries where people have it."

"I promise you that you don't have tuberculosis. But if you want me to make an appointment to go to the doctor's tomorrow and be tested, I will."

"Please do. I could be contagious."

He shook his head. I retired to the bedroom, once again, to collapse into sleep.

The next day, Frédéric valiantly drove me down the mountain to the doctor's office. In the waiting room, I imagined the sickness hovering as a phantom inside my chest. The doctor walked in, brisk in her high heels, and called me into her office, where she placed a stethoscope against my chest and listened.

I informed her that I probably had tuberculosis.

"I'm fairly certain that you don't have tuberculosis," she countered, moving the stethoscope around on my chest.

"I'm exhausted all of the time. It's not normal."

"Didn't you have shots?" she asked.

I sighed.

"I'm going to give you a pulmonary exam. It will show whether you have any blockage in your chest or lungs. But before I start, I need to ask you a few questions. Is there any chance that you could be pregnant?"

Enceinte. A wall protecting a castle. Or to be pregnant with child.

"I suppose there's a chance," I conceded. "There's always a chance."

"Have you missed a period?"

"I have no idea."

"When do you usually have your period?"

"I have no idea. I never even know what day it is."

She gave me a look of disdain that seemed to have been perfected by certain French women. "Why don't you take some blood tests and then come back in a few days?" she suggested. "In the meantime, I'll make the appointment to check your lungs."

"Okay," I said. At the same time I was thinking, *My God. When was the last time I had my period?*

We took the blood tests. They called us with the results that evening. But by then, I somehow already knew that we were having a child.

———◆———

A few days later, we returned to the clinic to have my lungs x-rayed. This time a much kinder doctor was on duty, and we informed him that I still wanted to be screened for tuberculosis, but that in the meantime we had learned that I was pregnant. He told me that the first doctor had been wrong, and that the x-rays in this case would do me no harm. He checked my lungs first. When he was finished, he did an ultrasound. He covered my abdomen with a clear, thin layer of gelatin, cold to the touch, and instead of searching for disease, he went searching for a child. And there you were. Sleeping. Already fully formed, your small head facing skyward, cradled into the placenta as though resting in a small raft set out to water, your tiny feet just visible, and indentations of eyes and mouth, small thumbprints.

Frédéric gasped.

I realized that I had already known in some part of me, for you were not a stranger to me.

In his office, the doctor handed us two sets of images. The first showed my lungs, free of consumption. The second held a body sleeping in light, with ribs pronounced, like a white harmonica.

"When was your last period?" the doctor asked me.

"I have no idea," I answered.

He sighed, as French doctors do, and then he measured the length of the cranium, which told him how many weeks along I was. Then he consulted a chart, turning a dial forward on the calendar until it arrived on my due date. He showed it to Frédéric and smiled.

"*C'est le vingt-sept—non, le vingt-cinq décembre. Joyeux noël!*"

I looked up at your father.

"It's the twenty-fifth of December," he translated softly. "Merry Christmas."

———•———

The world changed overnight. Or so it changed for me. It collapsed into something infinitely smaller, a thin and fractured crust of earth, floating on lava and fire, continuously worn down by water, and I was afraid.

Christmas. I imagined Mary's moment with the angel who slipped into her room.

"How can I be pregnant, if the pregnancy test said negative?"

———•———

When we ascended again to the mountaintop, I became aware for the first time that there was not enough air. I imagined the baby's lungs as two small moths, trapped beneath a tiny, overturned glass.

"I'm an awful mother," I fretted to Frédéric as the village came into view. "I carried a child for three months, and I didn't even know that he existed. Then I took him to a place where he couldn't breathe. I managed to neglect my child before he was even born."

"Look on the bright side," he answered. "Everyone says that the first three months are the hardest. And they're already gone."

"Oh God. I never should have bought the pregnancy test on sale."

"You just took the test too soon."

"And there was the wedding we went to. Do you have any idea how much I had to drink? I have no idea, because I can't remember any of it."

"He'll be fine. It was just one night."

"I was already…five weeks pregnant that night. My God."

"Do you have any idea how much alcohol French people used

to drink? They drank wine instead of water because the water wasn't clean. They smoked through all of their pregnancies. And yet somehow the French as a people survived."

Somehow, the survival of the French people was of little comfort to me.

———————

It was already July. We had planned on spending only two months in the mountains and then returning to Jerusalem at the end of August, only now there seemed little incentive to go back. We had yet to discover our bearings completely in Jerusalem. Frédéric, who had finished his high school diploma before our wedding, had spent the time since finishing a college degree in Islamic studies, and was hoping to continue on to a graduate degree. I reasoned that this would be best accomplished if we remained in France. I was certain that Frédéric would be only too happy to remain in his own country. But instead he was already figuring out which of our eleven rooms on Nablus Road would be the nursery.

"Are we really going to go back there to have a child?" I asked.

"Of course we are. You're due at Christmas. You can't be due at Christmas and not have the baby in Bethlehem."

"Bethlehem? Are you serious?"

"Yes, I'm serious. There's a very good French hospital in Bethlehem."

This almost made me smile. The French desire to maintain everything French—even to the extent of seeking out hospitals in conflict zones—was nothing if not admirable.

"But I have to go through a checkpoint to get to Bethlehem," I objected. "Every mother's nightmare is to be caught at a check- point while in labor." This was my suspicion, at least. In reality, I didn't know any mother who'd had to go through a checkpoint to give birth.

He shrugged. "It's your first baby. You'll have forever."

Oddly, the idea of having "forever" at a checkpoint didn't make me feel better. "How do you know I'll have forever?"

"Everyone knows that the first baby takes hours."

"But we could just stay here in the Alps."

"Being on top of a mountain in the middle of winter with meters of snow is a little bit like being stuck behind a checkpoint."

He had a point. "We could rent a home."

"Where? Do we want to be in some random rented house in the middle of the French countryside after we have a baby? Don't you think we'll want to be in our own home?"

Was it home, those rooms in Jerusalem? "Frédéric, I don't think I can go back there now. Don't you remember how all of the children play with toy guns? I don't want my son to grow up playing war."

"You don't even know if it's a boy."

"Okay, I don't want my daughter playing war."

"But I played war growing up. All boys play war growing up. It's completely natural."

"You did not play war. You played Zorro."

"No, I played cowboys and Indians."

"That's different. In our neighborhood they play Israelis and Palestinians. You pretended to shoot someone imaginary. They pretend to shoot their neighbors."

"You can do what you want. But boys will play war."

"This from a former novice monk."

"Yes."

"No toy guns in the house."

"He'll just use sticks and pretend they're guns. But agreed: no guns in the house."

I could tell, in that strange way, that the baby did not fully exist for him yet—that he had not fully internalized the anxiety of being responsible for a human life.

"Aren't you scared of raising a child in a country that seems to go to war every year?" I finally asked.

"Listen, Stephanie," he said, quietly but with assurance. "Whoever that baby is, he or she is going to be strong. You're strong. Anyone who goes almost four months without knowing she's pregnant is strong."

"Or stupid."

"Can you try for me? Then, if Jerusalem doesn't work out, we can come back to France. But I can't keep floating around like this. We need to plant roots somewhere. Let's just try. See how it feels when we go back."

I never expected that my very French husband would be coaxing us to go back to Jerusalem, while I pushed for us to say in the Alpine countryside. How things had changed.

That night I phoned my father.

"Hi, pregnant girl," he said.

"Hi, Daddy."

"Is everything okay?"

"I think so. Dad? I was just wondering… Was Mom in labor for a long time before you went to the hospital for the first child?"

He laughed. "Are you kidding me? Your mother didn't even know she was in labor! She made us go to see my mother to make sure. My mom opened the door, took one look at her and said—my God—why aren't you in the hospital? You're in labor!"

He laughed. "She had your sister while I was still signing in."

I was lying in bed the next day when Frédéric tiptoed in. I still had not fully forgiven him for his fearlessness. Earlier he had reminded me that women had given birth since the beginning of time, after which I had reminded him that they had also died in childbirth.

Now he lay down beside me. He gently placed his hand on my belly and whispered to the baby, "*Bonjour, toi.*"

Then he seemed to say it almost to himself. "Five and a half months left," he whispered, finally. "I needed more time."

And I forgave him. He was just as terrified as I was, the way every character in the Bible—Abraham, Sarah, Mary—is terrified when an angel appears and announces that a child will be born. Sarah even laughs out loud. It is so absurdly ridiculous.

You will have a child.

Me? Do you know how old I am?

Mary doesn't even say a word.

You will have a child.

We had missed his earliest heartbeats. We would never have them, like lost pieces of music. Now Frédéric would come and place his head against my belly, and whisper: "*C'est mon bébé, ça!*" You're my baby, you are.

We remained in France until August, long enough to see the very first leaves falling. Seasons always come to a mountaintop early, and there is a peculiar joy in descending a mountain in a single day and falling into a different season at the bottom, defeating fate. Yet the opposite is also true, and we seemed to move ahead in time, the year collapsing upon us. Autumn came early, and we watched the cows ambling toward lower pasture in search of life, the top of the mountain razed of its wildflowers.

Then it was time to go back to a place in the world where we were strangers, but strangers together. I packed a bag, and the pictures of the baby asleep in the raft of my body, taken alongside the large black sheet meant for finding broken bones or disease, which instead had discovered life.

I had never considered how many sharks slept in water, or how sidewalks could narrow beside a street, or how strong the sun was; I had never registered how frail bones are and how easily they might break. There were poisonous berries, small plastic parts that might be swallowed. The air was too thin in the sky, and the earth was too fragile, and I had no idea, from the very first day, where in the world to place you. To what thin crust of earth we could possibly belong.

My dearest Joseph, I will always believe that I brought you twice into the world; once in a hospital room in Bethlehem, and once on that day, when we drove down the winding road of the mountain, your father slowing at every turn to keep you safe—when we abandoned yellow flowers and eglantine bushes and sky, when we descended into the skyless patch of earth that we had chosen, and we placed a child into it.

There were brakes that could fail, or turns that could be missed. I could not build your body. There would be no clocks within it, and no knives or compass; there were not even words, only vowels and consonants swimming in water. You waited in my womb, saturated in water and sounds, to be released. We would bring you into war. I had lived enough on the periphery of it to know that it was terrible, and that it could burn up the soul of a man.

But lemon trees can only grow at low altitudes, and fig trees, and even most birds do not venture so high into the air as we had escaped. We carried you down into the inhabited world, into the river of air—or I carried you—for this is the same in all three languages: to bear a child; to *haml*, in Arabic; in French, to say *je porte ton enfant*, I carry your child—as in a cross, as in a burden, but also the word for a tree bearing fruit.

This much I have always suspected: everything that is beautiful must also have a weight.

It was late August when we arrived in Jerusalem. The neighbors were exactly where we had left them. They stared at us as though we were ghosts.

Jamil, the gardener from the neighboring convent, was standing in front of the gate. He ran to meet us.

"You came back!" he shouted.

"Yes, we did."

He shook his head. "Nobody ever comes back," he said.

Mary of the Shattered Ones

A WEEK LATER, I SET OUT FOR MY FIRST DOCTOR'S VISIT in Bethlehem. As I watched the walls of the Old City disappear behind me, the land gradually changed from treescape to barren desert hills, and I was once again amazed at how quickly the earth shifted in those parts. Bethlehem was only seven kilometers away by bus, but it was also on the other side of the separation wall, so that entering it meant passing through a border. Though Palestine was not officially a country, Bethlehem was not mixed between Israelis and Palestinians like Jerusalem. It was firmly in the Arab world, with the only Israeli presence being the soldiers who manned the checkpoint to enter it, and the settlers who lived in the settlements scattered around it.

There was something altogether concrete about needing to travel to a more dangerous place in order to give birth to a child. I remembered the song that we used to sing at Christmas mass every year in my childhood:

> *O little town of Bethlehem,*
> *How still we see thee lie.*

Above thy deep and dreamless sleep
The silent stars go by.
Yet in thy dark streets shineth
The everlasting Light.
The hopes and fears of all the years
Are met in thee tonight.

Even as a child I recognized something in those last lines: an entire lifetime collapsed into a single moment, when a child is born.

There is no better way to describe being pregnant than to say that the hopes and fears of all the years have somehow been given body: that when hope takes a body, that body is a child. There is also no way to avoid saying that it scared the shit out of me. My own "all the years," beginning with my childhood, had not been easy. I had battled depression for much of my teenage years, so much so that I eventually ended up in the psychiatric ward of a mental hospital for two weeks, recovering from a suicide attempt when I was fifteen years old. I was not the first in my family to do so: my mother's mother had suffered from depression and finally committed suicide as an adult, and my mother's father had been mysteriously murdered in his own home, with his own shotgun. My mother's sister had been tragically run over and killed by a bus. My own experience of my mother was that of a woman who loved us, but who had also spent years doing battle against the hellish circumstances of her own past. *The fears of all the years…*

I had moved forward, somehow, miraculously. I had never forgotten Frédéric's accusation: *You don't believe in resurrection.* So I had searched for it. Insisted upon it. Held onto it like my life depended on it, because, quite frankly, it did. And in the midst of so much fear, marriage had already felt like a miracle, less my own doing than that of an angel who had wandered onto a train, who had moved my life in a direction against gravity—a life full of fear now edging carefully toward hope.

But to decide to have a child! To think that I should be entrusted with a person! This was to choose to leap into the abyss, and to take another human with me. There was something about that decision, set against the reality of my family's past, that seemed altogether reckless. To have managed some happiness for myself was already lucky, but to think that I could pass on happiness to another generation was chutzpah. I remembered the words of Franz Kafka to his friend Max Brod: "Oh [there is] plenty of hope, an infinite amount of hope—but not for us."

And it would have been enough had I decided to give birth in a suburban house in Texas, or rural France. But I was going to have a child in a region of war.

After twenty minutes, the blue-and-white-striped minibus from Jerusalem stopped beside the separation barrier: a gray slab of concrete crowned in snarled barbed wire, with a military watchtower at the center, circled with small windows. The separation wall began in Bethlehem and stretched as far as the eye could see, a brutal interruption in the landscape. I descended from the bus, walked inside the checkpoint, and flashed my passport for a soldier waiting at a window who breezily waved me through a turnstile. So it was in the West Bank—nearly anyone could enter. It was the leaving that was difficult.

In front of me stood another pair of turnstiles, then a vacant lot separating the checkpoint from yet a third set of turnstiles, and then the concrete wall. For a brief moment, walking through the vacant lot, I wondered in which country I was standing. An elderly Palestinian man crossed my path, putting on his belt again after passing through security. The metal made a small, almost imperceptible tinkling sound like a bell. In front of me, hanging over the wall, a banner read: "Welcome to Bethlehem. Peace Be with You."

And in all of this, I was aware of the child I was carrying inside me, moving and swimming and breathing within the raft of my body, crossing a checkpoint for the very first time in his life through the vantage of my womb. I wondered if he could sense the quickening of my own heart. It was the end of summer, and soon I would be six months pregnant.

The Holy Family Hospital was set high on the slope of a hill looking over the entrance to the city. On the roof, a statue of the Virgin Mary stood, cloaked in a heavy, folded robe and with her hands outstretched, oddly familiar. I entered and approached the reception window, where the secretary peered down at me. He attempted to speak to me in English first, and then Arabic. At eight thirty in the morning, I did not feel up to the task of speaking any language at all.

"Do you speak Arabic?" he asked.

"Sort of," I apologized. "I speak Syrian Arabic."

He laughed. "What's your name?"

"Stephanie Saldaña." He appeared to ponder my name for a moment before turning to the documents and scrawling from right to left: some invented, transliterated version of my name in Arabic.

"What is your husband's name?"

"Frédéric."

"What?" He leaned into the counter.

"Farid, you can call my husband Farid." He carefully wrote this out in Arabic letters, and I decided that it would have to do. Farid meant "the unique one" in Arabic. Frédéric would appreciate that.

"How long have you been married?" This seemed totally irrelevant to the task of signing up to give birth, but it was a Catholic hospital, so I humored him.

"One year."

"Have you been pregnant long?"

"Is it that obvious I'm pregnant?" I teased.

He shifted uncomfortably in his chair.

"Yes, six months."

He wrote that down. "*Khamsin* shekels," he ordered, and I handed him the rough equivalent of twelve dollars.

The doctors' offices were around the corner, but there was no real waiting room. Instead, women filled the seats and the hallways in a somewhat chaotic assemblage: poor women from the surrounding countryside with drawn faces trying to keep their children from running around, wealthier local Christian women adorned in chic dresses with crosses conspicuously displayed around their necks, women in headscarves and others in short sleeves with perfectly styled hair. A doctor called a woman's name, and her entire family of children and sisters and aunts and mother and grandmother stood with her and moved toward the doctor's office, an entire village that appeared for an update on news of the coming member. I looked at them all, and it dawned on me that we had all once swum in our mother's wombs, that we were now carrying children, and that in some way we all inhabited the same country.

A doctor peeked out the door and called my name. I entered the examination room and handed him an envelope of papers from

France: the image that contained not a disease, but the black-and-white outline of a child swimming in my body.

"Don't tell me if it's a boy or a girl," I insisted. "I don't want to know."

He laughed. "Really? You're the first. Here the women only come to see me twice when they're pregnant: once to find out if it's a boy or a girl, and a second time when they're in labor."

I remembered the crowd in the hallway and reasoned that they had all assembled for exactly such news. "I don't want to know," I repeated.

"Okay, I'll try not to forget. But it might accidentally slip out. When was your last period?"

Since we had been to our first appointment in France, Frédéric had been the designated supplier of information. He knew when my last period was, what my weight was in kilograms instead of pounds, and my family illnesses. Since he was not with me, I shrugged. "In France they said that the baby is due on Christmas day."

"We'll see." He attached me to an aging sonogram machine. We were quiet. I could hear the crowds of women chatting in the hallway outside. I looked to see a single heart beating, an oval, a ribcage like a round harmonica. I gasped.

"There's the baby."

I kept staring. There were the hands. The feet. The indentation of eyes, nose.

The doctor wrote down an address. "That's my private clinic. Come and see me there in two weeks."

"That's all?"

"Here's a prescription for vitamins. That's all."

It was finished, after only five minutes. I had traveled such a long journey for something so brief. I walked into the hall, and the crowds looked up at me expectantly. I smiled at them, and we shared the secret shared between women across time.

I have someone alive inside of me. And so do you.

I thought of Mary, rushing after learning of her pregnancy to see her cousin Elizabeth, just so that they could marvel at each other, so that the babies in their bellies could bounce and wave in greeting, recognizing each other already.

From the garden, women were visible in the glass-walled hallways walking back and forth in their slippered feet, holding newborns.

I sat down at a table beside the olive trees, under the protective gaze of the statue of the Virgin Mary, took out a notebook and a pen, and wrote a letter to my unborn child.

> *Dear* _____ ,
> *It's so hot today. I was thinking of you, my beauty, my little one…*

When I was finished, I tucked the blank book into my purse and walked up the hill into the ancient city center, through the narrow streets, down the bustling markets of the mostly Muslim town. There was a sweetness to Bethlehem, the sidewalks packed with village women selling dried yogurt and plums and great piles of sage. Unlike Jerusalem, which was torn between so many fighting identities, Bethlehem was surer of what it was. As I ascended the hill, the main street branched off into two, and then everything descended, running beneath ancient stone arches until it led to Manger Square, where a stone basilica towered above the cave where Jesus was born.

The first church at the site of the Church of the Nativity had been dedicated in 339, but the present-day basilica dated from the reign of Justinian in the sixth century. Since then, it had almost miraculously survived in a world of vanishings. Tradition said that in the seventh century, when the Persians set out to destroy churches all over the region, including the Holy Sepulchre, they allegedly refrained from tearing down the Church of the Nativity because they saw a mosaic on the facade of the three magi, dressed as men from Persia and arriving to pay homage to the infant Jesus. Today, it is still visited by Muslims and Christians alike, who come to honor the son of a virgin named Mariam: the Prophet Jesus, who according to the Quran spoke from the cradle, healed the sick and raised the dead, breathed into clay birds and released them into the open air. In a region where religions so often fought over holy places, it was a relief to enter into a Christian basilica that was nonetheless the pride of a largely Muslim city.

Like the monastery in the desert, the Church of the Nativity's entrance was a miniature door of humility. I kneeled to make my way inside. The church opened into a magnificent nave, and on each side, two rows of pillars barely revealed the ghosts of ancient, painted saints staring out. Oil lamps swung from the ceilings at intervals. I descended the stairs to the cave beneath, where dozens of candles were burning among the stones blackened with centuries of smoke, and I knelt on the ground and kissed the star where a child was born.

Dear God, if you can do me just one single favor, then let my child live.

There is nothing like having a child to knock the shit out of you, to break any nonsense ideas that you are well, and healed, and competent. No, a child awakens every doubting voice within.

"How can this be, since I am a virgin?" Mary asked.

How can it be true, if I don't even know what day it is, if I leave my laundry undone for weeks, if I still use a mattress on the floor as my bed? If I don't know how much I weigh, if I don't even know when my last period was?

How can it be true, when I have spent so much of my life afraid—not just of angels, but of everything?

How can it be true, if we live in a place on the verge of falling apart?

<hr />

If any city reminded me of falling apart, it was Bethlehem. I had first traveled there when I was twenty-two years old, a young student just out of college on a scholarship to journey through the Middle East and Europe for a year. I had walked from the Old City of Jerusalem, during a time when the only border between the two cities had been not a wall, but a few orange traffic cones on the road and a handful of soldiers lazily watching the cars pass by. Once I'd walked passed them, I approached a small shop on the side of the road.

"Do you know where Bethlehem is?" I had asked the man working there.

"Wait five minutes, and I'll take you there!" he'd responded.

Sure enough, five minutes later I had found myself in the front seat of his car heading toward Bethlehem. Eventually, he had dropped me off in the middle of Manger Square. I had centered my backpack on my back, entered the first souvenir store I saw, and asked the owner: "Do you know of a place where I can stay the night?"

He had smiled. "Just wait five minutes, and I'll take you there!"

That was how I found myself, walking next to the owner of a souvenir store, knocking at various convents and asking if they had vacancies. After several tries, we arrived at a large yellow door and rang the bell. A young Palestinian nun in a gray habit opened the door with a beaming smile. Her name was Hannah.

"Do you take guests for the night?" I asked her hesitantly.

She grinned. "We always thought that we might. I guess that you will be our first."

It was an encounter that would change the course of my life—much like the angel who had appeared on Frédéric's train. I spent the following week in Bethlehem, and it was in those streets, among that particular wind in the alleys where Muslims and Christians had lived side by side for centuries, that I decided to give my life to studying the Middle East. I knew, then and there, that I would research Islam and Eastern Christianity and learn to speak Arabic—a total shift from the life I had imagined for myself as a writer and poet. It was a choice that would eventually take me to Syria—to Father Paolo, an expert on Muslim–Christian dialogue, and then to the man who would become my husband. Every evening in Bethlehem, I would end my day by walking to the cave beneath the basilica and kissing the star on the ground where tradition said a child had been born. It was 1999, and the city was re-cobbling the streets to celebrate two thousand years of Christianity.

Nine months after I left, Israeli opposition leader Ariel Sharon visited the Temple Mount in Jerusalem—known to Palestinians as the Al-Aqsa Mosque compound or al-Haram al-Sharif—an event that helped set off the Palestinian uprising known as the Second Intifada. The following years would see massive demonstrations, invasions, suicide bombs, and battles, as a slowly simmering war between Israelis and Palestinians finally exploded into the streets of Israel and the West Bank, resulting in thousands of deaths. Bethlehem became the first city that I'd known intimately to collapse into war.

In time, a dozen other cities would follow. I would look at the news and remember that star on the earth, among the dying, and think: *A child was born into this.*

The hopes and fears of all the years
Are met in thee tonight.

I grew tired. On the way back to the bus, I passed the hospital one more time. I looked up at Mary on the roof, her hands held out. Then I recognized her.

Where had I seen that face before? After I spent a year working as a journalist in Beirut in 2001, I had returned to the United States for graduate school. One day in the library, I had come across a photo on the front page of the newspaper from the recent fighting in Bethlehem: the image of a statue of the Virgin Mary, radiant in white, with her arms stretched out, shot clean through with bullets. When fighting broke out in the city in 2002, her body had been decimated by shrapnel, one hand torn off, and her nose broken. I had torn the picture from the newspaper and carried it with me, calling her Mary of the Shattered Ones.

Unknowingly, I had sat beneath that same Mary's protective gaze in the hospital garden that morning, minutes after I had seen my child's beating heart, as I sat down to write a letter to my unborn child.

Now I thought of her again, her outstretched hands, and the terrors she had passed through, of war and bullets and tanks moving through the streets. Her wounds had been patched over, the shrapnel removed. Was she truly made new? How much of the past do we carry with us as we stumble forward, waiting to give birth?

Rilke wrote that "every angel is terrifying." But surely none is so terrifying as the one who appears to every mother who will give birth, in spite of her past and her wounds, who tells her that out of those wounds an infant will arrive: hope in the form of a body.

I made my way back to the checkpoint, again passing through three turnstiles, metal detectors, barbed wire. I found my way onto the waiting bus. And as Jerusalem appeared again in the distance, I removed the small book from my bag and read the letter I had written to my child that afternoon:

> *Dear _____,*
>
> *It's so hot today. I was thinking of you, my beauty, my little one, as I walked into the parking lot of the hospital. You aren't even born. I thought: Why? Why am I even bringing you into this, already?*
>
> *This is the life I have chosen, my love. Forgive me. It's the only life I know how to bring you into.*

Umm Yusuf

I HAD ALWAYS EXPECTED THE DIVISION BETWEEN PREGNANCY and childbirth to be neat: first there was no child, and then one arrived. But it was not that way at all. The baby was already very much with us, every day, in the swelling of my breasts, the rounding of my womb, the shoes that no longer fit. Even the neighbors acknowledged the presence of a new person within me before he arrived.

It turns out that the easiest way to make your neighbors stop thinking that you are a spy is to have a baby. Every trip up the stairs with a crib to install or paint for the nursery seemed to confirm in our neighbors' eyes that spies do not have children, so all of their suspicions about us were likely unfounded. The last lines of resistance were quietly crossed, and we became part of the neighborhood at last.

The old men sitting on the front steps and smoking cigarettes would part when I opened the front door, to let me pass. Abu Hossam would nod solemnly. "We're praying for you!" he would say, before handing me sesame bread and refusing to let me pay. I encountered Sister Pascal at the Freij grocery store, who had now transformed into the kindest nun in the world, in her white habit. "*Nous prions pour vous,*" she whispered quietly. Sheikh Mazen, descendant of the Prophet Mohammed, announced solemnly: "*Nusallee mishanik.*" Surely there was no other unborn child who had so many prayers protecting him.

In the mornings, I would cross Mother Superior Maria, who lived beneath us, as I headed to the front door to buy bread. "*¡Estoy orando por ti!*"—I'm praying for you!—she would call out in Spanish, hastily making a sign of the cross in the air. Then she would sweep the space in front of me, as if blessing the earth so that I could walk on it.

In Arabic society, a mother and father adopt the name of their oldest son as their honorific title, a symbol of the importance of having a child and a tradition reminiscent of the name changes we see repeatedly in the book of Genesis to signal major life events. It seemed odd to me that I could live for thirty years and then suddenly have my name changed to that of someone I had, for most of my life, not known existed.

It did not come naturally to me. When Frédéric and I married, I had changed my last name on the French marriage certificate, but then had not been able to bring myself to use it. It had felt too strange, too forced, like taking on an identity that was not truly mine—to overnight become French instead of Spanish. And maybe I was scared. My parents' marriage had ended in divorce. So had his parents'. To keep my own name was to keep one extra skin of resistance to the possibility of loss.

But now I no longer had the choice. The neighbors did it without asking me. Once they learned that, if we had a boy, we wanted to name him Joseph, the entire neighborhood began calling me Umm Yusuf, which meant "Mother of Joseph."

"Umm Yusuf! Your bag is open!"

"Umm Yusuf! Let me carry that for you!"

"Umm Yusuf!"

It took some getting used to, and more than once someone shouted after me, "Umm Yusuf!" and I forgot to turn around.

I didn't even know if the child was a boy. But even this did not matter. A Palestinian friend informed me that, now that the neighborhood had decided that I was going to have a boy, there would be no changing my name. They would persist in calling me Umm Yusuf, even if I had a girl. In fact, they would continue with the name until I had a boy, as a reminder of the boy I had not yet conceived. And she would know: when she was pregnant with her first child, the entire neighborhood began calling her Umm Faris, until she had no choice but to name her first son Faris. I had to admire a society in which the neighborhood had a say in such matters.

But what if something went wrong? I was uneasy about naming a child who was not even born. Every step that we took toward investing emotionally in this child meant more pain if he or she were lost.

My Israeli friend Karen seemed to understand this intuitively when she called me to congratulate me on the pregnancy.

"Do you need anything?" she asked.

"No, I think I'm fine."

"Thank God," she said. "Because I know I'm supposed to ask, but I don't actually want to get you anything until he's born. It's a Jewish thing. If you give a baby something before he's born, then you might give him the evil eye." Many Jewish people take this so seriously that they will not even tell a pregnant woman *mazel tov*, or congratulations, lest they jinx something; instead, they'll only say *b'shaah tova*—may you give birth in an auspicious time.

"Oh God, don't give him the evil eye," I begged her.

"Yeah," she confirmed, "I thought that there probably isn't anything you need so much that it's worth risking the evil eye for."

———————

Ramadan came in September that year, and the street crowded every day with worshippers ferried in by bus from the West Bank to attend prayers at Al-Aqsa Mosque, so that the space in front of our house was transformed into a carnival. It was too hot to not eat all day, and among the fasting crowds, men snapped at one another and longed for their cigarettes. The buses that dropped them off and picked them up parked on either side of our house, and at night the air swelled with men shouting out destinations to those passing by: "Ramallah, Ramallah! Ramallah!" The bus to Issawiya, a Palestinian neighborhood in East Jerusalem, parked directly beneath the balcony.

"Issawiya! Issawiya! Issawiya! Issawiya! Issawiya! Issawiya!" the drivers shouted.

"Issawiya! Issawiya! Issawiya! Issawiya! Issawiya! Issawiya!"

Frédéric and I sat beside the breeze provided by the open window, listening. I had my baby book open, which informed me that by six months in the womb, a baby could recognize his own name if you spoke it aloud often enough. I turned to Frédéric grimly.

"Our child probably thinks that his name is Issawiya."

When the cannon shot fired, the long day of fasting was over. The sun set, and over the street a thousand lights were illuminated in the dusk, complete with crescent moons fastened to the lampposts. Only the poorest street vendors did not return home to eat with their families, huddling together to share hummus instead, unable to abandon their vacuum cleaners and blenders and tanks of fish and bags of chocolate to take a meal elsewhere. Ramadan was the busiest time of the year for street vendors, and they would likely earn more in a month's time than they would for the rest of the year. I watched the young men huddled in a circle on the pavement across the street.

For the first time, they did not seem like strangers, but part of my own field of belonging. Yes—I looked at them and, oddly, sensed, from the deepest part of me, that we belonged to one another, despite the fact that we had never met.

"Do you think we might bring them some fruit?" I asked Frédéric hesitantly.

"Why not?"

I rushed to assemble what we had in the kitchen—apples and bananas, a few ripe peaches and dates—and I placed them in a pile on a platter, together with two knives. I hurried down to the street and shyly offered the platter to the men circled around their meal. They looked up in surprise, and then one reached out and gladly accepted. I disappeared upstairs.

From the window, we watched them eating the fruit, peeling the apples with the knives as though engaged in a ceremony. Twenty minutes later, a knock at the door. I ran downstairs. One of the men handed me the platter and asked, cautiously, "Do you think we could we have some coffee?"

I ran upstairs. "They want coffee," I announced.

For some reason, this request gave me immense joy—where we lived, it was only the owners of the house who offered coffee, and the guests who accepted. A few minutes later, Frédéric appeared on the street with a tray full of small cups of Arabic coffee and a small bowl of sugar. The men drank them on the spot, thanked him, and put the glasses back on the tray. Had I known how to inspect the grains they left behind, I might have, in the local tradition, known all of their futures.

And I marveled. Marveled because of something new, something that had caused me to recognize men who had always been strangers in the street. Some new way of being in the world had touched me. It wasn't me. It was the child in me, the child who had told me. And it occurred to me that the greatest gift a child might give me would be to release me from the burden of myself. For the first time in my life, I felt like I might actually have it in me to be a mother—not because I was any good at taking care of anyone, but because this child, even from the womb, seemed determined to teach me how.

The next day, I invited Umm Hossam, the wife of Abu Hossam, over to drink tea. She had raised eight children, exactly like my own grandmother, and I was hoping that she might be able to give me some advice.

She arrived in the afternoon wearing a long navy coat, her hair veiled, and made a place for herself in the salon. Her youngest son, just under a year, lay beside her on the cushion. I brought her tea, and then the two of us sat down to drink together.

"Umm Hossam," I began, "I'm having a child in three months, and I have no idea what to do. I was hoping that you could help me."

She laughed. "What do you want to know?"

"Everything."

She touched my hand. I knew that her life had not been easy. But she was made of something more solid than I was, more resilient.

"I had my first child when I was sixteen years old," she began. "I was so worried. I asked myself: How will I know how to feed him? How will I know how to put him to sleep? But then Hossam was born, and when he was hungry he told me he was hungry, and when he was tired he cried until I helped him to sleep.

"Don't you worry," she said softly. "Our children know far more than we can ever know. Just wait, and your child will teach you everything."

Linea Nigra

LATE SUMMER TURNED TO FALL AND THEN TO WINTER, IN that curious time in the city during which three seasons seemed to overlap. The intense heat faded, and migratory birds began their journey overhead to seek shelter in Africa for wintertime. Then winter approached, and the leaves of the Great Tree drifted onto the balcony, until all that remained were the empty branches staring back at us.

My own body also passed through seasons. Dark rings formed around my nipples. I was stunned to discover a long brown line, called a linea nigra, appear seemingly overnight on my abdomen, like a border, marking the passage from one stage of my life to the next. From where had it come? What other parts of myself lay there, dormant and unrecognized, ready to ink themselves to the surface with this child?

Everything seemed to be in movement. I looked at Frédéric in the morning, still in his monk's cassock as a robe, handing me a cup of tea, and I was astonished to think that this frail and imperfect love we had built between us—a love on pilgrimage—had created a child. Had taken a form: hope in a body, with arms and legs; the sum of us and yet surpassing us; both entirely ours and entirely other.

"Do you know that you have a soul inside of you?" Frédéric asked at breakfast. "What does that feel like?"

"A small, white bird, nesting."

In late September, I headed again to the Holy Family Hospital, where I had signed up to take classes that would help coach me through the labor process. While in America these would have been couples' classes, among Palestinians childbirth was seen as a woman's business, and men were largely relegated to pacing back and forth as they waited in the wings, or nervously smoking cigarettes outside.

Immediately following the class, I would have my first meeting with Dr. George, my obstetrician, in his private clinic.

By now I had reached the exhausted, very cranky stage of pregnancy. When I arrived at the other side of the checkpoint in Bethlehem, I waved to a taxi driver immediately, shouted out the price, and hopped inside his car before any other driver could speak to me.

"*Mustashfa francowi*," I barked. The French hospital.

He turned around from his seat to examine me. "Are you Arab?"

"No."

"Your mother?"

"No."

"Your father?"

"No." Then, despite my attempts to be bullish, I fell into the Syrian habit of melodrama. "Just my heart."

He smiled. "That's the most important part of the body, the heart." He turned back toward the road. "Why are you in Bethlehem?"

"I'm having a child."

"At the French hospital?" he asked. "I have eight children. I had all of them there. I didn't pay full price because I'm from the camp. A *lehje*. How do you say that in English?"

"You're a refugee," I said quietly.

"Yes," he said. "What's the name of your doctor?"

"Dr. George."

"Ahhh, yes," he answered. "He delivered one of my children too."

He slowed down now, aware of the invisible life in his taxi, and he maneuvered the vehicle around every pothole so that the taxi wouldn't bounce, until I arrived at the hospital gates.

"*Khaleenee*," he said as I placed the money in his hand. I insist: take it as an offering from me.

"Next time," I said, and closed the door before he could hand the money back. "*Allah maik*," he called out the window as I left. God be with you.

<hr />

By the time I arrived at the hospital, a small class of nervous-looking Palestinian women had assembled in a room on the far side of the hospital courtyard.

A nurse bounced in, all energy in her uniform. She asked for our names, which we called out, one after another, as she checked them against a list on her clipboard. Then she announced, rather abruptly, "So, you are all going to have babies."

A murmur of giggles responded.

She clarified. "Each one of you is going to have a baby come out of your vagina."

There was an audible gasp. To be fair, she did not actually say "vagina," which is really only used in Arabic as a curse word. She used a term that meant something like our "hidden place." But we knew what she meant.

She smiled through her teeth. "Here you are going to learn everything you need to have a natural labor. If you have any questions, you can ask me. Now listen. I know your mother thinks she knows what you should do when you go into labor. I know that your grandmother thinks she knows what you should do when you go into labor. I know that your husband's mother thinks that she knows what you should do when you go into labor. But they are not a nurse or a doctor, so if you have a question, ask one of us."

There were nods of recognition around the room, from women who had clearly been getting an earful from the women in their families.

She continued. "So everyone in this room is at least five months pregnant. Now, how many of you have ever taken a mirror and looked at your 'hidden place'?"

Horrified silence followed.

The nurse repeated herself, forcefully now. "I want all of you to go home, get out a mirror, and look at your 'hidden place.' Because whether you like it or not, a baby is going to come out of there."

And on that point, there was no arguing with her.

———————

When the class was finished, I walked up the hill toward Dr. George's private office. Behind the secretary's desk, the door to the doctor's office was open, and inside I could see Dr. George, with his wide belly, busy leaning back in his chair and smoking a cigarette.

"Come in! Come in!" he called.

I pointed. "I'll come in when you put out your cigarette."

He smiled. "You should come more often. Maybe I'd quit." He put out his cigarette in the ashtray in front of him, and I waited for the smoke to clear before I sat down. I noticed a Virgin Mary calendar prominently displayed behind him, with Arabic writing spelling out the feast days, a hint that he was part of Bethlehem's ancient Arab Christian community.

"You're Christian?"

"Greek Orthodox," he said.

"I'm due on Christmas day," I reminded him. "Will you be *working* on Christmas day? Or will you take the day off because it's your holiday?"

"Don't worry, don't worry," he assured me. "You're due on December twenty-fifth, right? Greek Orthodox Christmas isn't celebrated in Bethlehem until the sixth of January. You have an extra twelve days to have the baby." And I was momentarily relieved that at least the schism between the Orthodox and Roman Catholic Churches in 1054 meant that my doctor would be with me on the day my child was born.

But a seed of doubt had been planted within me. "So you'll work on Christmas," I prodded. "That's good. But what if I give birth in the middle of the night? Will you be there, then?"

He sighed and nodded. "I don't know what it is about women. But you are always having your babies in the middle of the night."

We moved to the neighboring room, where he hooked me up to an ultrasound machine. He rubbed cold gel on my stomach, and I waited for the baby to appear on the screen.

"Don't forget, I don't want to know the sex," I reminded him.

Then you were there. Swimming. Enormous. Kicking to get out.

"Looks like he's going to be a little football player," the doctor said.

I grimaced.

"Nope, a ballerina," he corrected himself.

There was the hand. And there was the heart. It sounded like horses running next to the sea.

He printed out the two photos and put the date at the top. I could not stop staring at them as I walked back to the bus: the smudge of eyes, the dent of a nose.

It was alarming, really, to contain an actual living person. Once, years before, I had seen in the Byzantine monastery of Chora in Istanbul a mosaic of the Virgin Mary frowning, with the baby Jesus in her womb. She held out her two arms, seemingly in a look of exasperation, as if to say: "What do you want me to do? Smile all the time? There's a baby in my womb!"

Unlike the images in my sonograms, that Jesus sat upright and stared straight ahead, out of her belly, through the fabric of her blue gown. He looked like a toddler, completely aware, with a halo, and he appeared to be eating a popsicle and wearing golden pajamas. Mary's hands were outstretched to two angels, who paused in midflight beside her. And beneath her was written in Greek:

The Mother of God, the dwelling place of the uncontainable.

As I walked back toward the checkpoint, holding those photos in my hands, a man who sold jewelry chased after me, his bracelets clinking in his hands as he tried to catch me.

"I know you," he said. "Do you know me?"

"Yes." I had often seen him selling bracelets at the checkpoint. "But not today. I can't talk to you today."

"Don't you want to help me?"

I tried to think of what I could say to him. "I'm pregnant," I announced.

He stopped in his tracks.

"*Mashallah! Mabrouk.* Congratulations!" he said, beaming at me. Then he quickly added, "*Inshallah*, it will be a boy."

Ze Christmas Tree

WAITING FOR CHRISTMAS BECAME WAITING FOR THE baby to arrive. I thought of those Advent calendars of childhood, the windows we opened every day with a picture inside, as Mary and Joseph approached the stable in Bethlehem. Now every day opened to another list of things we needed: a doctor's appointment, a package of newborn diapers, a bag now fully packed for the hospital, with socks and a sleeping cap and something to read, an overnight bag for the most unpredictable journey.

Frédéric nested. All of the small, attentive gestures he had paid toward me, the cup of tea or the shoes placed next to the fire—were now extended to a child not yet born. He bought a new woodstove, afraid that the petroleum fumes from the old one would harm the baby. He asked his mother to mail a sheep's hide for the baby to sleep in, having heard that the wool would soothe the baby much like the warmth of the mother's womb, and he placed it in the empty crib expectantly. I told myself that this was what happened when a girl from the city fell in love with a Frenchman from the Alps: there were bound to be sheepskins and woodstoves involved, at one time or another.

And I marveled at how much a child made each of us want to offer up our most authentic selves. Although Frédéric had always spoken to me in English and done his own dreaming in French, now in the night he placed his face against my belly and whispered, "*C'est mon bébé ça!*" in his own language, and we were no longer separate. There was a country between us now that spoke both of our languages, waiting to be born.

At night I would wake up with the baby kicking and pace back and forth, holding him in the salon, letting him swim, as the floorboards trembled with the nearby call to prayer.

The winter so far had been bitingly cold and soaked with rain. But in the mornings, I would peer outside the window to the lemon and orange trees in the garden of the nuns below, swelling with fruit and aglow with water, and they offered strange comfort. I could never have believed that objects so bright could be borne out in such coldness: the miracle of oranges and lemons at a moment when everything else that grows seemed to die. But there they were.

Time worked differently on Nablus Road. It was a culture in which seasons were marked out by crops and winds, the passing of birds, in which holidays were initiated by the appearance of the moon. A pregnancy was watched with its own calendar. No one ever asked me when the baby was due. Instead they seemed to inspect me each day in order to do their own calculation.

"Still no baby?" Abu Hossam would ask me each time I opened the front door to buy bread in the morning.

"Still no baby," I would sigh.

"*Inshallah,*" he would say helpfully.

A young boy who worked shelving groceries at the next-door grocer's asked, "Umm Yusuf, where *is* Yusuf?"

"He's coming," I assured him. "He's on his way," though I was becoming less and less certain of that with every passing day.

As Christmas approached, the visits to Bethlehem changed from every three weeks to every two weeks and finally every week, and as I surveyed each new sonogram, the memories of war in that city were slowly replaced with weight charts, blood pressure numbers, baby books on nutrition, rosebushes in the garden, the miracle of the ordinary. Dr. George reminded me to be certain that the baby was moving. And so I did, every movement a prayer, a promise: *You are still alive.*

Two weeks before Christmas, Frédéric accompanied me to Bethlehem to buy our first Christmas tree.

"Why don't we just buy a Christmas tree in Jerusalem?" I complained.

"There are no Christmas trees in Jerusalem. Besides, I know a guy in Bethlehem."

You know you have lived in the Middle East for too long when you will purchase something from an entirely different city because you know the guy selling it.

That afternoon we found ourselves inspecting Christmas trees, surrounded by dozens of poinsettia plants, in a plant store that stood not fifty meters in front of the separation barrier. I suggested something small, but Frédéric would have nothing of it—a house with high ceilings required a monumental Christmas tree. He pointed to a pine tree the full height of his body, more than six feet tall. Someone clearly needed to ask the question of how we would get a six-foot Christmas tree from Bethlehem to Jerusalem without a car, but I decided not to be that person, and so we paid, and Frédéric grabbed the trunk and dragged the Christmas tree down the busy street, past the jewelry seller and the swarm of taxi drivers awaiting passengers.

"*Mabrouk!*" they called out. "Congratulations on your purchase!" We waved. Frédéric beamed. I remembered that his national service had been to work in the French forestry service, clearing trees along rural roads.

We walked the length of the separation wall, toward the first set of turnstiles at the checkpoint. I cheerfully showed our passports. Frédéric lifted the tree up vertically and pushed it through the turnstile, letting the tree fall on the other side before he followed it. The soldier on duty stared.

By now the Christmas tree was becoming burdensome. Frédéric continued dragging it through the parking lot and into the building that held the final checkpoint to Jerusalem. The line stretched for some twenty people. We took our places: me, Frédéric, the baby in my womb, and our six-foot Christmas tree. I was nine months pregnant.

"I feel like we're a piece of Dadaist art," I sighed.

Just then, the light on the checkpoint, which turned from red to green as it allowed each person through the turnstiles to pass security, stopped working. It hurt to stand. I was nauseated from the prospect of being trapped in a military zone in a long line full of people, stuck behind a Christmas tree.

Someone started laughing. Someone else. A man snapped a photo of us with his cell phone. I smiled, despite myself.

At last, the light began working again, and we reached the front of the line. Frédéric patiently pulled the Christmas tree through. I pushed it from the top, where the star would have been. The floor of the checkpoint was littered with pine needles. The soldier on duty didn't know what to do. He was tasked with checking if we were carrying anything dangerous.

"*Ma ze?*" he asked in Hebrew. What's this?

"*Ze* Christmas tree," Frédéric answered cheerfully.

The soldier, bewildered, waved us through. We waited for the white-and-blue bus on the other side, then Frédéric convinced the driver to cram the tree in the back, and we made it home with the smell of pine lingering among the plastic seats and rows of passengers. It was our first Christmas miracle.

The Hopes and Fears

My sister arrived a week before Christmas and settled into one of the many rooms of the house, and we waited. Even my maternity clothes no longer fit. I ate everything I could think of to make the baby want to come out early: pineapple, hot peppers, salsa, Thai food. I tried tango dancing at two in the morning. I ended up with heartburn, swollen feet, and still no baby.

Every day my sister would ask: "Do you think you'll have the baby today?"

"Yes," I would answer, as though positive thinking were enough to induce labor.

It was not. The baby earned his first nickname: No Show.

Finally, Frédéric and I decided upon a foolproof plan for bringing the baby on time: we would walk the seven kilometers to Bethlehem on Christmas Eve. I had read that walking was an effective way of bringing on labor. More importantly, if I were to go into labor in Jerusalem on Christmas Eve, the crowds of pilgrims traveling to Bethlehem for the holiday would make it almost impossible to reach the hospital in a taxi. But if we *walked*, not only would I almost certainly go into labor, but I would also conveniently end up right next to the Holy Family Hospital, where I needed to give birth. Genius.

On Christmas Eve, Frédéric, my sister, and I met up with a group of French nuns and a priest we had recruited to make the journey with us. As we set out along the road toward Bethlehem, I searched the sky for a star more radiant than others—one that might guide us.

I was already thinking of what a wonderful story this would be to tell my child. In retrospect, I had succumbed to the great writer's fallacy of believing that, if there is a story good enough to be told, then everything in the universe will come together to tell it.

The first mile was magnificent. By the second mile, I was becoming slightly resentful of the buoyant energy of the French nuns, who kept breaking into song. I had forgotten how swollen my feet had become with the additional weight, and they started developing blisters. When the French priest disappeared to relieve himself on the side of the road, it dawned on me that fate was not writing the romantic story I had hoped it would.

By the time we arrived in Shepherds' Field, the field where tradition said that the shepherds had seen the star that led them to the manger, I was sore and cranky and certainly not in labor. Around me were the caves that locals believed that the shepherds had once dwelled in, sleeping when they were not keeping watch over their flocks. A volunteer was assigning caves to the different pilgrims arriving for mass. We were in Cave Number 3. This struck me as utterly depressing, as though I had arrived at the megamall of biblical caves. The site was swarming with tourists wearing Santa Claus hats covered in flashing lights.

I found a chair at the corner of the very crowded Cave Number 3. The priest who walked with us now appeared at the altar, transformed in his liturgical vestments, and though he was speaking French, I understood. He read out from the gospel of Luke:

> *While they were there, the time came for her to have her child,*
> *And she gave birth to a son, her firstborn. She wrapped*
> *him in swaddling clothes,*
> *And laid him in a manger because there was no room*
> *for them at the inn.*

Frédéric reached for my hand. The priest looked in our direction. Then, I watched him gather his breath before he turned to the expectant faces in front of him.

"Brothers and sisters," he began. "You've just heard me read from the gospel of Luke. And like all of you, I've listened to this story, year after year on Christmas Eve, all of my life. I've gotten used to it." He paused and looked at the crowd, assembled in the cave. "But then tonight, something happened. I walked to Bethlehem with a man and his wife, who is nine months pregnant, waiting for their first child to be born. And suddenly, the story became real to me again. I remembered that it isn't only a story in a book, but that it actually happened, to people like you and me. That it isn't over. It continues to be real, even today."

I could feel myself trying not to cry. All that had transpired—and had not transpired—that night was a blessing. Life is messy. It is full of bathroom breaks, and swollen ankles, and bad calculations, and Christmas trees dragged through checkpoints: apparently it is even full of Santa hats with flashing lights. It is a story that we do not get to write ourselves. Why else are we so moved when Mary calls out to the angel: "How can this be, since I am a virgin?"

"How can this be?" What a perfect way to begin the quintessential story of childbirth, with a mother who learns that all bets are off, that this story will not be written on her terms.

To say yes to this, to this miraculous, messy, untimely act of creation, is all that we can ask of ourselves.

That Christmas Eve, I sat there, in Cave Number 3, somewhere nearby the place where a star had appeared two thousand years before, and I did not have a child. But I was part of a mystery borne again and again: broken and burnt out and imperfect as I was, inheriting still this "How can this be?"—this impossible gift.

The hopes and fears of all the years
Are met in thee tonight.

A World Made New

CHRISTMAS CAME AND WENT, AND THERE WAS STILL NO CHILD.

"*Nu?*" my friend Benjy wrote me, asking in Yiddish where the baby was. I looked up a phrase and wrote him back.

"*Der mentsh trakht un Got lakht.*" I responded. Man makes plans, and God laughs.

My sister stayed on in the house, but now my father and stepmother arrived, having originally booked their tickets to fly in a week after the birth. When I opened the door to buy bread in the morning, Abu Hossam just shook his head and sighed.

Ten days after Christmas, Dr. George ordered us to the hospital to have the baby induced. It was not the way I had imagined the story for myself. I had spent four months worrying about passing through the checkpoint during childbirth, but since I was not in labor, we had plenty of time, calmly arriving at the Holy Family Hospital at midday.

Dr. George came as the nurses were checking to see if I was dilated.

"Still no baby?" he asked.

"Still no baby."

There comes a time in a pregnancy when the fact that the baby hasn't arrived feels like a personal failure, as though that baby would rather do anything in the world other than be born and spend time with you.

"You know that when you're ten days overdue, we have to induce."

"I know, doctor. That's why I'm here."

"On the other hand, as you said, you're here. Nothing can happen to you once you're here, and we can keep an eye on you."

"That's good to know."

"You're not at all dilated. I know that you want to have a natural birth, that you don't want me to induce—so I need you to tell me what to do."

I had become accustomed to the fact that nothing in this pregnancy was happening on my terms. I looked up at him curiously. "Really, doctor?"

He nodded. "Really."

In fact, all I wanted to do was sleep. There was no longer a checkpoint between my house and the hospital room. Someone else was cooking my meals. My room was not crowded with family. I was suddenly not in any hurry to have the baby. I was exhausted— from waiting, from the stress of not knowing if I would arrive at the hospital safely, from my family hovering over me and looking for indications that I might go into labor, from the street vendors and nuns and relatives of the Prophet Muhammad watching me for signs of an infant.

"I'm so, so tired. If you induce me now, I don't think I'll have the strength to make it through the labor. Is there any limit to how long I can stay here?"

"You can stay here as long as you need to," he said.

"Can you induce the baby tomorrow?" I asked. "Tonight I just want to rest."

He patted my head. "Sleep, then. We just have to keep checking on the baby's heartbeat every few hours to make sure that everything's okay."

The hospital grew dark with the silence of winter. Bethlehem lay on the edge of the desert, and January took on a stillness I remembered from the monastery in Syria, a certain quality that made objects come into focus. Outside, in the courtyard, the statue of Mary remained aglow, holding out her arms, and beneath her the orange and lemon trees weighed down with fruit, that same miracle following me from Nablus Road, trees bearing fruit when everything else that grows was dying, color bearing forth in this coldness.

Frédéric and I found my room, at the very end of the farthest hall of the hospital. I watched the women we passed as if they were returning pilgrims who might give me some secrets of the coming journey, some lying down and holding their babies wrapped in thick blankets, others pacing with them up and down the halls. Grandmothers handed out chocolates to relatives assembled at bedsides. Everything was in Arabic, everything beyond language.

In the middle of the hallway, a room held rows of newly born infants asleep in plastic beds. At the window, two men, who clearly had never met before, stood shoulder to shoulder and shyly pointed out their babies through the window, whispering.

"*Haitha ilee.*" This one is mine.

We entered my room, and within a moment I had collapsed into bed. Frédéric kissed me on my forehead and left me to rest. To preserve the intimacy of the hospital for the other women there, Frédéric had used his church connections to arrange for a private room on the other side of the hospital—this man always had ways to secure houses, hospital beds, and Christmas trees. He would come when I needed him. But now I was glad to be left alone.

I pulled the covers over my head, and a minute later I fell into the sleep of the dead. I had never slept like that before, and I never would again. I disappeared, taken out of the world momentarily. When I awakened, I suspected that days had passed. It had only been four hours.

I called the nurse. She led me into another room, and Dr. George was there again, checking me.

"What happened?" I asked him.

"You're three centimeters dilated now," he said. "You don't waste any time, do you?"

I was confused. I was just asking why I had fallen into such deep sleep. "What does that mean?"

"What it means is that you'll give birth tonight or tomorrow."

I had been waiting so long to go into labor that now, when it was happening, it seemed to be a mistake.

"I'm having a baby?"

He laughed.

"How will I know if I'm giving birth today or tomorrow?"

He pretended to think for a minute. "Today, there were only boys born in the hospital. If you want a boy, then you have to give birth before midnight. Otherwise, if you give birth tomorrow, who knows what you'll have?"

He left. I lay there in the bed, staring at the ceiling, and then the nurse arrived again to give me a CTG and listen to the heart. She attached the monitor to my womb and then turned up the volume. The room resonated with the sound of the beating heart: horses galloping near the sea, forceful and muffled at once. She left the room and the sound remained, galloping.

When she returned, she moved me to my side and then began speaking to me in Arabic.

"Where are you from?"

"I'm from America."

"America! My son just got engaged to an American Palestinian."

"Congratulations," I managed. I was still not fully awake, but she clearly needed to process, and as any woman knows, this urge must be acted upon.

"I hope they get Jerusalem ID papers," she continued. "At least then maybe they'll stay here. My other son has already left. What are they supposed to do? There's no life here."

I kept listening, and trying to look past her in order to see the lines of the heart, moving regularly up and down on sheets of paper.

She unhooked me, and the beating stopped.

"Everything's normal," she announced. "We'll check you again in a few hours."

The sheet of the baby's heartbeat was still hanging from the machine, with the lines drawn out on it, like an SOS from another world, my child trying desperately to contact me.

"Do you think you can give me the sheet?" I asked her.

She tore it off, wrote my name at the top of it, and handed it over. Then she reconsidered, took it back for a moment, examined it, and scribbled a note across the bottom.

"No contractions yet," it said.

———◆———

The sky outside had grown dark. I opened the window in my hospital room, and there was rain, a single olive tree. Silence.

I called Frédéric. "We're having a baby tonight," I said.

I could hear him smiling. "Should I come?"

"Not yet. We have time."

A friend had warned me: once you have a child, you are never alone in the world again. I would take advantage of my last hours of solitude to reflect. It seemed too immense to even comprehend. Beginning in a few hours, even when I was alone at home, part of me would always be with another human being—worried, anxious, proud. I would no longer be my own.

I was too nervous to sleep. Eventually I sorted through my bag until I found the book I had, for some reason, chosen to bring with me: *Into the Wild*, the story of a young man named Christopher McCandless who decides to brave the Alaska wilderness alone, and ends up dying, his decomposed body discovered by a moose hunter. I knew the contractions were coming, and it did not help that I was reading the story of a young man who is facing the wild alone. I could not remember what had possessed me to bring such a book to the maternity hospital.

I continued to read. Christopher, now going by Alex, was determining that if he ran into a bear, he would climb a tree. I fell asleep to the patter of rain falling outside.

I woke up to knocking. Frédéric was standing in the doorway alongside Father Peter, a Jesuit priest who had lived in the Middle East for more than four decades. Peter possessed a kindly, wrinkled face, and a habit of giving away everything that he owned, except for his books, which he guarded with a vengeance that endeared him to me. There were kind men and there was Father Peter, who was something else, who carried himself with a simplicity belonging to those who are holy, but who do everything in their power to lead you to believe that they are ordinary. And you might even be convinced, were it not for the local people always running up to him in the street, beaming with joy upon meeting him. Peter was patient and yet sometimes cranky—especially if you tried to compliment him. He had a love of Hemingway, Faulkner, and the poetry of Gerard Manley Hopkins, and had managed to read more books than anyone I'd ever met. In other words, he was my kind of saint.

He was older than Father Paolo, but a friend of his, from a generation of Jesuit priests from long ago, fluent in Arabic and living throughout the Middle East, from Baghdad to Egypt, taking both Muslims and Christians as their students. And if Paolo had been our spiritual father in the desert, then Father Peter was our spiritual father in Bethlehem. He entered the room and patted my shoulder. Frédéric leaned down to kiss me.

I was pretty sure that they had already started celebrating the baby.

"It's not every day that a man becomes a father," Father Peter announced.

I groaned. "How did you even get into the hospital? Visiting hours are over!"

"Peter says the Mass here every morning," Frédéric beamed. "He can come in whenever he wants."

I had to laugh. I sat up in my bed, and Peter handed me a small donkey made out of olive wood.

"I wanted to give you something. A present for the baby."

"A donkey?"

"Not just any donkey. This is Telhami." *Telhami* meant "Bethlehemite" in Arabic.

Father Peter leaned in to tell his story. "They say that when the time came for Mary and Joseph to travel from Nazareth to Bethlehem for the census, Mary found a donkey in Nazareth to carry her on the journey. She rode him all the way to Bethlehem, and he remained with her until it was time for her to give birth. That night, on Christmas Eve, the donkey wandered off from the stables and met another beautiful donkey from Bethlehem, and they fell in love and conceived a baby donkey that night."

He held the small wooden donkey in his hand. "After Jesus was born, Mary's donkey had to go with the family to flee to Egypt, leaving the donkey he loved behind, still pregnant with their baby. In his absence, she gave birth to a donkey named Telhami, a reminder of the union between them."

I had anticipated many things on the night I would give birth, but not a tragic donkey love story. "Whatever happened to Telhami?"

Father Peter smiled. "He grew up in Bethlehem and remained in the area, taking the name of the village. And then, do you remember when Jesus rode a donkey into Jerusalem on Palm Sunday? That donkey was Telhami, returning to carry him after all of those years."

I placed Telhami next to the bed. Peter tousled my hair, Frédéric kissed me and made me promise to call him the moment I needed him, and they left. I closed my eyes and tried to sleep.

But it was time.

I slid on my slippers and crept into the hallway. The world was fast asleep. Even the nurse on duty had fallen asleep over her papers. Only Mary was awake, all aglow in the courtyard, peering down at me.

I leaned against the windows and tried to breathe through the contractions.

I returned to my room and attempted to sleep again. It was now impossible.

I walked out to the hallway, and paced back and forth beneath the statue of Mary. Every few minutes, the contractions came, and I placed my hands against the wall and breathed to keep myself from buckling under the weight. The pain was excruciating. I considered that my mother had also gone through this for all four of her children, and it occurred to me that I was a terrible and ungrateful daughter for not thanking her every single day for the pain that she had borne for me. I said a silent prayer to her in the night.

Mother, if you had to go through this for me, then I forgive you for anything you ever did wrong, and I forgive you in advance for anything you might ever do wrong to me in the future. I had no idea.

The pain was blinding. I leaned against the wall again. My mood shifted: now I raged against history, angry at the women in my life, angry at Hollywood filmmakers. There must have been some conspiracy of silence since the beginning of time that had allowed women to continue to have children, despite the impossible pain. We had all been tricked. For surely if women knew how painful it was, we would collectively refuse to ever have children again. *How do women all over the world not know about this? And how did we as a species survive?*

I was, very briefly, honestly confused about this point.

I promised myself that if I survived, I would immediately set out to warn the women in the world that childbirth should be avoided at all costs, even if it meant the end of the human species.

The contractions stopped. I walked over to the nurse on duty and shook her awake.

"I want my husband," I said.

"*Haraam*. What a pity!" she answered wearily. "You have a long time to go. Let him sleep."

She took my blood pressure and steeped a cup of sage tea for me. It was named *mariamiyya* in Arabic, after the Virgin Mary, who according to the local Islamic tradition used sage leaves in order to soothe the pangs of her labor in the desert.

I remembered that, in the book of Genesis, birth pains were the punishment for mankind's first sin. That in the Quran, Mary is overcome with anguish as she waits to give birth to Jesus. This all made sense now.

When I finished drinking, I looked at the nurse steadily. "Thank you," I said. "Now get my husband."

And this time she didn't argue.

———————◆———————

Love happens in hospitals, the way prayers happen in churches—the walls are filled with stories of the born and the sick and the dead, with so much fragility, and then we walk in it, in our slippered feet, trying not to do too much damage. That night, Frédéric took my hand and we paced down the hallways of the Holy Family Hospital. All night, the statue of the Virgin looked down on us, she who had been through so much, torn open, now healed, carrying the memory of her wounds. The lemon and orange trees glistened in the rain and light. We had traveled so far, the two of us, from Syria to Aleppo to France to Istanbul, to a house on Nablus Road, but there was no journey like the one we made that night in the dark, that painful passage from one kind of life to another. I was aware of being taken over by forces within me that were controlling me, and I tried to breathe and remember what I had learned in birth classes, but it was all gone now, and I was stumbling in the dark.

Is it too much to ask for a child to heal some of what has been broken? To believe that the new life coming was not only that of the child, but also that of the parents, entrusted now to travel the fragile crust of the earth with this impossible gift, this life? As I gave myself over to the pain, I kept thinking, *On the other side there is beauty, there is beauty, there is beauty.* Frédéric whispered to me. I had not imagined that such pain could exist. One hour, two hours, five hours, eight hours, nine hours. *Breathe. Breathe. Ferry that soul to this side of the water.*

Frédéric remained beside me, reminded me to do the most elemental acts that I had somehow lost hold of: *to walk, to breathe, to breathe.*

Time moved in two opposing directions, stretching on endlessly and condensing quickly, long silences punctuated by intense pain, contractions moving closer together. In the early morning, the nurse measured me, and I was almost fully dilated. She pushed me in a wheelchair to a delivery room upstairs. All of my natural child-birth books had made me frightened of giving birth in beds, which symbolized the horrors of traditional births, but I was much too tired to remember what I was supposed to do instead, so—scared as I was of the bed but incapable of imagining any alternative—I collapsed on the hard floor in pain. It was January fifth, the night before Christmas Eve celebrations in Bethlehem.

At five thirty in the morning, Dr. George arrived. By that time, I was no longer on the floor, but leaning into the wall.

"January fifth," he announced, clucking. "You see? This baby knows exactly when the *real* Christmas is!"

I started crying. "I want an epidural. I know I said I wanted a natural birth, but I changed my mind. I didn't understand. Please give me one. Give me anything."

He shook his head.

"Tell him, Frédéric," I begged. Frédéric tried to tell him.

"It's too late for an epidural," Dr. George announced. Then he called out to the nurse in Arabic. "Move her to the bed. She's ready."

And after months of reading books learning how to give birth in water, or standing up, or lying on my side, or even squatting, I was too exhausted to argue. I didn't care anymore where I gave birth. I climbed onto the bed. The nurse hooked up the monitor to the baby's heart, turned up the volume. Pounding.

"Push," the doctor ordered.

I started to push. Nothing happened.

Push.

I held Frédéric's hand and squeezed it tightly. He tried to speak to the doctor and I punched him in the stomach.

Push.

Dr. George was standing at the end of the bed, hoping for a baby to appear. Seeing that my pushes were coming to nothing, he turned to the nurse on duty. "How much did you pay for carrots yesterday?" he asked her in Arabic. "Because I paid seven shekels for a kilo. Can you believe that? Seven shekels for carrots? Who pays seven shekels for carrots?"

Push. I pushed again. All became a blur. The baby's heartbeat. Screaming. Morning light streaming through the windows.

A boy. You. Joseph.

———•———

I looked up in a haze. There were nuns gliding into the room who blessed you, left. A dream.

I cradled you in the space between my cheek and breast. You seemed designed to fit into the space precisely. *Fearfully and wonderfully made.*

Dr. George approached the bedside. "Okay, enough time has passed now," he said. "You need to push out the placenta."

I almost burst into tears again.

I had convinced myself that I was done. I knew from my books that I would have to push out the placenta eventually. But I had secretly hoped that they had all been wrong, and that I was the unique case of a woman in labor who didn't have a placenta left after I gave birth. In my defense, no one in the movies ever gives birth to a placenta.

I pushed. Nothing happened. I had exhausted every ounce of energy I had.

Dr. George tried to soothe me. "You did everything naturally until the birth, and that's what's important. But now you need to let us give you some anesthesia."

I nodded and turned to Frédéric, scared. "Please take him," I whispered, handing you to him. "I don't want the first thing in the world that he feels to be my fear."

"Shhh. It will be okay."

They wheeled me off for surgery to remove my placenta. I turned and there was Frédéric, visible through the frame of the doorway, holding you in his arms. I had never loved a man as much as I loved him at that moment—he who was holding the world in place in my absence. They wheeled me to a freezing room, and I shivered. The anesthesia numbed me until someone covered me with a blanket. Then they were wheeling me down another hallway.

"When will it be done?" I asked the nurse.

"It's already done," she said.

Reality is messier than we realize until we live it. The day you were born was a disaster and a terrible, unbearable pain, before the world broke open to something else. I looked up and there was my first-born son, now cradled in my father's arms, my father who had rushed over from Jerusalem after Frédéric called him during my labor, without me knowing it. He peered down at me.

"Hey, Daddy," I whispered.

"Hey, little girl," he whispered back. "How do you feel?"

I smiled weakly and sighed. "I feel like a mammal, Daddy."

And there were tears in his eyes, and the world was made new that day, and it was good.

You slept in the clear plastic bed next to me, dressed in giraffe pajamas and a yellow Winnie-the-Pooh hat. You had the hiccups. I held you and you hiccupped in bed. And then you fell asleep with your face against my chest.

Dr. George came in and sat on the edge of the bed.

"Is everything okay?"

"Everything's fine. Only I can't believe that you were talking about carrots when I was giving birth."

He laughed. "Was I? Giving birth is what I see every day." He looked down at you, asleep. "When are you thinking about going home to Jerusalem?"

It seemed too soon to ask. "I thought I might try to go home in three days."

"Good. That's what I was hoping for—because tomorrow and the next day, the roads between Bethlehem and Jerusalem will be closed so that pilgrims can come for Orthodox Christmas. Then later in the week, President Bush is traveling to Bethlehem, and all of the roads between Bethlehem and Jerusalem will be closed again for his visit. You can *only* go home in three days."

I considered this mess of history that we had just placed a child into.

"Then that works out well, then."

"You probably won't see me tomorrow," he added. "But another doctor will come and see you."

"That's right," I smiled. "Merry Christmas."

"Merry Christmas."

He left. Night fell. Frédéric knocked quietly at the door and tiptoed in, barely lasting a few minutes before he nodded off in a chair to sleep.

I stayed awake to watch you, your eyes closed in the plastic bed. There is something unique in the first night of a child's life in the world. You had been inside of me for nine months. Now, a part of me, until now invisible, was made visible. Here was part of myself, given a body, in front of me. And yet altogether other than me: mine and not mine, mysterious.

My dearest Joseph, to have a child is not only to change history, but to defy gravity. Everything shifts, not only the future but also the past, because everything in the past, every street I had walked upon, every word I had spoken, every angel who had appeared on a train, every fragment was a detail that led to you. And roads your father had walked upon in India, and men he had spoken to, and prayers he had uttered in the desert, mysteries that I would never know or even conceive of—they had led to you too. And even with this, you were entirely your own self. And I knew that my parents had felt the same way when they had given birth to me, that I, too, was built of their past lives, and yet I lived my life forward. Every child is this.

I sorted through my hospital bag, until I found again the notebook I had kept during my pregnancy. I turned to the last blank page and wrote a single letter.

Dear Joseph,
On the night before you were born, I looked outside to see a statue of Mary, with her hands out: once torn open, now fully healed. There was an orange tree and a lemon tree in full fruit in the middle of winter. I took that image, and I sewed it into your heart, so that you would be born with it inside of you.

Part Four

The Magical Hours

"A pearl buried deep in a field is not visible."

—*Simone Weil*

The Things
of This World

WE RETURNED TO JERUSALEM DURING THE WINDOW BETWEEN
Orthodox Christmas and the visit of George W. Bush, this time with
a tiny human creature tucked against me. I was anxious to rest, but
Nablus Road had other plans, and the house soon filled up with an
assembly of guests: Abu Hossam and his wife and all of their sons
carrying a plastic bouquet of flowers, the entire Freij family, Mexican
nuns carting baby clothes, and a local tailor offering winter pajamas.
Sister Pascal arrived on the first day, followed by a line of Franciscan
nuns in blue habits.

"Joseph is from *our* house," she proudly announced to the
assembled visitors, as though she were the one who had just suffered
through ten hours of labor. Then she cradled my son in her arms until
he cried, and she carefully handed him back to me.

I was grateful now for such a cavernous house, and while she
had been right in the beginning to warn us that it was much too big
for two people, now it was just big enough to accommodate the ever-
swelling crowds from the street. The front-porch gang made their way
upstairs, with bags of onesies and hats and baby shoes, and my friend
Karen, who was relieved that she could now bear gifts without giving

me the evil eye, arrived with a Noah's Ark wall hanging inscribed in Hebrew. I wondered how such a terrifying biblical story, of a family surviving mass death and an entire planet being submerged in a flood, had inspired so many children's decorations. My father watched, dazed at the French and Arabic and Hebrew speakers ascending and descending the stairs.

As the poet Richard Wilbur wrote, "Love calls us to the things of this world." Joseph, still not fully awake, pressed himself into the indent of my arms, and he cried when he was hungry and whimpered when he was tired, just as Umm Hossam had promised, and though he didn't teach me everything, he taught me enough to get by. At the end of every day, I would be relieved that the guests had come and more relieved that they had left, and I would settle with Joseph into the cocoon that we inhabited together, two bodies still functioning as one. I had been traveling for too long, and now I felt some force stronger than gravity pulling me down to that house on Nablus Road: love and family and the discovery that my existence was now bound up, inextricably, in the bodies of two other people. Every hour or so, Frédéric would tend the fire in the woodstove. Joseph would awaken in the middle of the night, and Frédéric would wake up just to lift him from the small wooden crib next to our bed, out of the woolen sheepskin and into my arms, where he would drink from my body. I was still weak from surgery, and Frédéric would wake again when I finished, just to lift him and ferry him back to the crib to sleep. My breasts filled and emptied and filled again for a child; my husband kept a vigil of holiness he had never expected, lying in wait. Entire stories were written in those brief encounters. I watched a man become a father, lifting a child and placing him back again in a brief ceremony that Joseph would never remember, but which meant everything.

I called those hours between midnight and six in the morning the *magical hours*. I had known about them for years: from Muslims who believed that those hours before dawn held silence during which one would grow closer to God; from Jews who awakened an hour before sunrise to bind tefillin to their arms in prayer; from monks in the Eastern churches who arose early for the matins, ending at sunrise. A chapter in the Quran is called "The Morning Hours," and my Quranic teacher in Syria had awakened each morning to pray in that brief window before the sun rose. In Jerusalem, pilgrims spent the night inside of the Holy Sepulchre and referred to those hours— when the world was silent, save for the lighting of candles—as the Magical Hours.

So it was, at four in the morning, when Joseph cried, and Frédéric lifted him from his crib, and it was just the three of us in the stillness of the city, the birds above and the dead below and this little life, calling out, in the magical hour. Time stretched out, so that I often did not know if a few minutes or several hours had passed. The city carved out the smallest space of light and silence left in it, and allowed us to inhabit it, and for the first time I understood what it was to occupy sanctity in time. Then the three of us collapsed into sleep. In the morning, I would awaken in a bed damp with my milk.

The rhythms of motherhood emerged, and I ate when Joseph ate and slept when he slept, and a world shifted in focus. My life, which had already transformed beyond imagining with marriage, now changed shape again, which is the case when any two strange humans, be they thirty years old or three days old, encounter each other and decide to fall in love. The world must realign itself.

Frédéric, who had always been the calm, steady presence in our marriage, was not so in parenthood. He worried incessantly. When Joseph slept too long, I would find Frédéric next to his crib, checking to make sure that he was still breathing. When he was finally convinced that the baby was merely asleep, he would pull the blue knitted blanket up to his chin to keep him warm, but then a few minutes later—worried that he would overheat—he would return to pull it down again.

He acquired the habit of pacing back and forth with Joseph draped over his shoulder, patting his back softly in time. He would pass hours of every day in this routine, as a father who understood that he could not rid the world of every danger it would pose for his son, but that he could at least hold the gas at bay. A few days into Joseph's life, I awakened wearily in the morning, to see Frédéric pacing back and forth in front of the window with his son nestled against him, barely visible beneath the folds of his little blue knitted sweater. I had stopped nursing hours before, and it occurred to me that Frédéric had been up since then, pacing back and forth in front of the window, singing softly...

> *Au clair de la lune*
> *Mon ami Pierrot*
> *Prête-moi ta plume*
> *Pour écrire un mot.*
> *Ma chandelle est morte*
> *Je n'ai plus de feu*
> *Ouvre-moi ta porte*
> *Pour l'amour de Dieu*

I rubbed my eyes. "How long have you been awake?"

"A few hours." He grew quiet again, continuing to hum softly. He seemed to be pondering something while he continued his steady line of walking back and forth in front of the window.

"You know, all of those years, when I was a novice monk, I tried to wake up in the middle of the night to pray, and every time I fell back asleep. I can't tell you how many times I tried!" He blushed. "I guess that it took a child to make me be able to stay awake all night!"

He continued pacing until I pointed out that Joseph was sleeping, and he softly lowered him into his crib. In the garden beneath us, the tinkle of the bell summoned nuns to their sunrise prayers.

Memory

THE FIRST WEEK OF MOTHERHOOD PASSED IN A HAZE OF feeding and sleep. When Joseph turned seven days old, I called Dr. George to schedule my son's first-week checkup.

"Is something wrong?"

"No, the hospital just said that I should come for a checkup when a week had passed."

He snorted. "I don't understand. If there's nothing wrong, why would you possibly bring that baby out in the cold?" Palestinians, from what I could tell, were generally terrified of cold weather, much like Texans. Dr. George seemed to be under the impression that if I took Joseph outside then he might freeze to death.

I insisted. "I really think that I should bring him for a checkup."

"But nothing's wrong with him. Is anything wrong with *you*?"

It was the first time anyone had asked about me since the birth. "No. I mean, not really. I have hemorrhoids."

"You're hemorrhaging!" Dr. George screamed.

"No, no, no. I have hemorrhoids."

He sighed. "Oh, that's totally normal. Go to the pharmacy and buy some medicine, and then bathe in some chamomile. It's good for you."

Then he hung up the phone.

Three days later, despite the biting cold and my own doctor's advice, I decided to take Joseph to the hospital. What if he hadn't gained enough weight? What if his umbilical cord had become infected? I bundled him up in three warm winter blankets and descended the steps, to the clucking of neighbors assembled around the front door, who could not believe that I would bring a child out into the cold.

"*Haraam, haraam,*" two women said under their breath as I passed them by. "What a shame."

I caught the minibus to Bethlehem as quickly as I could, finding a seat in the back next to an elderly woman, balancing baby Joseph across my knees. I fixed his blanket, ran my finger across his mouth in fear that his breath might grow cold. I was just anxious to get there and get home again. We were halfway to the checkpoint when an Israeli soldier on the side of the road signaled to the driver to pull over for no apparent reason. Two soldiers sauntered onto the bus. The one in front had a rifle that swung low and loose from his shoulder, so that when he came to inspect my passport it hung over Joseph's head and brushed against my legs. They pulled two passengers off the bus for not having the right papers and then waved to the driver to carry on.

Tears rolled down my cheeks.

"What is it?" the elderly woman asked me.

"He's only ten days old," I whispered.

I arrived at the doctor's an hour later, and she checked us quickly, confirmed that there was nothing wrong with either of us, and sent us on our way again into the cold.

For many days, I could not shake the image of that gun, hanging over Joseph's head. I had taken him to the hospital in the hopes of keeping him safe, and instead I had exposed him to his first glimpse of violence. The world was full of such dangers, light sockets and drunk drivers and objects he could swallow, and at that moment it seemed a miracle that any of us had survived.

They say that we are only able to have children again because we forget the pain of childbirth. So it is, also, with the first, anxious days of parenthood. Frédéric and I stumbled through each day. We hesitated to give Joseph his first bath, afraid that he might slip and fall somehow into the small puddle of water we had put into the plastic container. I fretted over diaper changes and late-night wakings, and Frédéric paced next to the bed, in a world suddenly full of sharp corners and flights of stairs, the realization that a child is not only a human being, but contains with him an entire world, and the possibility of losing it.

It was also a season of remembering. At night, reserves of knowledge from my own childhood arrived. I somehow knew how to change a diaper. I knew how to rock an infant to sleep, how to cradle the head. The words to lullabies came unsummoned. It turns out that we do not forget our infancy, but that it simply lies sewn into our hearts in wait until we need it again, to help us guide our own children, to help us understand our own parents. Now I knew that my own mother must have awakened in the night to feed me, that my father had taught me lullabies, that it was only because of a thousand forgotten hours of being cradled that I understood how to do it now. They had stitched those lessons into my heart, and I was astounded to find them there, unblemished after thirty years. It is one of the greatest tragedies that the moments in our lives in which we are with our parents the most correspond with the very years we cannot remember. But Joseph gave me back those moments. I understood not only who he was, but also who I was.

"How many nights did I fall asleep in the rocking chair with you on my shoulder!" my mother exclaimed when I described a sleepless night to her on the phone. I wondered if thirty years after the fact was too late to say thank you.

Our lives took on a monastic rhythm, of nursing and sleeping, singing and sleeping, changing and nursing and sleeping. One day, when Joseph was several weeks old, he gazed up at me, examined my face, and he recognized me. He looked at me, and I looked back at him, with all of the curiosity of two beings who, out of billions, ended up together.

So it's *you*, after all? *You*, after all of this time?

The Language
of Childhood

I WAS STARTLED TO AWAKEN ONE DAY AND DISCOVER THAT my child had turned eight months old. Weeks and months had disappeared, marked by milestones of sitting up and rolling over and sleeping three hours in a row, by the discarding of smaller clothes for larger sets, in a world in which each month, representing such a small part of my own life, was a doubling and tripling of his. For the first months, I hid out with him in our house, sheltering from the cold. Then the winter subsided, and we left the cocoon of our house and entered into the world, with its viruses and pollution and birds and miracles.

There are those children who grow up in the countryside, who can wander through the woods and recognize the smell of pine needles and the earth after rain. Joseph would not be one of those children. I could only bring him to Nablus Road, a street without playgrounds, its only nature the remnants of a valley so buried beneath the city street that it no longer resembled a valley at all, where the noise of traffic distracted from the swallows and sunbirds in flight overhead.

But Nablus Road still contained its own magic: for in the mind of a child, our street spoke every language in the world. Every afternoon, I would carry my son carefully down the flight of stairs outside, at the bottom of which his stroller would be waiting—*arabaye* in Arabic, which also coincidentally meant "chariot," a distinction too appropriate in a culture in which children were afforded almost royal status. As I adjusted the straps, inevitably we would cross paths with Mother Maria, busy sweeping away the pink bougainvillea petals from in front of her door. She would lift him up to kiss him on the cheek and speak to him in Spanish. "José," she would coo affectionately. "*Dame un beso.*"

Eventually, she would turn to me in apologetic explanation: "I asked Joseph to give me a kiss."

It was, at first, bizarre to me that she expected Joseph to understand what I could not, but eventually it dawned on me that we all believe that children are born knowing how to speak every language in the world. I'm not sure at what point the rest of us forget how to speak so many languages, but it must belong to the years in which we stop believing in Santa Claus and fairies, in which we cease to have access to a wonder that transcends the laws of the possible. The tragedy of growing up is that we forget not only our languages, but also that we belong to everyone. Yet we retain enough of that wonder to know that children exist in another space. That is why, I presume, each time we meet a baby, we cannot help but speak to him or her in our mother tongue, certain that he or she will understand.

Perhaps we are not wrong. I saw Joseph, moving in for a kiss.

Abu Hossam and the front porch gang would speak to Joseph in the thick Hebronite dialect of Arabic before tousling his hair, and he would react with the same utter familiarity. Several times a week I would bump into Abu Ines, the street cleaner whose job it was to walk up and down Nablus Road in his fluorescent worker's vest, sweeping up garbage and piles of rotting vegetables into cardboard boxes. Whenever he saw Joseph, he would prop up his broom and dustpan against a wall and run over.

"Zouzou!" he would exclaim, using the Arabic diminutive for Joseph. "*Keef halak, habibi?*" Then this street sweeper, who before now had no reason at all to speak to me, would turn to start a conversation. "Have you been to Bethlehem lately?"

"I just took Joseph to the doctor there," I assured him.

Then he would lean over to whisper in Arabic to Joseph in a conspiratorial voice: "*Inta Telhami*. You're a Bethlehemite, just like I'm a Bethlehemite. I love your whole family, but I will always love you, Joseph, the most, because you're from Bethlehem. There's no place in the world more beautiful than Bethlehem."

Apparently, my toddler already belonged to a tribe.

Once a month, I would carry Joseph to the convent of the Franciscaines de Marie at five o'clock, just before supper, so that the elderly French nuns could pass him around the room and fervently make the sign of the cross on his forehead, repeating again and again with pride that he had come from "their house" and so was part of their family. When I appeared in the door, one of them would call out excitedly to the others in French, "*Viens! Viens ici! C'est Joseph, le petit Jésus!*"—Come! Come here! It's Joseph, the little Jesus! Then they would huddle around him, exclaiming how *mignon* he was, as he clasped their rosary beads within his tiny fist.

It had not occurred to me when we named our son Joseph that we had settled on the one name that seems to exist in almost every language, common to Christianity, Judaism, and Islam. He was José to the nuns downstairs, Joseph—but with an emphasis on the "e"—to the French nuns beside us, Yosef to the Israelis, Yusuf to the Palestinians, and Giuseppe to the Italian monks in the Franciscan churches. I was not even fazed walking in the Armenian Quarter of the city, when a local referred to him as Hovsep.

Naturally, Joseph relished the attention and soon learned to turn his head in response to all of them.

Only our neighbor Michel insisted on talking to him in English.

"You're going to ruin your child!" he muttered. "French, English, Arabic—he's going to be completely confused! This child will have no idea who he *is*."

I would be lying if I did not admit that this concerned me.

Still, this mess of identities was the city in which we lived and also a great gift of childhood—that briefest of windows, in which no one could convince us that there was anything dividing us from each other. Through Joseph, for a few months, a sectarian society so often ghettoized into religions and classes and family feuds, was made whole in the body of a little boy.

As the days and then weeks passed, every afternoon we would take our walk through East Jerusalem, as much a routine as his morning nap. When I opened the door to Nablus Road and lowered the stroller onto the sidewalk, the old men smoking cigarettes on our stoop would part ways for him, and Hossam—Abu Hossam's oldest son—would lift the stroller gently over the piles of sesame bread, so that Joseph's legs briefly dangled in the air. In time, Joseph would hold out his hand for the traditional greeting, and in return Hossam would place into it a round pastry filled with date paste, which Joseph would hold protectively by the hole in the middle, the way most children might cling to a rattle. As we continued down the street, women would stop to grab his bare feet or tousle his sandy hair, and whisper in Arabic: "May God protect him."

Though it was easy enough to become accustomed to strangers loving my child, it was infinitely harder to get used to them raising him. The American boundaries between family and stranger did not exist on our street, which is perhaps why Arabic children are taught to refer to adults close to the family as "auntie" or "uncle." I could not walk Joseph through the neighborhood without him being overwhelmed with gifts from his many dozen "uncles." Omar, two shops down, would shake Joseph's hand and then give him a small mountain of chewy Turkish candies; I would wait until we were out of eyesight and then immediately confiscate them, worried that Joseph would choke. Next, the vegetable vendors, upon seeing his tears, would break off a banana from the bunch and open it carefully before trying to place it into his fist, which was very often still clutching the date bread from Abu Hossam. Men working the counter at the coffee shop would sneak him chocolates wrapped in colorful foil that he would stuff into his mouth, foil and all, before looking at me guiltily and appealing for help. Souvenir store owners would run inside to fetch him stuffed camels with small bells around their necks. He collected bracelets with the word "Palestine" sewn into them, olive-wood crosses, and plastic packets of chocolate coins that had been manufactured for Hanukkah but were now many months out of season and somehow marooned among the Muslims of East Jerusalem.

"Umm Yusuf," the storekeepers would shout when they saw me alone. "Where is Yusuf?"

It took me time to notice that those men, too, were missing parts of themselves. Loneliness reveals itself in details: a street of men who commuted early in the morning to arrive at their stalls at eight o'clock, where they swept the sidewalk in front of them, beneath the glow of the Old City walls and to the chanting of the Quran. They did not go home again until late at night, which meant that they rarely saw their families. We were surrounded by convents, shops, and vegetable stalls, with no other houses on the street but ours, and so

Joseph had no other children to compete with for attention. He was a chance for all of those men to have a child to dote on, a momentary stand-in for their own children, amid the heat and exhaustion and tension of the workday, an opportunity for tenderness.

Still, we could only handle so many camels.

One afternoon, the three of us returned home from a walk around the neighborhood, piles of plush sheep and chocolates and plastic key chains collected in the basket beneath Joseph's stroller. At the front door, Abu Hossam reached to hand Joseph date bread. Frédéric cut him off. He had reached his limit.

"Please stop," he begged. "Otherwise he'll be spoiled, and he'll think that he can have whatever he wants, whenever he wants it."

But then Abu Hossam looked at Frédéric with a rare expression of reproach. "This is between me and your son," he insisted, and handed Joseph the date bread.

Humbled, Frédéric went inside.

Later that afternoon, Abu Hossam felt the need to explain himself. He told Frédéric, "If you give a child something each time you see him, then he will grow up thinking that giving things away is the most natural thing in the world. Giving children gifts is how we teach them generosity."

Dear Joseph,

This is how I remember the first year of your life: I read and wrote and sang you to sleep, memorized the grasp of your fingers and your calls in the night, practiced the balance of holding you close and letting you go. In the mornings, I would let you nod off in my arms, where I could be certain of your breath and your heart beating; but in the late afternoons, I would always release you into Nablus Road, where we strolled through love and languages. And often, by evening, after so many salaams *and so many gifts, you would have drifted off to sleep in your stroller, your head nuzzled against the sheepskin, a toy camel in your clenched fist. At the door, I wouldn't dare wake you. So I would unlock the door, and Hossam would lift you up—stroller and all—and carry you inside, all the way up the great flight of stairs, raising you high into the air and then placing the stroller gently on the floor in front of our front door.*

And then he would tiptoe down the stairs, so as not to undo his work, turning to me before closing the door.

"Ma salama, Umm Yusuf," he would mouth softly. Good-bye, mother of Joseph.

Lessons

LOOKING BACK, I CAN FORGIVE MYSELF FOR MAKING THE amateur mistake of believing that we might fully *belong* to the city, and that the piles of candy and camels meant that the ordinary rules of conflict did not apply to us. I had forgotten the primary rule of the Middle East—that everything hangs on a thread. So much depends upon what moment you decide to leave the house to buy the vegetables.

Joseph was nine months old on the afternoon that Frédéric and I diverted from our normal stroll around the immediate neighborhood and instead took a walk near Damascus Gate, just far enough from our house that we were no longer in a zone of protection. We had been walking only a few moments when I saw something land on the ground nearby. I jumped. Stones began raining down around us. I turned to see a gang of young boys chasing us up the hill, each of them with something clenched in his fist. No one was stopping them. We ran. I could hear the stones landing behind us. A stone fell dangerously close to Joseph's head, and Frédéric tried to push the stroller faster. As we fled, I thought better of it. Frédéric continued on with Joseph, but I turned and sprinted toward the boys in a rage.

"What do you think you're doing?" I screamed in Arabic. "He's just a child!"

They continued pelting stones. Tears burned my eyes. I fled up the hill again, defeated.

It had happened less than a hundred meters from our front door.

We continued our walk, but something had been severed, and soon we made our way back home. On Nablus Road, we stopped into the shop of Sheikh Mazen and his brother Omar and told them what had happened. They shook their heads sadly. "They would have thrown stones at us too," Omar said, but it was only out of kindness.

For months, I had sustained myself with the belief that some magical membrane had protected us because we had a child. But that night, I placed Joseph in his crib with a sense of a fragile world. For centuries—and perhaps still longer than that—mothers have tried to prepare their children for pain through story and song: a rock-a-bye-baby about a tree bough that would eventually break and send an infant tumbling to the ground; a ring-around-the-rosy about flowers placed in a pocket, perhaps to ward off the black death; a mockingbird promise about a bird that might not sing, a diamond ring that might not shine. London Bridge fell down; Humpty Dumpty couldn't be put together again. Perhaps if we slowly inoculated our children against this reality with melody, with gentle rocking, then the violence would not sting so much when they came upon it.

I kissed Joseph on the forehead and left him to sleep.

Later that night, I sat with Frédéric at the kitchen table of our house between countries, chastened and afraid. "I don't know what we're doing," I confessed. "The longer I live in this city, the less any of it makes sense to me. Sometimes I think that after all of these years, I've learned less and less, until finally I've learned nothing at all."

He was quiet for a moment. Then he said softly, "That's not true, Stephanie. This city is teaching us humility."

War

WAR CAME THAT SAME WINTER. IT WAS ONLY A MATTER of time. Ours was a reality that was bound to shatter—as inevitable as the fact that we grow up and forget our languages, that the bough breaks and the cradle falls.

We had flown to America to visit my family for Christmas when the news came that Israel and Hamas had gone to war in Gaza, in an operation that would be known as Operation Cast Lead. As with most things in the Middle East, the details of the war were disputed, with Israel claiming that they were responding to rocket fire into their territory, and Hamas insisting that they were responding to the breaking of a cease-fire and ongoing border closures. It did not much matter now. We watched from across the world as the first images of rockets appeared, soon followed by bodies and hundreds of casualties in Gaza, many of them children.

We had started our life in Jerusalem during the war with Lebanon, and the civil war between Hamas and Fatah had broken out the next summer. I had lived on the periphery of war in the Middle East for years, in the tensions of a post-9/11 world, and in Damascus as it flooded with refugees from the 2003 U.S.-led invasion of Iraq. But to be a mother during war was altogether different.

"Are you sure you're going back?" my father asked me.

"Gaza's far away from Jerusalem," I assured him, even though it wasn't, and he didn't try to dissuade us because he knew there was no use.

Now that I had a child, I began to understand how much pain I had put my father through by living in war zones. Now he would also worry about his grandson. I had spent the last two weeks watching a complicity build between my father and Joseph. Every morning, I would awaken exhausted to Joseph's cries, nurse him in bed, and then stumble with him down the stairs. My father would be waiting at the bottom, his arms already out, to take his first grandchild and feed him oatmeal.

"You know my grandfather died when I was six years old," my father explained to me. "My most vivid memory of him is of eating oatmeal with him, every single time I saw him, for the first few years of my life." He spooned some into Joseph's mouth. "You're grandpa's oatmeal boy, aren't you?" he asked.

And I watched how eternity enters into time through bowls of oatmeal, the clink of bowls against spoons linking the span of more than half a century.

We passed the holidays as the deaths mounted on the television. I went through the motions of making a birthday cake, and let Joseph blow out the first candle, and that is how our son turned one year old.

A few days later, my father drove us to the airport, where he slipped twenty dollars into my pocket, in a habit he had never been able to shake. He held Joseph and clasped my hand and kept catching Frédéric's gaze for assurance. It turns out that one never stops being a parent.

We said good-bye. We moved ahead toward airport security. I

turned around, to see my father's tears streaming down his face. He let out a single sob.

I had no idea anymore if our choices made any sense at all.

———•———

It was freezing when we arrived on Nablus Road, almost exactly a year after I had arrived there with Joseph from the hospital in Bethlehem. Now new life cohabited with death, and we awakened the next morning into war—both far away, and at the same time on Nablus Road, pulled to our front door by gravity. War is a poison that infects the air. It was difficult to part the space in front of us with our bodies. The men in their storefronts labored in the simple acts of unlocking doors, making change. Televisions and radios played nonstop out of kiosks and falafel restaurants.

I awakened on our first morning back and opened the door onto the balcony overlooking Nablus Road to count as many soldiers as I could see. I stopped at fifty-seven. That afternoon, I sent Frédéric down to buy milk and eggs. I would not leave the house with my son.

———•———

The next morning, I looked down from the balcony to discover that a temporary checkpoint—called a flying checkpoint in that particular poetry that belongs to war—had been hastily assembled in front of our house, just beside Abu Hossam's front steps. Soldiers manning it busily inspected passports and stopped men from entering the Old City. It was confirmation of what we had always known: that our house marked a border. I left Joseph with Frédéric and exited the house to write at a coffee shop at the end of the street. I returned three hours later to find myself at the end of a line of men trying to pass the checkpoint. I waited for my turn. The soldier demanded, "What are you doing here?"

I pointed to the front door behind him. "I live here," I said with steelier confidence than I knew I possessed.

He let me through.

The wind had stripped the Great Tree in the courtyard bare of its leaves, and there were only resident birds, left behind when the others migrated farther south, exposed on the January branches, staring out in full feather. In the mornings, collared doves, startled, would catch my gaze from the balcony before flying off to leave the tree barren. The bougainvillea shed its color and stained the stairs with wet, rose-hued petals, and the sky clouded over into gray. The newspapers showed the bodies of the dead collapsed into rubble. Only oranges came into season, and in the mornings I could look down from our balcony and see the branches of the orange trees awash in green leaves and weighed down with color, the fruit afire. I remembered that promise to Joseph, one year before, from the night before he was born. But now these same oranges made me angry, for it seemed to me that they had been placed there as some sort of joke, promising everything and offering nothing, for despite their fire it was still January, and the world was still cold.

War is always terrible, but the full horror of death was only made apparent to me now that I was a mother, forced to confront the way in which it contrasted with the innocence of childhood. This death, this killing—this was not who we were born to be, but who we had become. I meditated on the amount of time put into creating a single life: the nine months in the womb, the nights awakening with early contractions, the vitamin supplements and doctor's appointments, the excruciating labor. Then the life after, the rousing from sleep every few hours in the night, the suckling from the breast, the crawling, sitting, standing, walking, the first words, the vaccinations, the attention to allergies and sleep patterns. Bowls of oatmeal. Running to be sure that a blanket has not fallen.

All of this life snuffed out, in a single instant: with a bullet, a bomb, a collapsing house. The physics of it seemed impossible—that so much time could be placed on one side of the balance, only to be erased in no time at all. The contrast between the time it takes to create a life and the time it takes to destroy it.

The ancient Greeks and Romans knew this: in *The Odyssey*, Odysseus descends to the underworld only to discover that his mother has died of a broken heart, waiting for her son to return from battle. In *The Aeneid*, the mother of a soldier named Euryalus loves her son so much that she follows him to battle, only for him to sneak away in the middle of the night to die with his best friend. Her words, immortalized in Latin, are reminders not only of the futility of war, but also of the invisible scars it leaves on mothers:

> *Thus, then, my lov'd Euryalus appears!*
> *Thus looks the prop my declining years!*
> *Was't on this face my famish'd eyes I fed?*
> *Ah! how unlike the living is the dead!*
> *And could'st thou leave me, cruel, thus alone?*
> *Not one kind kiss from a departing son!*

There is no choice, in such times, but to try to continue to live. Joseph had started day care before we traveled to America, so two days after we returned, I awakened, forced myself to dress, bundled him up in layers of winter clothes, and strapped him into his stroller to drop him off in the morning. When we arrived, I noticed that his babysitter, Anoush, had replaced the cartoons in Arabic that she regularly had on the big-screen television in the mornings with the news, and in the midst of the day care, there were tanks exploding and missiles raining down from the sky. A voice in Arabic announced the day's dead, numbers so high that the children would not learn to count them for many years. The Christmas decorations were still up, a green plastic tree decorated with red garlands. And there was Joseph among the toy plastic balls, with Snow White on the wall nearby, a bluebird perched in her hand, and he sat and tried to put wooden puzzle pieces into places where they would not quite fit.

I did not feel that I could tell Anoush to turn off the news. I asked her to silence it.

I walked home in the cold. The death count was approaching a thousand people. Abu Salaam was still on the corner of Nablus Road selling newspapers, and the boys were still calling out the prices for round sesame bread, but somehow it didn't feel like my street anymore; it had become heavy and strange and steeped in winter in our absence, and I understood that death can be a palpable weight in the air when it comes, that it saturates everything it comes in contact with: glasses of water, swaths of fabric, dreams. When I walked into the house, the sink was full of dishes, the water freezing cold, and I left the kitchen and sat alone at the table and no longer recognized my own life. I had a one-year-old child. I was sitting nearby my second war in three years—my third if you counted the summer's civil war in Gaza.

I thought of the line from the gospel of Luke, when the angel Gabriel appears to Mary and asks her to change her entire life. Against her fear, she finally says yes.

"And the angel left her," it concludes. Exactly when she needed an angel most.

I closed myself into my office. On the shelf was a book that a Palestinian ornithologist had given me about the wildlife of Gaza. I turned the pages from right to left, still unaccustomed to Arabic books that seemed to read from the future to the past.

I sat down at my desk and scrawled out a list of names of birds:

Bluethroat
Song thrush
Stonechat
Chiffchaff
Graceful warbler
White wagtail
Yellow-vented bulbul
Crested lark
Common swallow
Little ringed plover
Night heron
Glossy ibis

How were they faring in this war, this winter? Would they, who knew by instinct how to make their way home from the cold, know how to navigate this?

Less than a mile away, Joseph was piling up wooden blocks. I wondered how anything survived these brutal human seasons unscathed.

———◆———

That night, Joseph burned his hand. It was late, and he had not adjusted to the time change back from America and so would not fall asleep. I stayed awake as long as I could, and finally drifted off. Frédéric paced back and forth, listening to Joseph calling out for him.

Hours passed. Frédéric was worried that, with his blanket off, Joseph would catch cold. He could not leave him to stand at the edge of the crib. Finally, he gave in and took Joseph into his arms, held him against the heat of his body. He settled in the warmest place in the house, near the woodstove.

He held him for hours, the boy nestled in the nook between his father's neck and shoulders, the two of them awake. I lay fast asleep in the bedroom. Then at some point, Frédéric must have drifted off.

I awakened to screaming. Joseph had somehow pulled away and placed his hand directly on the stove. From his high vantage point, on his father's shoulder, he had reached above the protective screen around it. The flesh on his hand was burning. He did not know how to walk yet and could not stand without holding onto something, so he did not know how to take his hand off the stove—equally afraid of the burning and the falling down.

I ran to them. I sobbed. I held Joseph, and said again and again: "It's okay. It's okay. I'm sorry. I'm sorry. I'm sorry."

In a time of war, everything collapses into a single trauma. I wrapped his hand in a towel, and we rushed down to the street and caught a taxi to the hospital. I knew that the stove had burned him, but something kept making me think that it was because of the war. I shouted at the driver to go faster.

If we had not returned here, then my boy would not have burned his hand.

The taxi pulled up to the hospital curb, and I fumbled in my bag but could not find the twenty-five shekels to pay the fare. The taxi driver waited. Every moment that passed was another moment that my son was in pain. All of the rage I felt at the world was directed at the driver now. Couldn't he see that my child was hurt? Couldn't he just let us go, for Christ's sake?

I found the money, gave it to him, rushed inside. I am not sure that I have forgiven him, even today.

It was four in the morning when we signed in at the window and waited. Joseph was wailing. Many of the doctors were gone, having been called up to serve in the war.

A doctor arrived, inspected Joseph's hand, cleaned it, and bandaged it.

"You're lucky," he said. "It didn't penetrate the second layer of skin."

I sobbed.

The nurse attending us looked at me callously. "Why are you crying?" she asked. "It's only a burned hand."

She was right: it was only a burned hand. Perhaps she had a son too, and he had been called to the war, where the stakes were much higher. At that moment, around fifty miles away in Gaza, people were killing and dying on both sides—children, really—both killing and dying, and my son had only burned his hand. She was not wrong. But a child is a child, and he was mine.

It was early morning when we emerged from the hospital to make our way home again, Joseph's hand bandaged, proudly clutching a white doctor's glove inflated as a balloon. The sun was rising over the Old City walls. A group of workers, who awakened early to commute, huddled together in the cold and drank coffee, their breath visible in the morning air.

Abu Salaam was putting out the first newspapers. I glimpsed the headline from *Al-Ahram*, an Egyptian newspaper, about the war in Gaza. It said, in English: "Raining Death."

———————◆———————

I have never understood whether the impulse to continue with the ordinary during times of conflict is resistance, or denial, or a kind of magical thinking that makes us believe that if we pretend that everything is normal, then it will be. In Arabic culture, *samoud*—or steadfastness—is recognized as the highest virtue, the will to continue living in the midst of despair. And it was true, that life could only become normal again through toothbrushes and pasta and the passing of time. The next day, I bundled Joseph up and brought him to his day care in the Old City. It was Friday, and soldiers were already setting up barricades outside Damascus Gate for the clashes in front of our house. On the way out, I crossed Mother Maria, who asked if I would be home in the afternoon.

"I want to drop a bag of oranges and lemons in front of your door," she said. I thanked her, remembering the line from the gospel of Luke: "And Mary pondered all of these things in her heart." The small details that take on greater meaning for a mother, contemplating her child. I would live the rest of the day for the lemons and oranges, waiting at the entrance of home.

The clashes at Damascus Gate usually took place in the early afternoon. Nablus Road was so dangerous during such moments that it was safer for Joseph to be at day care than in his room, vulnerable as it was to tear gas that could waft up and into the rooms through the cracks of the windows. When I opened the front door, Abu Hossam's stand was locked firmly shut.

So Joseph and I climbed the long hill toward day care. When I arrived, scenes from the war were playing again on the news. I watched Joseph piling blocks with his bandaged hand, and I worried that it might hurt him to touch the world.

"Will you call me if there are clashes in the Old City?" I asked Anoush.

"Why? He's safer here than at your house."

This was true.

"Don't worry," she continued. "I'll pull the metal blinds shut, and no one will even know that the children are inside."

It was the most absurd idea, that we could somehow make our children invisible if we needed to, but I chose to believe.

———

It was our darkest period in that city. We had built our life on a street of great beauty and great violence, but on those days it often felt like the violence was the stronger of the two. I would write in the afternoons. Frédéric, who now worked on a development project in the West Bank, would cross the checkpoint in the mornings and then again in the afternoons, and come home exhausted. In the evenings, my husband and I would sleep on the western half of the house, holding each other on the narrow mattress, and Joseph would sleep on the eastern half, but in truth none of us slept much at all.

At night, I sometimes dreamt that we had made our life somewhere else. In the image, Frédéric was holding Joseph on his shoulders, and there was a wind. I had a writing desk facing the sea. I looked much younger. In this dream, there was never war, because war came only in other dreams; they were careful not to mix, and I believed that this must be the kindness of God.

Time passed slowly. I finished the last edits on my book. I stood on the balcony, waiting for birds. And I remembered.

I remembered falling in love, the leaves changing colors.

I remembered reading books in the library all afternoon.

I remembered climbing into the ruins of an ancient Roman city under the full moon.

I remembered a silence in the desert penetrating my bones.

I remembered sleeping on my roof and staring at the stars.

I remembered living slowly enough to memorize language.

I remembered gathering rain in glass bottles.

I remembered the Aztec Theatre in San Antonio and double features and kissing my first boyfriend in the back of a movie theater when I was fourteen years old.

I remembered the voice in the dream I had once, when I almost became a nun, warning me: "You cannot take the piano with you."

I had not become a nun in the desert, and still I had not bought a piano, afraid as I was of owning anything too large to throw in a suitcase in the middle of the night, lest we need to escape.

I sat in my office, for a long time, staring out the window. I remembered an elegant potted plant with red spiky flowers that my friend Karen had given to me as a gift for my birthday the week before. I had already completely forgotten about it, abandoning it on the windowsill looking down at the nun's garden. Surely it had died by now.

I rushed out of my office, poured water in a glass, and hurried to the flowers. Keeping this single plant alive took on a sudden urgency; it wasn't much, but it was something I could *do*. I rushed to the window, where I found it blooming on the windowsill, tiny drops of water already gathered inside of the spiky leaves.

Frédéric walked into the room.

"Frédéric, did you water my flowers?" I asked.

"Of course I did," he said and looked at me curiously. "I always do. You never noticed?"

The world was mine already, and I hadn't even known.

———◆———

Then we woke up, and the war was over.

Later, only the most terrible and most beautiful parts of that season remained in my memory: an image of a Syrian woodpecker, with black plumage and a red shock of feathers on his head, staring back at me from the barren tree; Joseph leaning against me at night when I changed the bandages on his hand, his cheek touching mine. Three o'clock in the morning, when again he called my name, and I ran to him afraid, only to hear him ask, in French, for a glass of sparkling water—some of his very first words.

That morning I rushed to Abu Salaam's to see the news. And instead of headlines of war in Gaza, they were of a plane in New York that ran into a flock of birds and lost its engines. The pilot made an emergency landing on the Hudson River, and everyone survived.

Oranges and lemons left on the front doorstep, oranges we peeled by hand, so that the smell of them remained on our skin for hours, even as we read the newspapers.

Frédéric slowly repairing the gate around the woodstove, making it higher, so that no one would be burned again.

Hospitals

A FEW WEEKS AFTER THE WAR ENDED, FRÉDÉRIC DESCENDED the stairs from our house early in the morning to buy bread and returned with a stricken look on his face.

"What is it?" I asked.

"Hossam and Saleh were stabbed."

It had happened late the night before, according to our neighbors. Hossam and Saleh, the two oldest sons of Abu Hossam, had finished up their work selling hats and umbrellas in front of our door and packed up their merchandise in boxes. Then they had driven to the nearby Flowers Gate of the Old City to pick up a delivery. When they arrived and opened the car door, local boys ambushed them, pinning them down and stabbing them, repeatedly, in the back.

"We have to go to them," I said.

They had been sent to separate hospitals, so we went to find Hossam first, who was in more critical condition. We traveled to a hospital across town, and there we saw him: handsome Hossam, pale in a white hospital gown, strapped to tubes in a bed.

Umm Hossam held her oldest son's hand.

"Thank you for coming," she said quietly.

"Of course," I answered. "You're our family here."

Joseph reached out to touch him. Until now, he had known Hossam only as the young man who had carried him, like a prince, in his stroller up the stairs a hundred times since he was born. Hossam, with his hands full of tubes, wrapped his fingers lightly around Joseph's small hand. I was relieved that my son was still too young for me to have to explain. Hossam glanced at me. It was a culture in which men and women kept a distance from each other. Now he held my gaze for an instant, and I nodded at him, and thought that this eighteen-year-old boy who stood outside of my front door every day would never be a stranger again.

Umm Hossam had become pale. "This hospital," she told me wistfully. "I haven't been here since I gave birth to Adam." Adam was her youngest son, a year older than Joseph.

I remembered what someone had told me once about Jerusalem, that the city is divided, but at least everyone comes to the same hospitals to be born and to die.

When visiting hours finished, Frédéric and I walked outside. I pulled Joseph against me and turned to Frédéric. "They're so lucky that the knives just missed their spines."

He looked at me, sadly. "You don't get it?" he asked. "That wasn't luck. They missed the spine on purpose. These attacks were a warning. They were meant to wound both of them as much as possible without actually killing them."

A friend of mine once described life in conflict zones as a violence that begins at an infinite distance and creeps in closely. First it happens on television to a city nearby. In the newspaper, you glimpse the bombed-out picture of a place you once visited. Then the relative of a neighbor is killed. A distant cousin is next. Then a cousin. A neighbor. Finally, a parent, a child. But once it enters into your intimate circle, it never leaves again.

Our street changed for me when Hossam and Saleh were stabbed. Now the conflict had come to our front door. I had steadied myself for the conflict between Israelis and Palestinians, but not for the more confusing part of the conflict: how violence seeps into daily life, how people who appear to be on the same side turn against one another.

A week later, I walked downstairs and Hossam and Saleh were working at their old stand, wearing new clothes, masking their wounds.

"You came back?" I asked Saleh.

"Of course," he said. "I couldn't let them see me not come back."

What Passes
and What Remains

A MONTH LATER, I ACCEPTED A TEACHING JOB AT A university in the West Bank, and the confines of my life changed. Now I would no longer pass my days on our street and in the Old City, but in Abu Dis, a small village on the opposite side of the separation wall. In the mornings, I would drop off Joseph at his day care in the Old City and then set out to campus, which, though it should have been only ten minutes away from our front door, took me nearly an hour to get to by bus, since we had to travel until we reached an opening in the separation wall, miles away, that would allow us to cross to the other side and circle back again. By the time I finally arrived at the university, I could stand at the highest point of the hill on which it stood and look down over the wall, where I could see the place from which I had set out nearly an hour before, almost right in front of me.

It was also a reminder of how cut off I had been from the real violence that inflicted the region. Though East Jerusalem was difficult, it was mild compared to the tension in the neighboring West Bank, where checkpoints separated the major cities, military incursions into villages were regular events, and an entire generation—racked by the violence of the Second Intifada and a stagnant political process, many cut off from ever visiting Jerusalem and their holy sites, their physical landscape closing in on them— had grown up without hope. They had also, due to war, missed critical parts of their educations.

I taught two classes: English Composition and Introduction to Literature. My students did not care much about learning to write essays, but they fell in love with literature. It was an oral culture and we read the stories out loud, and I savored the sound of words in air. On the first day, I selected a quote by Yevgeny Yevtushenko from the very opening of their course packets: "Poetry is like a bird, it ignores all frontiers."

"What does that mean?" Nada, a student from Bethlehem asked. She was tall and thin, with her hair purposefully pulled back in a way that reminded me of college freshmen the world over. The girl sitting beside her turned. "It means that poetry is free," she explained in Arabic. "It doesn't have checkpoints."

There is much to be learned about a generation from teaching them literature, about what it feels like to live life in the passive tense. Students who could not easily travel from city to city because of checkpoints and had no way to encounter others in the wider world learned to find their companions in books. They became kin with those exiled in pages: with Kafka's character Gregor Samsa in *The Metamorphosis*, turned into a vermin, who sees all of the possessions of his life taken from him even as he stays watching in the room. Or Odysseus, surviving war and exile, who does not believe, when he finally returns home after so many trials, that it is possible that home could still exist. Students who lived in refugee camps connected with Milton's Satan in *Paradise Lost*, exiled from heaven, the paradise that should have been his, given over to others so that they might live in it. A former prisoner found himself in Walt Whitman's "A Noiseless Patient Spider," an insect left alone, his soul trying to connect to the outside world, reaching out filament by filament.

I would take their suffering and their laughter into my body in the mornings. When class was finished, I would catch the bus home to hold my son in my arms. The separation wall butted up against one side of the campus, but the other side offered a view out to the desert and sky. As the bus started, I would watch the clouds moving over the wall. I decided then that it was the sky that made the wall look so ghastly—like two windows put up against each other, only one was moving and the other remained still. In the sky, the birds passed over, the clouds passed over, and the light and shadows passed over. But on the earth, no one passed over.

Sometimes miracles come to us in people we meet. Sometimes they come to us in orange trees, in full fruit in the middle of winter. And sometimes they come to us in books. I have always believed that a book that arrives in one's hands at a certain moment is a message from another space and time.

That winter of 2009 in Jerusalem, in the wake of the war and teaching, I was in need of such a book. I found myself suspended between realities increasingly difficult to reconcile: a husband I loved; a son learning to walk and speak his first words in French, English, and Arabic; and a world stumbling from one war to another. I was more and more uncertain of how to navigate between them.

One morning, I climbed the hill with Joseph and dropped him off at his day care. I continued on to Jaffa Road, at that hour already alive with cars and construction, and then onto a quiet alley descending the hill, to an English used bookstore, the way others might look for a chapel in a moment of grief. I slipped inside, nodded at the woman working at the front desk, then disappeared among books. It was as though I were seven years old again, completely lost. I passed an hour that way. There was nothing I wanted to buy. I just didn't want to be alone, and I longed to be in my own language.

After an hour, I stood up to leave. Outside the entrance to the store, I noticed boxes of books lined up beneath the window and a sign in front of them advertising: "Books, 2 shekels." It was the equivalent of fifty cents. I sorted through them absently. Among the volumes, I spotted two that were clearly left over from someone's old British collection:

> *Pears' Cyclopaedia: Twenty-Two Complete Works of Reference in One Handy Volume of Nearly 1,000 Pages*
>
> *The English Flower Garden and Home Grounds, Part II: Containing the Flowers, Flowering Shrubs and Trees, Evergreens, and Hardy Ferns for the Open-Air Flower Garden in the British Isles, with Their Cultivation and the Positions Most Suitable for Them in Gardens.*

The forty-ninth edition of *Pears' Cyclopaedia*, issued in 1938 by A. & F. Pears, a soapmaking company, wore a rich red cover, the binding long ago taped from overuse. I could almost imagine some young boy in England, stealing off beneath a tree, to study the maps among its pages.

I opened *The English Flower Garden* to page upon page of black-and-white illustrations of flowers. I turned absently to page 691, where a delicate etching of *Lonicera periclymenum*, or the honeysuckle, covered almost an entire page.

I paid the woman four shekels and carried them home.

———

That night, when the house was asleep save for the call of birds outside, I escaped to my office and opened the books, in the magical hours.

The flowers in *The English Flower Garden* appeared beside their scientific names in alphabetical order: *Adiantum*, or maidenhair fern; *Adlumia*, or climbing fumitory. *Adonis*, pheasant's eye; *Aesculus*, horse chestnut. Every name seemed more delicate than the last: *Anomatheca*, flowering grass; *Carbenia*, blessed thistle. The author had painstakingly sketched out every turn of leaf, so as to capture each vein. I absorbed myself in reciting the names out loud—an inventory of the beautiful.

Memories flashed back: my father kneeling beside my childhood bed, talking me through my nightmares by describing a green field, awash with flowers. There are moments when there is so much horror that you have to willfully summon beauty into the world, say its name out loud, in the hopes that you might replace one with the other and tip the balance, so that the world might be made right again.

Lilium canadense. Gladiolus. A world healed with the particular.

I picked up the second book, the red-bound encyclopedia of that little boy from long ago: *Pears' Cyclopaedia* from the year 1938.

On the opening page, a colored painting depicted a young boy blowing bubbles. It was a child's book, once owned by a little boy in England, his name still stamped in the cover: "Eli Strauss." I ran my finger over the stamp of his name.

It recorded, year by year, a world on the edge of collapse.

By 1939, the world would tumble into a war that would destroy a continent, lead to millions of deaths, and decimate the Jewish community to which that little boy belonged. But he did not know that yet when he stamped his name on the inside cover.

I turned to the chapter titled "Events." As promised, it was an attempt to explain in child's language all of recorded history, from the beginning of civilization to the moment in which the encyclopedia was published. The earliest entries were only a single line.

> 2234 — *Chaldean astronomical observations began.*
> 2200 — *Hia dynasty founded in China.*
> 1273 — *Assyrian empire founded.*

For pages, the descriptions continued—entire histories condensed into single lines: Alexander was born, as was Jesus Christ. The First Crusade merited only a few words. But as the book tumbled toward the present, lines turned into paragraphs, the ordinary mixed in with the terrible, a world about to go mad.

> 1935 — *Miss Amelia Earhart flew from Honolulu to California in 18¼ hours. A chimpanzee was born in the Zoological Gardens, the first to be born in captivity in London. The swastika became the German National flag.*

*1936—Much rain caused widespread flooding in
England. Mr. Roosevelt reelected President
of the U.S. Germany repudiated the water-
ways clauses of the Versailles Treaty.*

*1937—Three wolves escaped from the Oxford
Zoo and after several days of roaming
free were shot.*

*1938—January 20: A brilliant display of the Northern
Lights was seen from all over England.
January 25: The Falls View Bridge at
Niagara collapsed under the strain of
piled-up ice. Drastic changes made in the
control of the armed forces in Germany.
Herr Hitler became chief of the supreme
command of the armed forces.*

History in the present does not know what will become of it.
I thought of that boy, reading his encyclopedia beneath a tree, and
wondered if he had been aware of how much more terrible the
world was about to become, before it got better. In the section titled
"Prominent People," Adolf Hitler was listed with Auguste Rodin, John
Keats, Beethoven. In the section showing maps of the countries of the
world, I mouthed the names of places that would soon no longer exist.

On the final page of the encyclopedia was a blank calendar for
1940 and 1941, both waiting to be filled.

There was little comfort to be drawn from such a book. I
wondered if I had brought my son into a similarly unsustainable
world. Surely things would get worse before they got better—not
only in Jerusalem, but in the entire Middle East. In the midst of the
daily obscurities, day care and sesame bread, things were shaping up

to spiral out of control. I somehow knew that my little boy was that little English boy, now asleep in his bed, but positioned at the edge of a world that was about to unravel.

I prepared to put the books away, the solace of flowers gone.

But then something made me turn one final time to the opening two pages of the encyclopedia. The early pages were illustrated with the flags of the world. There is something that appears so permanent, so official in a flag that one forgets that it is only temporary. Here, first, were displayed the "Flags of the British Empire," then the "Flags of Foreign Countries." I examined them. United States. France. Italy. Belgium.

Then I stopped. There, among the familiar emblems, was the Nazi flag, the swastika, with the name Germany typed under it, placed securely among the other flags of Europe. Even seventy years later it was shocking, the swastika a claw in its center.

But something had been written over it in ink. I squinted to read it. The little boy, Eli, had not thrown his encyclopedia away during the war. Instead, he had held onto it. When the war had finished, he had returned to the pages of the year 1938, now in his past, and in black pen had drawn a single line in ink through the center of the Nazi flag to cancel it out. He placed brackets around the flag itself, as if to signal that it was temporary. And beneath it, that boy, who had returned to his childhood book as a man who had lived through war, had written in English cursive:

No longer existent.

I ran my finger over his words: "No longer existent."

For a moment, I felt as though that boy had also traveled through time to whisper to me.

And I sat in my office, alone in the middle of the night, and I wept.

———————◆———————

Simone Weil wrote, "All the natural movements of the soul are controlled by laws analogous to those of physical gravity. Grace is the only exception."

I had spent years trying to understand what she meant, but I think I was beginning to comprehend now—that there are those supernatural physics that allow for a flower to be stronger than an entire war. We can call that flower beauty, or grace, or hope. What is sure is that which is beautiful not only saves us, but it also belongs to the eternal, while the terrible passes away. Borders do not last. The names of countries do not last. And the names of flowers, they, too, do not last. But flowers themselves remain. Music remains. Certain phrases from childhood, sewn into our memories, passed down imperceptibly in the way we speak to children, they also remain, and will continue to after we are gone.

Childbirth remains.

Lemon trees. Fig trees. Stories remain.

I had seen jars from the Roman period, unexpectedly lifted up from the bowels of the sea, intact, after two thousand years.

Love remains, above all.

That night, while my husband and son were asleep in their beds, I made a list of what lasts: snowdrops and periwinkles, lullabies and prayers. And I knew that we don't just carry beauty but that we cling to it, as a resistance against gravity. That perhaps, in the end, that is the single task we must set out to do in our lives.

We lived in a terrible time. Perhaps it was only going to get darker. But to have a child was to have faith that the world, against all logic, was moving toward something better, eventually, even if horror came first. That the future could also transform the past, like that man, who had returned to comfort his childhood self in the only way he knew how, by writing in his book.

I prayed that our lives would also be written down in a book, and that one day my son would return to the book of my life, after these wars were over, and whisper the beautiful parts out loud. And then bracket out the worst parts with a pen, and write:

No longer existent.

Part Five

Sirens in Jerusalem

————————◆————————

"Here is the time of the Sayable, here is its home."

—*Rainer Maria Rilke*

Afternoons
in Eternity

I HAD OFTEN THOUGHT THAT TO VISIT JERUSALEM WAS TO participate in sacred space, to witness the Dome of the Rock where Mohammed ascended through the heavens, the remaining wall of the Temple, the narrow alleys where Jesus dragged his cross on the way to his crucifixion. Every corner remembered the past: where a battle once raged, a saint once slept.

But the more time passed, the less I took notice of these physical places, for to *live* in Jerusalem was to be drawn instead into holiness in time—in the hours siphoned off by the call to prayer, the church bells marking off vespers or matins, the traffic dying off as the sun set on the Sabbath day, its onset marked by the wailing of a siren. We were living not only in a place, but in a moment in eternity, a single swath of time suspended between a past already gone and a future not yet realized, both of which were embedded in the present in a way I did not yet grasp.

By the time Joseph was two years old, his day care—with its two simple rooms—was much too small for a boy who wanted nothing more than great open spaces and rocks to climb on. In the absence of nearby parks and playgrounds, we headed each afternoon to the nearest open space we could find: the Church of the Holy Sepulchre.

It was a difficult route by stroller. Dozens of stairs descended through the Old City marketplace and down into what was once the valley beneath Golgotha, the mountain where tradition held that Jesus was crucified, which now was a square perfectly situated halfway between Joseph's day care and our house on Nablus Road. I learned to balance two of the four wheels of his tiny black stroller on the ramps made for produce carts and to carefully slide Joseph down the stairs toward the church. He squealed in delight, gripping the side of the stroller with one hand, waving to all of the shopkeepers with the other, Prince Joseph in his chariot.

I came to a stop at a souvenir shop beside the courtyard at the entrance to the church, where a Greek Orthodox shopkeeper sat on his stool, smoking a cigarette among piles of candles and wooden icons and glow-in-the-dark rosaries for sale. He couldn't have been more than twenty-five, and I didn't know his name, but he knew Joseph's, and every day at three thirty sharp, he waited for us with a bundle of five white candles in his hand. Joseph reached out from his stroller and shook the man's hand seriously, and he grinned in return. "*Habibi, inta*," he declared. You're my sweetheart. Then he handed over the candles and said, to both of us: "Say a prayer for me."

I don't know why he singled out Joseph for this daily ritual, or why, day after day, he refused my entreaties to pay him. When I tried, he rebuked me sternly. "This is between me and Joseph," he insisted. He seemed to have assigned some power to the prayers of a little boy. Joseph held the bundle in his fist as we said good-bye and rolled through the tiny arched entrance marked "Holy Sepulchre."

If the Church of the Nativity in Bethlehem was the place where eternity entered into time in the form of a child, then locals believed that the Church of the Holy Sepulchre contained eternity itself. First built by Constantine the Great beginning in AD 326 to mark the place where his mother Helena was said to have discovered the "true cross," the vast stone church at the heart of the Old City was perhaps the holiest place in the Christian world, where pilgrims believed that Jesus of Nazareth was crucified and buried in the tomb of Joseph of Arimathea, before he was resurrected three days later. For centuries, Christians have journeyed toward the omphalos, the navel of the world on which they were certain that the rest of the universe spun, so much so that medieval maps placed the church directly in the center of the world. And at the center of that center was the Anastasis, the empty tomb where Christians believed that Jesus was raised from the dead, defeating not only death but also time. Once a year, on Holy Saturday in the Greek Orthodox calendar, thousands of pilgrims wait outside of the tomb for the Holy Fire to miraculously appear at the moment of the resurrection: proof that the past had been shattered, that we are all travelers in eternity, still participating in a moment that came two thousand years before us. *As it was in the beginning, is now, and ever shall be, world without end.*

Today it remained a complicated space, a church holding many different denominations of Christians, each in their respective corners, praying in their respective languages, a maze of Greek Orthodox and Armenian Christian, Syrian Orthodox and Ethiopian Orthodox, Egyptian Coptic and Roman Catholic—an arrangement that led to spectacle and chaos and the occasional fight between clerics wielding candlesticks. But for Joseph, the Holy Sepulchre was like being set loose in a carnival, dense with religious men wearing colorful, hooded costumes, many of whom seemed to play with fire; with bearded priests waving censers that released clouds of incense smoke into the air; and with roaming choirs singing in Greek or Armenian as they slowly walked in procession from station to station. As we approached the towering wooden doors to the entrance, Joseph leaned out of his stroller and caressed the stone pillars on each side, their surface covered with hundreds of names carved in Syriac, Greek, and Arabic, left by visiting pilgrims over centuries. He kissed his hand and planted a kiss on their names with quiet reverence, as he had watched a hundred visitors do before him. I tried not to think of all the germs he was putting into his mouth.

Then we were pulled into a church so vast that it felt as though a piece of sky had been siphoned off to make room for it. Joseph motioned to me to unstrap him from his stroller. He climbed out on wobbly legs, straightened his shoulders, and strutted straight ahead to the Stone of Unction, the long marble slab in front of the entrance where Christians believed the body of the crucified Christ was laid out by his followers to be anointed and blessed with oils before burial. Around him, Russian pilgrims pressed their rosaries against the stone. Joseph knelt beneath the eight hanging lamps and kissed the stone. For added effect, he climbed onto it entirely and lay prostrate, pressing his forehead against the perfumed surface. It was only a matter of seconds before cameras began flashing.

"*Bambino!*" Italians gushed, rushing over to take a photo of the blond child in the midst of worship. Joseph lifted his head before dramatically kissing the stone again. I gave him a minute or two to charm tourists before lifting him off, his forehead smelling of roses.

Then we turned the corner to the Anastasis at the heart of the church: the place of rising. I remembered a lifetime of Easter services, hearing as a child the priest describe Mary Magdalene arriving at the tomb to find the stone pushed aside, the space empty. Her anguish, until Jesus appeared and asked: "Woman, why are you crying? Who is it you are looking for?"

Now, I stood with my own child beside the tomb. Joseph surveyed the rows of candles in awe. Afraid that he would burn his fingers or set his hair on fire, I tried to move quickly. I lifted him up and held him, squirming, in my arms, and we reached out and removed the five candles, one by one, and set them alight with holy fire.

"Papa," he whispered. "Mama. Grandpa. Anoush." Then he paused. "Thank you."

We always ended with a prayer for the man outside, the man whose name I did not know, who asked us to pray for him.

I was surprised how much this short prayer, whispered in the space of a minute, moved me. For our years in Jerusalem, I had grown resigned to simply going to church on Sundays at the Syrian Catholic parish around the corner, where I was often too tired to concentrate on understanding the difficult language of the sermon.

My prayer had become this: *Dear God. I keep showing up, at least. Does that count for something?*

But now I prayed with Joseph. There is something about praying with a child that is life stripped bare—pure reverence, a boy close enough to his emergence from eternity that he still might remember something of it, and offer it to me.

Thank you. I love you. I have not forgotten you.

When we finished lighting candles, Joseph wriggled out of my arms and ran to the chapel behind the tomb, where an Egyptian Coptic priest in a flowing black robe, a pointed hood, and a beard was waiting. On a good day, he spirited a small wooden rosary from one of the many pockets of his robe and place it into Joseph's hand.

I thanked him, and he nodded his head, and I wheeled the empty stroller over the uneven stones of the church floor, while Joseph raced ahead to the Catholic chapel.

When the Franciscans came into view in their brown cassocks, Joseph's face became overcome with wonder. He ran to them and quietly bowed his head. Then he whispered, in solemn greeting, "Heigh-ho. Heigh-ho."

I was not certain how Joseph got it into his head that the Franciscans at the Holy Sepulchre were the seven dwarfs from *Snow White*. It could be that they seemed to be plump and balding, with beards and belted robes, or that more than once we had come across them in midsong, so that it was not impossible to imagine that they were heading home after a long day of work at a diamond quarry. It was part of a growing dilemma in a city in which it was difficult to know who was in costume and who was simply dressed in his daily clothes; the week before, Joseph had pointed excitedly to an ultra-Orthodox Jew with an enormous, bushy beard, convinced that he was Santa Claus, just as he was certain that a statue of Saint Bernadette in prayer was playing patty-cake.

A smiling young Franciscan who recognized Joseph opened his arms in greeting. Joseph rushed into them, and the priest lifted him up and swung him around.

"It looks like this little one might grow up and be a Franciscan!" he exclaimed. I only smiled, trying to decide whether Joseph thought he was Dopey, Happy, or Sleepy.

We continued on to our final stop, and Joseph's favorite chapel of all: a space entered by exiting the humble far door of the basilica and sliding into a barely noticeable courtyard, with nothing more than a square of tiles and a flight of steps leading up to the bathrooms. At the bottom of the steps, a kind Palestinian man in worker's overalls stood vigil, waiting for the pilgrims to finish using the toilets so that he could enter the stalls and clean up after them. He was never without a mop and a bucket of soapy water.

Joseph rushed over. "*Selem*," the man teasingly ordered, forcing Joseph use his manners, to slow down and shake his hand. Then he obligingly handed over his mop, and with great delight, Joseph set out to do his favorite activity in the whole world: mopping the floors of the church courtyard. The mop was twice his size, and he had to drag it behind him, his young, uncertain steps leaving uneven lines of water along the tiles. But he was a grown-up now, cleaning the holiest site in Christendom, making the navel of the world a little bit shinier, and as he marched up and down, there were birds overhead and candles visible through the door into the church. I sat on the steps and watch my son to the sound of monks singing, barely audible beyond him, drowned out as they were by the sound of pilgrims flushing the toilets.

Children will always know better than we do who saints are anyway. They will know without being told that the man we should be seeking may not be lighting candles inside of the church, but cleaning toilets beside it. Joseph understood where holiness was in that church in a way that I never had before, and he led me to it. In the center of the church, the face of Jesus in mosaic looked down on us from the ceiling, majestic and golden. When he had finished mopping the floors, Joseph took me there because birds liked to fly in the dome, the flapping of their wings echoing in space. If I have known holiness in my lifetime, it was in standing in that chapel, with Joseph's face flushed with excitement as he pointed to the roof and shouted: "Look, Mom! Jesus! Birds!" He said it with the same excitement of a boy who sees a very low-flying airplane and reaches out in the hopes that he might catch it in his hands.

On the way out, there were broken Roman pillars to climb on, which might almost replace another boy's jungle gym. If we timed it well enough, we could just intersect with the Armenian Orthodox seminarians on their way through the front door, boys in their twenties in long black robes, solemnly singing as they walked toward the tomb, many who couldn't resist breaking file for an instant to wink at Joseph and stick out their tongues.

Then he kissed the door one last time, and I kissed him too, still smelling the roses in his forehead, and we entered the streets blessed. I wheeled him home. For us, there was only resurrection. I never took him up the stairs to Golgotha, to visit the chapel of the crucifixion, where Jesus suffered on the cross before crying out. It was there, always, hovering over us, and yet I stayed away, in the same way other mothers protected their children from small objects that could be swallowed, or locked away cleaning products in the cabinet at home. My instinct was to shield him, for now at least. The stairs up to the chapel were slippery, and he might fall. Besides, he was barely two years old. Now was the time for sweetness. There would be time, and only too much time, for sorrow later.

An Unexpected Battle

I HAD BEEN WAITING YEARS FOR OUR LIVES TO FALL APART on Nablus Road. I had watched the long and toxic violence accumulating, expecting the day when it would boil over into full-fledged war, in an alley so accustomed to battle that it wore its scars on doors and windowpanes. I had learned to brace myself, for what would happen when bombs returned to cafés in the city center, a few blocks away. And for years I had lain wait for what would happen on the day when we would, most certainly, have to pack everything into our bags and leave.

Instead, while I was keeping watch on one front, my life shattered from somewhere else.

My father Skyped us one Sunday afternoon, and instead of asking to speak to Joseph as he always did, he asked me to call Frédéric to sit beside me. We stared at each other over video from across the world.

"I have cancer," he announced quietly. "Lymphoma." He had been gaining weight for some time and complaining of back pain, so he decided to see the doctor. Tests revealed his body swollen with tumors. It was the same disease that had taken his mother and his grandfather.

I couldn't breathe.

"The doctors say that it's very treatable," he insisted.

But the world as I had known it was gone already. I had been prepared for war, but the only thing I had known for certain in my life was that my father would live forever.

————————

There are those who might write the phrase "my father would live forever" in jest, but my father was not like other men. Since his childhood, he had decided that the ordinary rules of gravity did not apply to him. Unlike others, he did not have to grow up. He also did not have to accept our human limitations. In the earliest picture that I have of him, he is standing on a sidewalk in Texas, dressed in a Superman costume, staring fiercely at the camera with his cape swinging behind him, his two hands out in combat. He had set out in search of lonely neighborhood kids who needed help, even if it only meant being pushed on the swings.

Most of his life appeared, from the outside, like that of any boy who grew up in Texas: the second oldest of eight children, married at twenty, the assistant manager of a Sears department store. But his four children were well aware that he was a superhero in waiting. He would regale us with stories, late at night. Though he would continue to pretend to the world that he worked in a department store, he would always wear something red—a shirt, a tie—a reminder to us that he was Clark Kent, hiding his powers beneath moderately priced men's casual wear.

To us, he could cast out demons. He could race into my five-year-old self's bedroom and carry me off from a nightmare to another planet entirely.

By the time his three oldest children had left for college, he had abandoned obscurity and entered into his public role as president of Catholic Charities in San Antonio. In a matter of years, he set out to do what he had signaled to us he would accomplish since we were children: he began to rescue people. He discovered that the elderly were dying of heatstroke in their homes, so he created a program to deliver fans door to door. His programs fed the poor, sheltered the homeless, and gave aid to pregnant teenagers. History grew bolder, and so did he, coordinating relief efforts after Hurricane Katrina sent thousands of homeless victims to Texas. In the meantime, he founded the nation's largest resettlement effort for refugees without relatives, seeking out those at risk of death in Iran, Iraq, and the Sudan, in an act perhaps inspired by a Superman poster that had appeared in his childhood, when he was ten years old, urging children to be kind to refugees. Decades later, he helped find them refuge in our city, Baha'is and Muslims and Christians from worlds away, rescued from war or persecution, now walking dazed among the taquerias and Laundromats of San Antonio.

During all of those years, I could not remember a single instance in which I called him on the phone and he did not answer.

He continued to wear suits to work, but at home he could be found lounging on the couch in his Superman pajamas, for there was no need to hide his identity from us.

And now this: father of fathers, grandfather of grandfathers, a superhero. Nowhere did cancer fit into this story. Sooner would the earth break in two.

Frédéric, Joseph, and I caught a plane to Texas for my father's first chemotherapy treatments. My father, sleeping on the couch, looked so fully alive, even with his hair beginning to fall out, that I could not fathom the tumors inside of him. He awakened and kissed me on the forehead.

"You're my beautiful little girl," he whispered.

At night, I wept in the dim light of my childhood bedroom, which my father had still kept, with my bed, my trophies, my chest full of letters. Frédéric took me into his arms. And out of the darkness, we became one, and conceived our second child.

Sebastian

Four months later, Frédéric, Joseph, and I returned to France for a six-month break, escaping into the house in the high Alps to rest. I was deep in the nausea and exhaustion of the second trimester, and there was relief in climbing high above the world, into a village where nothing happened save for the drama of cows and the memory of the war dead from nearly a century before.

The baby grew inside of me, and as my belly swelled and the linea nigra appeared, Frédéric and I waited in the space between two spectrums of eternity, between my father's test results in Texas and the returning sonogram from the doctor in France: five toes visible, a clenched fist, the beating heart of our second son.

Across the world, my father fought a war: ingesting chemicals with names I could not pronounce, losing his hair and growing it back again, tumors swelling and melting. He had made me a promise—that he would be there to see the birth of his second grandson, even if it meant conquering death.

So that is what he did.

In late August of 2010, a week before my due date, my father and my stepmother arrived in France at the chalet in the high mountains, with instructions from his doctor to rest. In his rental car, he had stashed red wine and a Superman costume for Joseph. Joseph immediately pulled it on and began flying around the house.

On the last day of August, I was calmly soaking in the bathtub when I began to feel stabbing pains. I reasoned that they couldn't possibly be contractions, because my bath was so lovely, so I continued soaking and reading my book. Eventually I looked at my watch. Felt the pain. Looked at my watch. The contractions were only a few minutes apart.

"Frédéric!"

He rushed into the bathroom. I held out my watch for him to see. We stared at it for a few minutes, as though that would somehow slow down time.

Finally, I climbed out of the bath, threw on my clothes, grabbed the hospital bag, and handed Joseph over to my father before jumping into the car. He ran to the window and leaned over to kiss me.

"Good luck, little girl," he whispered.

I was fully in labor as we drove down the mountain. I had forgotten that the Alps were so high. The road curved every few seconds, until a moving truck came into view in front of us.

"Make him move!" I shouted at Frédéric.

"How can I?"

There was no room for passing him. I clung to the sun visor of the passenger's seat and screamed. We turned corners, descending, descending. I breathed, screamed, breathed. The truck eventually pulled away.

We sped all the way to the hospital.

"Give me an epidural!" I begged the nurse when we finally arrived at the emergency room.

She shook her head. "It's much too late." They moved us to the delivery room, where this time everyone was speaking French instead of Arabic, because I was destined to give birth only in immense pain in foreign countries, and in a haze of screaming and joy we brought forth our second son.

He looked up at me. I knew him.

"Sebastian," I whispered.

And we loved him. I had worried that, bound by the laws of matter in its finitude, I would never be able to love another child as I loved Joseph. How could I? Had I not used up every ounce of love that I had? Yet there he was, Sebastian, and the impossible miracle happened—that love is expansive and infinite, that the more you experience it the more there is of it, for here was a second child and I loved him just as much as the first, and I sat there in awe and wondered from what well it all sprang and how it was possible.

That afternoon, my father stood at the door of the hospital room, holding hands with Joseph. Joseph ran to me, crawling up onto the hospital bed beside his new baby brother.

"Be careful," my dad cautioned. "He's a little baby. He can break."

Joseph kissed him. I handed my newborn son over to my dad. He lifted him and cradled him in his arms in a way that I recognized I had learned, unconsciously, from once being cradled in his. In a single embrace, all of the promise and peril of life, all that could be loved and lost and gained back, was held in balance. And my father whispered to me, across generations: "You did good."

———◆———

The first instinct after giving birth to a child is the desire to bring him back home. But France was not home. It was easier than Nablus Road. But I missed the life that was ours.

So two months later, we journeyed down the mountain, this time with our two sons, to return to messiness, to neighbors gossiping, to the bullet-wrecked sign of Nablus Road and a country between.

Each time we returned to that broken city, it belonged to us a bit more.

In Jerusalem, Frédéric paced back and forth, singing to his new son. Joseph grew up. He sat next to the window, looking down at the nuns' garden, narrating to his brother, who lay on a striped blanket: "This is door, see? This is tree. This is bird. *Porte. Arbre. Oiseau.*" And so the world was created anew, and given names. And it was good.

The Piano

NOT LONG AFTER WE RETURNED TO JERUSALEM, WE WERE
walking near the New Gate in the Old City and came upon an old
German upright piano called a W. Hagemoser, made in Berlin and
with dark, almost black wood, sitting in the lobby of a music conser-
vatory and marked for sale. Beside it sat another piano, so worn down
that the bearded Italian priest in charge said he would give it to us
for free if we paid the price to ship it to the house. The German
piano was $1,000. I was so frightened of both of them, of the years of
memories they contained, that I hesitated.

"Sit," Frédéric coaxed me. "Just try it."

I had not played the piano for a great many years, and now I
heard the songs of my childhood emerging from beneath my fingers.
I was taken back to afternoons with my father, sitting on the couch
across from the piano when I was a girl, urging: "Play something for
me!" And I would begin, in a ritual of how a little girl tries to tell
her father how much she loves him in the language she knows best,
closing my eyes with that seven-year-old amazement that I could feel
my way through a song in the dark.

When I finished trying the German upright, I turned to the

free piano. The notes were tinny and worn out, and I could not bear to play for more than a few minutes before I returned to the dark wooden German piano again. I looked up at Frédéric. He nodded. There are a few times in life when you judge your own human value. We didn't have much money, but I could not accept a life in which I would play the free piano—it felt too much like succumbing to a broken version of my own past. The woman at reception said that we could pay it off over a year, a hundred dollars every month, and for the next year I would stop into the Magnificat music school on the first of the month to pay off what I would imagine was a pedal, some keys, some strings inside the body of wood.

It was the largest object I had ever owned, and the piano came to dominate our house. Everything in the living room was situated on the floor, including the Arabic-style mattresses that we used instead of furniture, and the piano towered over them, moving the house upward and bestowing on it a measure of grace. As the only European object in the room, it seemed an admission, after all of our years in the city, of who we really were. But for months, I would walk past it and refuse to play it.

One morning, when everyone else was out, I sat down and began. I had stopped taking lessons when I was fourteen years old, when my family had become too poor to afford the luxury, so I had only memorized a few songs in childhood. I was surprised that my hands could remember the keys. I kept returning to the same melody, ashamed at the expanse of years passed, with the knowledge of one who grasps that it is now too late to acquire what might have been taken.

Play something for me.

I was thirty-three years old. For almost half of a lifetime, I had become a connoisseur of bracelets from the Ottoman period, antique hats, prayer beads that could be slipped into a pocket. The Palestinian author Raja Shehadeh recounted how his father, after he had lost their family home in Jaffa during the war of 1948, managed to sneak back across Israeli lines a few weeks later with a truck, to collect their furniture. When he arrived at the house, all of the furniture was still there. But he was so paralyzed by losing a city, a life, that he left everything where it was. At the last moment, he grabbed a statue of a Buddha from a mantle and put it in the car.

Play something for me.

I had tried to keep my attachments limited to what I could throw into a suitcase. But it was no longer in my power. I had two children now, and a husband who had climbed down a mountain for me, and a father battling cancer. Loss would come, one day or another. Those are the wages of love. There is no holding it at bay.

After that, I would play every day after dinner. I played for Sebastian, struggling to scoot across the floor as his first months passed. I played for Joseph, who climbed onto the piano stool in his Superman costume and leapt down.

And at night, when Joseph was asleep, I would whisper over his forehead the blessing:

> *May you love something too heavy to carry,*
> *and may you lose it for half of your life.*
> *When you have it back again,*
> *may you play it alone in the dark, singing:*
> *"One day this all will be gone. Today it is not gone."*

Knocking on a Door

THE ADDITION OF SEBASTIAN TO OUR FAMILY SEEMED TO pull the various parts of us into balance. Frédéric and I had always spoken English together, but Joseph decided that he would speak French with Sebastian, and so our house settled into four languages: English and French among our family, Hebrew on the western side of the house, and Arabic on the eastern. I had once read that a child who grows up with several languages often begins to speak later than he might otherwise, struggling to understand how a glass on a table can be a *glass*, and a *kass*, and a *verre*. But, in time, he learns that it can be all of those things, and also that it is none of them, but something deeper.

I listened. And as Sebastian repeated words over and over again, *l'eau, soleil, viene.* I would repeat them in my heart, and then out loud. Umm Hossam had promised that my children would teach me everything. Well, now they were teaching me to speak French.

At night, I would watch Frédéric carry them to bed, one in each arm, in the home of love and language they built between them. I listened to him sing them to sleep in a language not yet my own.

Some details come into focus only over time in a marriage—and even as they do, they reveal all the more the limits of what we understand, like a vase emerging from the earth, inscribed in a language we cannot read. We know more for having found it. And yet.

As our boys grew up, I knew my husband more and less than anyone in the world. I could read his silences. I would awaken in the night to his slightest movements. He had held my hands as each child emerged into the world, and he still waited for me every morning with a glass of tea.

And yet. Love is to hold each other in that strangeness, and I loved him more than any other stranger in the world—enough to know that his heart still contained a vacancy in the shape of a monastery. I never forgot what he told Paolo, before he left: "Now I have to choose between love and love." He chose us. He loved us absolutely. But he never stopped loving all that he left behind. It took years to understand that the two were not in contradiction, as I learned with Sebastian and Joseph—that love does not diminish with the new but only expands to make room for it all.

Still, it was hard to accept that loving us had exiled him from part of himself. Once, a Turkish acquaintance told me that her father had met Frédéric and me together in Jerusalem, and then returned home to Istanbul to tell her, "My only hope is that you one day find a husband who loves you so much." This is true.

And yet, once, I also read a description by the poet Naomi Shihab Nye of her father, in exile from his homeland in Palestine, looking out of place at a lunch counter in Kansas, and I recognized my husband in the description of him. He was home to us, but he was never completely at home with us.

I would have done anything to make it better. I just did not know how.

"Don't worry," he promised me. "Nothing is ever lost. It is only transformed."

———◆———

Frédéric had still kept one ritual from his monastic life: every year he went on a retreat. That winter, Frédéric packed his bag for Bethlehem. He would meet every day with Father Peter, the beloved priest who had come to us on the night of Joseph's birth and who was trained in giving the Spiritual Exercises, the Jesuit retreats designed to help individuals make choices about their lives.

I remained in Jerusalem with our two boys. Frédéric read and prayed alone on the edge of the desert in Bethlehem, not far from the hospital where we had paced back and forth at night, waiting for our first child to be born. And during those days, the old emptiness came up, the sense that even with so much given, something more was waiting for him.

Father Peter asked, "Have you ever thought of becoming a priest?"

"You know I can't," Frédéric answered. "I'm married."

"I know," Peter replied. "But that is just the question that keeps coming to my mind."

Frédéric returned to his room to rest. But Father Peter's words would not leave him.

———◆———

In fact the answer "I can't" was not as obvious as Frédéric had made it out to be. Though Father Peter was a Roman Catholic priest, Frédéric, the boys, and I had always attended the Syrian Catholic Church in Jerusalem, where our sons had been baptized. This was because when Frédéric had wandered into a monastery in Syria ten years before, it had been into the mystery of a Syrian Catholic monastery, an Eastern rite church that was part of the Catholic Church, but that maintained some of the rites and rules of the Orthodox Church. One of those was allowing married men to become priests.

He now considered the possibility that Father Peter might not have suggested the impossible after all; perhaps he could be ordained a Syrian Catholic priest.

Two weeks after his retreat in Bethlehem, Frédéric went to confession in Jerusalem with Father Etienne, another Roman Catholic priest. In the midst of their conversation, Father Etienne turned to him and asked, "Have you ever thought of becoming a priest?"

"You know I can't," Frédéric answered again. "I'm married."

"Still," Father Etienne insisted, "I just felt that I needed to ask."

Frédéric walked home, placed a pot of tea on the stove, and sat me down at the table. He took my hand.

"I have no idea what this means," he told me. "I feel like I am being asked to do the impossible, to knock on a door that has no answer. I know that. But now I have no choice but to start knocking."

———

Two weeks later, Frédéric walked down the street to visit the Syrian Catholic bishop. He described his retreat and recalled the decision he had made, all of those years before in a desert monastery, to give his life to God. He confessed the fact that being married and having children had only deepened that desire, with the knowledge that love is not limited, but is exponential.

Finally, he asked if it might be possible for him to seek ordination as a married priest in the Syrian Catholic Church.

He knew that it would not be easy, or even straightforward. He would need to obtain an official change of rite from Roman Catholic to Syrian Catholic. Though he was already conversant in Arabic, he would need to learn to speak it so fluently that he could hear confessions and visit the sick. He would also need to learn Syriac, a dialect of Aramaic, and to complete four years of study in theology and philosophy, as well as engage in pastoral work. But the greatest challenge would be that of the imagination: if he set out to become a married Syrian Catholic priest, he would be entering what, for us, would be uncharted territory. Neither of us had ever been close to a married Catholic priest.

Frédéric later told me that the bishop looked at him without the faintest expression of surprise, as though he had been expecting this conversation for a very long time.

If someone had told me that life is unexpected, I would not have guessed that I might one day be married to a priest. But I had married a man who spoke to birds, who saw angels appear on trains, and I knew better than to think that life with him would be straightforward. He believed in the physics of grace—that the smallest amount of hope, balanced against impossible odds, was enough to conquer them. And if they were not conquered, even then, the process of moving forward was never in vain. I was reminded of the iconic words of Sister Maria from *The Sound of Music*: "When the Lord closes a door, somewhere he opens a window."

Frédéric entered the seminary a few weeks later.

The Love Stairs

A YEAR PASSED WITHOUT WAR, AND CALM SETTLED OVER the city. Security guards disappeared from the entrances to cafés. Customers forgot their fear of shattering glass and sat next to the windows. Arabic and Hebrew could be heard on Jaffa Road, as enemies brushed up against each other. The light rail, a tram which had been in construction for years, finally reached completion, and with it the impossible happened—that scar of no-man's-land in the heart of Musrara, between our house and the western part of the city, finally fell into movement, with Arabs and Jews climbing aboard the same compartments and riding side by side to their respective neighborhoods, the dinging of the bell audible from the rooms of our house.

And our life, in all of its complexity, began to form its own logic. Every morning we woke up, and I dressed the boys, and we dressed ourselves, and prepared our four separate bags. Frédéric headed off to the Catholic seminary in West Jerusalem, where he was studying for the priesthood, a lone married seminarian in a class of young Roman Catholics. Joseph was dropped off at the French lycée downtown, where he started kindergarten in French. I walked Sebastian to Joseph's old day care in the Old City, where he was learning his first words in Arabic. Then I boarded the bus and traveled to the other side of the separation wall, where I taught Palestinian students Kafka and Faulkner and Shakespeare. None of it made sense, but it made sense to us. And at the end of the day, we gathered our bags from our respective worlds, and came home.

Sometimes, on my day off, I would accompany Joseph to school, walking him across no-man's-land, past the tram station, and to a small set of metal stairs hastily built on the edge of a parking lot in the western half of our neighborhood of Musrara. These stairs were known as Chiara's Staircase, but locals called them the Love Stairs. A Jewish artist in West Jerusalem named Matan Israeli, who once had a girlfriend in the Old City in East Jerusalem, had grown tired of her having to circle all the way around the wounded neighborhood to meet him, because a wall still ran along the seam, separating the neighborhood in two. So he had built her a pair of wooden stairs over the wall, like a narrow Band-Aid right through the heart of the wound, where our neighborhood had been torn in half more than half a century before. She used this small flight of stairs to meet him. Soon Arabs and Jews, as they slowly became aware that they could venture into each other's neighborhoods without getting beaten up, began to use the stairs too. The wooden stairs were later dismantled, and metal stairs replaced them.

It was on the Love Stairs that I would lift Joseph when I traveled from our house on Nablus Road to his school in West Jerusalem, a fifteen-minute walk that took us across borders, wounds, and languages. Any outside visitor, had they seen us, would only have recognized a mother leading her child up a small flight of stairs, toward a parking lot strewn with trash. Yet so much depended upon those stairs: they anchored two worlds together in balance. I held Joseph's hand as we approached them.

"Do you know what these are called?" I asked him once.

"The wonderful stairs!" he exclaimed.

And I held him. I stood on the stairs and I held him. I had hoped for some grander meaning in life, but this was it, and in some ways it was grander than anything I could have imagined. All we can do is try to focus on the good and add to it. He was four years old, and on those stairs, we and the city and the entire world were made whole again, if only for a moment, if only in his arms.

The Invisible Man

THE PHONE RANG EARLY ONE EVENING IN JUNE. FRÉDÉRIC was away on a quick trip to France. The boys were asleep in their bedrooms.

My older sister Lisa tried to make herself understood through her crying. I should catch the next flight home to Texas, she said, because our father was dying. He might not survive the night.

I hastily decided to leave my two boys with a family friend, since children were not allowed in the intensive care ward of the hospital. By the afternoon, I was waiting in line at the airport. Horror piled upon horror: my husband in France, my children with neighbors, my father dying in a hospital a continent away.

When my plane landed in Texas the following morning, my brother and sister were waiting for me. My father was still alive.

We drove directly to the hospital, where I crossed the threshold into his hospital room. At the entrance, dispensers of antiseptic were available for visitors to wash their hands. He had little immune system left, and our germs could kill him.

Then I saw him: weak and wrecked and so thin I barely recognized him. Half of his weight had disappeared since the last time I'd seen him, a few months before. He looked up at me from the top of his sheets.

"You're here," he whispered.

"I'm here."

"Well, that was pretty scary for a moment." He tried to laugh, but coughed instead. Every word demanded the effort of what remained of his body.

I clasped his hand.

"Maybe it's because you came that I'm still alive," he whispered. "Maybe God knew."

This was exactly the kind of thing my father would say.

"You rest now, Daddy. You rest."

And he closed his eyes, as if the world were already too much for him.

There can be the urge, in the telling, to make sense of what is awful, but I will try my best not to do that here. There is nothing romantic about watching a parent die. Six years before, he had kissed me in my wedding dress. Now the room reeked of bleach and sickness. My father called out, and a nurse ran to grab a plastic pan so that he could urinate in it, and he nearly cried, doing that in front of his youngest daughter, and we looked at each other in that particular hell that is a father's body breaking down in front of his little girl, who he was meant to protect.

"I'm sure you wanted to see that," he joked, his voice rasping. I tried to hold myself together.

"I'm married and have two little boys, Daddy. I see it every day."

A nurse entered the room, took his vital signs, then left again. The door closed behind her. My father motioned for me to lean close to him. "In a second, she'll come back," he whispered, "and then she'll fill me full of poison."

I looked in his eyes, and he was afraid. My father was never afraid.

So began the magical hours, the hours I spent with my father in eternity.

We live with the illusion that there will always be enough time, and in the end, there are only fragments, moments. I had postponed so much, and now it would be too late. I was meant to be the family storyteller, the collector of histories. I was meant to learn how our family had sailed on ships fourteen generations before from the Canary Islands to found a city in Texas. I was meant to memorize the details of how his father was wounded twice in the Second World War, the only member of his unit to survive a battle in Luxembourg.

I was meant to learn the stories and details of my own childhood, from the years I was too young to remember. I did not know anything. Now the past was not worth the effort it would take for my father to tell it to me.

He was sixty-two years old, and it was too soon.

The nurse slipped in the doorway and administered the poison. He slept. We closed the shades and the room dimmed. This was what it was to look at the one you love, in the form of a soul. My two brothers stood by, and my older sister, and my stepmother, and aunts and uncles and priests who filed in and out of the room like shadows.

The last times I had seen my father in the hospital had been when Joseph and Sebastian were born. Those I loved, emerging from eternity and going back to it, among monitors and crisp sheets and the rest of us in our slippered feet, trying not to interrupt as we tiptoed past.

It can feel like an impossible cruelty to consent to the one you love being poisoned, to know that this poison is the only thing that might save him, but that in all likelihood it would kill him. In those days, I experienced what it was to have our roles reversed: for me to watch my father, shaking and feverish and afraid, waking in the night, trying to navigate his way through a nightmare. For two weeks, every morning, my siblings and I sat with him in the hospital. Some nights I slept there.

On those nights in the hospital, I would think of Joseph and Sebastian and Frédéric on the other side of the world. I remembered Nablus Road, the neighborhood boys fighting outside the windows, the soldiers setting up checkpoints, the tear gas rising to the cracks not sealed tightly enough in the windowpanes, the accumulation of exhaustion and violence on a single slender strip of land, and I thought that this was happening in my father's body now. His was a body at war with itself. I was hoping that beauty would be stronger than death. That was all. I remembered sunbirds and nightingales, pigeons in flight, circling over the fighting and the dead in Jerusalem, and I was thankful for Nablus Road and all that it had taught me. It was a school for a war that I had not anticipated—it had forced me to live and love within the face of death. I was grateful to Abu Hossam and Omar, and to Hossam and Saleh, with their backs full of scars, selling winter hats. They had taught me strength I did not previously have, to stare at the world as it is and to not turn away. I would depend on it now.

Before, I had only thought that every moment in my life had been a rehearsal, in some way, for my children's birth: that every country I had traveled, every language spoken, led me to them. And that was true. But now I knew that every moment had also been a rehearsal for my father's death. I had lived in war. I had stayed awake all night taking care of my sick sons. I had studied, imperfectly, the art of standing in front of the terrible, and waiting, hoping, that, in time, the beautiful would appear.

Yes, my father, when he had held my hand and guided me through my nightmares when I was five years old, was preparing me already—to outlast him.

———◆———

So much of parenthood is asking our children to continue a story that was gifted to us at birth, a chain that began long ago, with our own parents and their parents before them. It is a story composed not of language, but of the way an infant is held in the night, of lullabies sung to keep the danger at bay, of oatmeal for breakfast and kisses imprinted into foreheads, of love passed through eternity, gesture by gesture.

Perhaps the terror of parenthood is only compensated for with the comfort of knowing that we are no longer finite, but links in a story that began at the beginning of time, and that just as we carry the bodies and countries of those who came before us, we will be borne forward by those who come after us. My father had always been aware of that—that was why he needed to be in every hospital room when a child appeared. Those hospital rooms were ceremonies, transmissions.

Every moment, after all, is a lesson to be learned, and one to be passed on. It had taken me too long to understand.

But now I knew, and there was still a little time remaining.

My father could barely speak. When he could, he asked the nurse for a Coke float. He took the first sip slowly, and a flicker appeared in his eyes.

"You must understand," he whispered. "This is not just a Coke float."

I nodded my head. I knew what he wanted to say: that there was childhood hidden in it.

He gathered what was left of his strength: "Thank you so much," he called out to the nurse at the door, his weak voice breaking. It would be minutes before he would find enough strength to speak again.

I took notice. I would teach my sons. If we only have the strength for one prayer left, let it be gratitude.

———◆———

When my father no longer had the strength to teach me, I tried to give him back some of what he had gifted to me instead. I sat beside his bed, and held his hand.

There were monitors and tubes and a bag for his urine, machines to help his breathing, tumors in his lungs, a hell of violence and savagery upon a human body. I read to him from *Winnie-the-Pooh*:

> *"What about a story?" said Christopher Robin.*
>
> *"What about a story?" I said.*
>
> *"Could you very sweetly tell Winnie-the-Pooh one?"*
>
> *"I suppose I could," I said. "What sort of stories does he like?"*
>
> *"About himself. Because he's that sort of Bear."*
>
> *"Oh, I see."*
>
> *"So could you very sweetly?"*
>
> *"I'll try," I said.*
>
> *So I tried.*

I looked up. My father, smiling faintly, had fallen asleep.

Light fell in and out of the room. We drew the shades, opened the shades. For days it went on like that. My brothers and sisters and stepmother alternated staying beside the bed.

Then, he disappeared. For two days his body was in the bed, but he was gone. He stared out the window with blank, glassy eyes. Nurses checked his temperature, but he did not recognize their comings and goings. The archbishop came to bless him. He seemed to twitch in bed but remained gone. My brother put *Lois & Clark*, a TV series about Superman, on the small television in the room and left it to play on a continuous loop. His favorite nurse walked in.

"Do you know who I am?" she asked my father, and he shook his head.

"Do you know who I am?" my brother Steven asked him, and he was silent.

Then Steven pointed up at the television screen. "Who's that?"

"That's Superman," my father whispered.

"Who's he fighting?"

My father coughed. "The Invisible Man."

"What does he look like?"

My father looked up at his son, incredulous. "He's invisible," he answered.

Then he fell back asleep.

He was gone for hours. Awakened. I held his hand, and he pointed out the window. A bird perched on the windowsill. Light was falling outside. The physics of grace.

"Look," he whispered hoarsely. "Sunset."

———◆———

There are a few times in a life when you stay awake all night, watching someone sleep. The first night Frédéric and I ever slept in the same room, I had awakened to see him, bleary-eyed from watching me. "Where did you come from?" he asked. And I knew that I wanted to be with this man for the rest of my life.

Joseph, on the night he was born. The light of the moon outside, and the vision of the orange trees, and my boy, my very own boy, sleeping beside me.

Sebastian, in a hospital in France, with a wrinkled frown.

The last night I spent with my father.

———————

These are the magical hours, when time stretches out. You keep vigil. You recognize what is holy and unique in the one you love, all of the lives that existed before his and tumbled into making it happen, each body an entire country, and you stand in awe of it, and hold onto it while you can.

In each of these, you memorize: hands, eyelids, barely open mouth, the steady pattern of breathing. But only with a child and with the dying do you feel that they are hovering between two worlds, so you try to look through them—to glimpse some hint of the eternity where they have been, or the eternity where they are going.

Now and then my father awakened, whispered, "ice chips," and I spooned them into his mouth. Then he slept. In the middle of the night, the nurse came and put on a mask to help him breathe, and I stayed in the low chair and watched the lines of his heart move up and down, just as I had heard the steady beating of Joseph's heart as he emerged from within me, coming into the world from the other direction.

———————

At six thirty the next morning, the nurse came in to say good-bye before the shift change. The hospital rules said that I had to leave for the next two hours. Then I would have a few last minutes with him before I had to leave for the airport to return to Jerusalem, where I would have a day to pack my bags before all of us flew to France.

I held my father's hand. "Daddy, I just need to leave you for a little while," I said. "It's the rules of the hospital."

The nurse studied me. "Are you the daughter who is leaving today to fly across the world?"

"I am," I answered.

"You can stay," she said firmly, so that I would understand.

———

Then we were left alone. My father asked me to open the shades so he could see the sky. I opened the shades, and the sky had not disappeared overnight, and that was something. I sat beside him and pulled out my computer, and I set it up on the tray across his bed.

"I have something to show you, Daddy."

We waited until the film came on screen: my father in the hospital in France, standing next to a window flooded with light, holding Sebastian in his arms on the day he was born.

Joseph's voice was audible in the background, singing, and then he was visible, two-and-a-half years old, with his mop of blond hair, his body circling my father's legs. In the film, my father was fully alive, his face flushed with joy, and he lifted Sebastian up from the bed for the first time and rocked him, just barely, back and forth in his arms. Sebastian's eyes had not completely opened yet, and he looked up at my father, curious, blinking.

"Isn't he beautiful?" my father asked Joseph. "It's your baby brother." Joseph moved forward to touch the baby's face.

Then my father in the film turned to me.

"You did good," he said.

In the hospital bed now, my father sobbed. "I didn't know you still had that," he gasped, and he was no longer just talking about the film; he was talking about that image of himself, fully alive, holding a child. He held my hand and pleaded, "They'll have so many beautiful memories, won't they?"

"Of course they will, Daddy. I'll make sure that they do."

And it did not matter anymore that that had been one of the last times he ever held Sebastian, that he had been so sick since then that he could not hold him in his arms, because now we would fill up the space with that single moment of holding, until it stretched into eternity, my father holding his grandchildren, over and over again forever.

"Thank you so much," he whispered.

———— ◆ ————

My father died on a hot summer morning a week later, the day after the Fourth of July. They brought him home from the hospital, and my brothers and sisters lit fireworks above the swimming pool where he had once played Frédéric in a game of chess for my hand.

I was in France when it happened. There was no time for me to fly across the world to be beside him.

Instead, when the priest came to anoint my father, we said goodbye from across the world. We called on the telephone, and they put the speaker next to my father, whose eyes were closed, so he could hear us.

Frédéric's voice caught in his throat, so that he struggled to manage. "I know that on that first day I met you, I promised you that I'd take care of Stephanie," he said. "So you don't have to worry about that. It's okay to go. I'll take care of her now."

He handed me the phone. I looked outside. The two boys were playing on the front porch. The flowers were in full bloom. I whispered to my father the same words he had whispered to me as a child when I couldn't sleep at night:

"Close your eyes, Daddy. Now imagine a field full of tall grass, and flowers, and trees, and the sun is shining. Everywhere you look there are butterflies. Do you see the butterflies?

"Close your eyes, Daddy. Now go to that place."

Sirènes

THE NEXT YEAR WAS OUR LAST YEAR IN THE HOUSE ON Nablus Road. The French nuns, who had always been planning on properly restoring the house, finally asked for it back again, and we could not say no.

Every autumn we used to buy enough firewood to last us through the coming winter and beyond, but that year we bought no new wood. The wood that remained from the previous years would suffice. On the street, someone tried to speak to Joseph in Hebrew, and he answered, in English: "I don't speak that language." And I knew that he was growing up, for he no longer understood every language in the world.

In November of 2012, war broke out between Israel and Hamas in Gaza once again. In the past, the fighting had always been far away, but now Hamas was firing rockets into civilian areas of Israel, and the war that had felt at least slightly removed was finally coming to us. All day, the news lit up with alerts of rockets landing near cities: in Ashkelon, Sderot, Beersheba, as civilians fled to the closest shelters.

On the third day of the war, I was sitting in my office at home when an air-raid siren began wailing through the streets like a phantom. A rocket was falling somewhere nearby—the first time that rockets from Gaza had ever targeted Jerusalem. All over the city, thousands of pedestrians fled for bomb shelters.

I ran to the bathroom, huddled on the floor, and wondered where my sons were.

———

Downtown at the French school, Joseph's teacher was announcing to the bewildered class of five-year-olds that they, too, must run and hide. There were sirens in Jerusalem, she told them. But there was a shelter beneath the building, and if they stayed together there was no need to be afraid. Joseph clutched the hand of his best friend, Ulysses, and with the mass of children, they rushed to the shelter and sat on the ground, waiting. A second siren cried out—another rocket falling nearby.

I pictured them, somewhere across the city, crouching and shivering in the dark.

That afternoon, Frédéric ran to pick Joseph up from school, but amid the frantic parents and alarmed children, Joseph remained calm. Frédéric, not wanting to frighten him, took his hand and walked him home.

———

The next day was my turn to pick up Joseph from school. I remembered the story of how, during the Second Intifada eleven years before, a suicide bomber had blown himself up in front of the gates of the

French school. His severed head had flown into the air and landed inside the courtyard, among the children at play. It was hard to come to terms with ordinary childhood, marbles and jump ropes and arithmetic lived out in the midst of such possibilities.

I arrived early, peering through the windows of Joseph's classroom to watch him at his desk, attentive, working on the curve of his letters. At the sound of the bell, he jumped from his chair and fastened his oversized backpack to his shoulders.

We made our way down the long hill toward home, holding hands. We had been walking for several minutes before he pulled on my arm and motioned for me to lean toward him.

"Mom, did you know that yesterday, two mermaids came to Jerusalem?" he whispered, his eyes widening.

"Two mermaids?"

He clenched his fingers, his arms shaking with excitement. "And the teacher—she said that we had to run and hide. But that we didn't need to be afraid."

It took me a moment. *Mermaids.* I remembered: in French, the word for "siren" is *sirène*, also the word for "mermaid." When my son ran to hide in the shelter, he had thought that mermaids were heading toward the city.

"And do you know what sound mermaids make when they call?" he asked.

"What sound?"

"Whoooooo! Whooooooo! Whoooooooooo!" he sang out into the street.

"Tell me again?"

"Whoooooo! Whooooooo! Whoooooooooo!" He lifted his arms in flight, raising his voice above the incessant honking of cars.

"Whoooooo! Whooooooo! Whoooooooooo!"

We carried on down the crowded sidewalk, holding hands, walking against the line of traffic. I could not tell if the tears in my eyes sprang from sadness, or relief, or the love that wells up sometimes so that it physically pains the body. I imagined him in that dark basement, huddled with his best friend, Ulysses, whose name practically made him destined to live that moment, listening to sirens.

"And why did mermaids come to Jerusalem, Joseph?"

He shrugged. "You know, Mom," he said, "the sea is not very far away."

The Great Tree

Fall turned to winter, and the war passed. Log by
log, we used up our supply of firewood. Outside, vendors sold sage
leaves, as lemons and oranges came into season. The iced drinks
for sale were replaced by *sahlep*, a sweet, steaming white drink once
made of the root of orchid flowers, and Abu Hossam lined his stand
with winter hats and umbrellas and scarves. I tried to take notice
of every detail, knowing it would be my last winter in that valley of
birds and miracles.

One night in early December, I was kept awake by howling
winds from a storm so strong that it shook the house. The windows
groaned with the strain of trying to remain hinged. In the early
morning, Frédéric rose from bed to make his tea, reaching the largest
window just in time to see an incredible sight: the Great Tree from
the inner courtyard was lifting from its roots, at that very moment,
and crashing toward him. He ran. The tree collapsed into the courtyard below in a thunderous crash, crushing the pomegranate, orange,
and lemon trees in its path before punching a hole in the side of
our house. From the bedroom, I heard the impact and rushed to the
window. Half of the trees from the garden below were gone, along

with the leaf-laden boughs we had always lived among. It was as if, like Robert Frost wrote, "the inner dome of heaven had fallen."

For the rest of the day, great flocks of birds came to sit on the surrounding fence, looking down in disbelief, or perhaps homage, at the Great Tree that had sheltered them for a century, now fallen, a village gone. The next day, snow began drifting in the late afternoon and continued all night long, burying the streets and the fallen trees. The few standing orange trees were blanketed in white.

I thought of my father. I thought of the monastery in the clouds of Syria, where Frédéric and I had fallen in love. I thought of all of those enormous things that came before us, which we could not imagine inhabiting the world without—and then they are gone.

And yet the impossible oranges, covered with snow, remained.

That night, I held my youngest son, Sebastian, a long time before I put him to sleep. When it was time to put Joseph to bed, instead of leaving him, I remained and found a place to rest beside him. There are those moments when we stay with our children in bed to comfort them, and then there are times when we remain because they comfort us. We could hear the wind howling outside through the space where the tree had once been, through the hole punctured on the opposite side of the house. For the first time, I was glad that we were leaving the house, because I could not imagine it without that tree.

Joseph crinkled his brow as he lay in wait in bed. My little boy had grown up that year. Death will do that to a person. He had knowledge of things I had hoped I could withhold from him for a little longer.

I held his hand.

"Mom?" he said. His head was resting on his Spider-Man pillow. "When I grow up, I'm going to be your dad."

"What do you mean, you're going to be my dad?"

"When I get big, I'm going to be transformed into your dad. Because he's dead, but when I grow up I'll replace him, and then you won't be sad anymore."

I felt a sob collecting in my throat. "You'll replace him?" I asked.

"Yes. And you will be my little girl."

We held each other, listening to the wind. He was right. It would all come full circle. One day Joseph would be my father, one day I would be his little girl, and he would watch over me when I was afraid, passing from one eternity to the next. One day I, too, would lie in a bed while he watched me sleep, and read to me from *Winnie-the-Pooh*. One day would be his time for returning.

And I closed my eyes beside him, stunned by the enormity of all that was lost, and all that remained.

Afterword

"Tell me what you see vanishing, and I will tell you who you are."

—*W. S. Merwin*

MY DEAREST JOSEPH, THREE YEARS HAVE NOW PASSED since we left the house on Nablus Road, and nearly all that I described in this story has disappeared.

You were five years old when we began packing up those eleven rooms. Over seven years, we had managed to accumulate mountains of trinkets we didn't need—unnoticed because they were spread across so much space. It took weeks to empty them out.

There it was: the image of your body, asleep in the carriage of my womb, mistaken for an illness that might kill me. The piece of paper, with lines marking your heartbeats, with the handwritten note: "No contractions yet."

The green-striped pajamas that your brother Sebastian wore on the day he was born.

Frédéric's notebook from India.

Pour un moine, quitter à jamais son monastère
ne peut être qu'un acte de foi, ou une fuite.

For a monk, to leave his monastery forever
can only be an act of faith, or of running away.

As I packed the last boxes, I whispered, "Thank you."

On the last day, Umm Hossam climbed our stairs to say good-bye. I pulled the remaining teacups from boxes to make tea, and we sat on the few spare cushions left on the floor.

"I still can't believe that we're leaving," I confessed. "I have so many memories of this place."

"They won't just be memories," she insisted. "You must tell your children about this house. If you tell them stories, then this house will always be yours, because it will continue to live in them. Every time you walk past, point to the house and tell them: 'Here was where you lived when you were a baby. Here was where Abu Hossam and Umm Hossam came every Ramadan to eat a meal with us. Here was where you began to walk.'"

Among the boxes, I pointed to a tree that I had bought the first week we arrived in the city. Somehow it had managed to survive our summers away, the falling snow, weeks when I would forget to water it.

"I want you to have this tree," I told Umm Hossam.

"I'll plant it in our yard," she promised. "And anytime someone walks past, I'll say: 'That is Stephanie's tree.'"

Then she left. I closed the door to the street and walked up the stairs. In the outdoor closet, a dove had built its nest, perhaps some kin to the bird that had greeted us upon our arrival. I said good-bye.

Your father found us a new house a ten-minute walk away, up the hill and inside the walls of the Old City, just inside the New Gate. No longer would we be living in the valley where all things fall. Instead, we would move into a house nearby the Church of the Holy Sepulchre, to the alleys of rising.

When we went to visit, your father took my hand and led me inside to show me the Crusader archways. Through the window of our bedroom we could see an immense garden of olive and orange trees buzzing with sunbirds in flight.

"That's the garden of the monks of the Greek Orthodox monastery," he announced.

"Of course it is," I laughed, for only Frédéric would move our family from a convent to a monastery.

It was only four small rooms, but he had made sure that there was just enough space for the piano.

And he held my hand, and I told him: "This looks like home."

Catherine of Siena once said, "All the way to heaven is heaven." That's true, my Joseph, even if it's hard to remember sometimes. Everything that was difficult was beautiful in the end. Everything led to you.

Soon after we left Nablus Road, the disappearing began. Abu Salaam finally closed his newspaper stand at the corner of Nablus Road, after some seventy years, and a few months later he died. Then Sister Pascal, the cranky French nun who showed us our house, and later adopted you as her own, died too, until there was no one remaining on the street who remembered what it had been, when it was only a valley of birds and stars. The city municipality decided to repave the sidewalks, and the vendors with their fish and parrots and herbs and Mickey Mouse carpets left. Even Abu Hossam's falafel cart in front of our house closed, until the space took on some unearthly calmness of a country gone.

The English bookstore closed. So did your day care, where you assembled wooden towers with your bandaged hands. I tried to cross from east to west through the neighborhood one day, only to find that the Love Stairs had been torn down.

But on some afternoons, I would descend to the place where all things fall, and walk along the valley of Nablus Road. The remaining vendors would lean out of their storefronts and call: "Umm Yusuf, where is Yusuf?" And I quietly thanked them for the finest years of my life.

———◆———

By the time you were in kindergarten, the war in Syria had begun. We tried to serve you breakfast, to remember your winter jacket, as our minds wandered to distant battles. I tell you this so that you might forgive us one day, for a kiss forgotten, for hair left uncombed. We did our best.

During the first year of the war, Father Paolo criticized the regime of Bashar al-Assad and called for international intervention, so he was exiled from the country where he had lived for thirty years. Part of me was relieved. I had already lost one father, and I did not want to lose another.

But in the end, I think that he could not forgive himself for watching from a distance as his friends were killed. That July, he called us on Skype when we were in France. His eyes had grown tired, and his beard had turned completely gray.

It was time to finally finish our conversation.

"You look wonderful," he said, smiling sadly. "It makes me so very happy to see you so happy."

He had called to tell me that he would soon sneak back into Syria, into the war, to negotiate the release of hostages.

I was no longer a novice in the art of taking leave of those I loved. I tried to hold his gaze as well as I could. We spoke of what we always did, of books, of you and your brother, of the war. Then, he returned to our oldest conversation.

"Do you remember our talk?" he asked. "The one about crucifixion?"

"Yes," I whispered. "You quoted Simone Weil, who wrote, 'Every time that I think of the crucifixion of Christ, I commit the sin of envy.'"

He smiled faintly. "And you said that God does not want us to suffer."

I tried not to burst into tears.

He looked at me with tenderness. "Maybe you were right," he admitted quietly. "Perhaps God does not want us to suffer. But still, you stayed in Jerusalem for these seven years," he continued carefully. "You had children. You lived through war. You traveled through checkpoints. You made choices that were not easy. How do you think of our conversation after all of these years?"

"What do you want me to say, that you were right?" I whispered, trying to smile.

But he was waiting for something else.

I had stayed because everything that I loved was bound up in the staying. I tried to choose my words carefully. Simone Weil had believed something else: that the world is mostly darkness. But that grace, even if it is the size of a mustard seed, is stronger than all of the darkness in the world.

I paused. "I guess I believe that if we recognize beauty, then we make it real. And in this way, we can live in the kingdom already, no matter how difficult the reality."

He nodded. He was quiet for a long moment. My teacher then looked at me with a weakness I had never seen.

"I know what you're saying, and I believe it. But it's hard, isn't it?" His voice cracked with emotion.

"Yes, Paolo," I said. "It's hard. Sometimes it is almost too much to bear."

I wanted to ask him not to go, but I knew that he would not listen. So I told him that I loved him, instead.

Father Paolo crossed the border into Syria two weeks later, on July 29, 2013. We were later told that he asked to meet a man by the name of Abu Bakr al-Baghdadi, the leader of a group that was calling itself the Islamic State, in the hopes of negotiating the release of hostages. We never saw him again.

Nearly one year later, Father Frans van der Lugt, a Jesuit priest we had known in Syria who had stayed behind in Homs delivering bread on his bicycle amid the shelling, answered to a knock at the door. He was shot in the head.

Then our friend Father Jacques was kidnapped, his church razed, his parish taken hostage...

Roman cities I had once wandered through at night were bombed, markets that once smelled of bread reduced to rubble, bridges that I once stood on collapsed, students and teachers and friends fled into exile. Even the train was likely gone. But in my mind, Syria would always be a country with a monastery in the clouds, where your father taught me resurrection. Where we boarded a train, and he whispered those words:

Ami

Douleur

Chanson

As I finish this, bodies are floating up on shores and suffocating in trucks, thousands fighting their way onto trains. In our streets in Jerusalem, men are stabbing and shooting each another, and checkpoints are dividing the neighborhoods, as the war that had always been invisible now rises to the surface. My love, I fear that this will be the book of your life.

And yet, still. Woodpeckers. Song thrush. Warblers.

A few weeks ago, I gave birth to a little girl, your sister, Carmel.

My Joseph, I'm sorry if some of this is confusing. I would be lying if I pretended that it all makes sense to me. But it must be pronounced, despite that. Long ago, your father told me that during the Second World War, Radio Londres broadcast messages into Nazi-occupied France, secret codes played on the nightly radio. There, hidden among the sentences of daily life, lay secrets meant for the French Resistance. The news of a coming invasion was disguised as poetry. Men and women, sitting down to hear the radio after dinner, would be met with the sentence: "Before we begin, please listen to some personal messages…"

La villa est silencieuse.

L'étoile filante repassera.

Le chien du jardinier pleure.

La belle aussitôt la suit.

La belle aussitôt la suit.

La dernière heure a sonné.

Gabriel garde l'anonyme…

The villa is silent.

The shooting star will pass again.

The gardener's dog is crying.

Immediately, the beautiful follows her.

Immediately, the beautiful follows her.

The final hour tolls

Gabriel remains anonymous…

I often imagine those men and women, sitting down after their nightly meal, struggling to listen through the sentences to recognize some clue that might make sense of a world gone mad. I have often wondered if all of our lives in a time of war resemble that, our days full of moments concealing signs and codes we cannot fully understand, but on which everything depends. It will always be confusing to think that that which is terrible and that which is beautiful have the same materials to work with, the brick and mortar and earth and stars of our immediate world. There is that which can kill us, and that which will save us, and we live among them, struggling to discern our way through. And it is terrifying, my love. It has never stopped being terrifying.

Even now, I don't know how we can possibly be sure if the Love Stairs are only pieces of metal or if they contain some larger promise, if there is hope to be taken from where a bird leaves his nest. I do not know the meaning of the orange trees covered with snow, a book picked up, at the last moment, in a bookstore. Perhaps it is a way of imagining ourselves out of this darkness and into eternity. But it is all that I know how to do—to interpret the world, and hope that this act helps in saving it.

———◆———

My love, in the end, all of us live in a country between, in that fragile space between those events of the past that called us into being and those events in our lives that we push forward, participating in an eternity that we will not see. It is a country of violence and great beauty, of birds and the dead. Where the daily events of dishes and oatmeal become sacraments. In this world, I have lived the most immense sadness. In this world, I have received the gift that is you, and your father, and your brother and sister. I would not trade it for the world.

Joseph, you are now seven years old. Much has been lost in your lifetime. But as your father taught me long ago, nothing we love is ever gone. It is only transformed. Every child is part of what remains.

If I can ask you to remember only one thing, then let it be this: keep watch. You have not been born into an easy world. But every now and then, in the midst of our daily lives, a miracle strikes.

An angel appears on a train.

A handwritten sign, with the name of a city.

A crowd of men, praying on the filthy streets.

A little boy's encyclopedia.

A flight of stairs.

Sirens in Jerusalem.

We cannot know what any of it means. Still, everything depends upon the noticing. They are ruptures in eternity, I think. You will see for yourself.

I don't know when this book will find you. But if it is in a dark time, know that the beautiful will come. Sometimes you'll have to stand in front of the terrible for a long time before it appears—sometimes it will seem like whole spaces of your life are filled up with that standing. But beauty will come. I promise you that—and the long expanses without it will help you know when it happens.

There might be years in your life when you forget how to see it. But if you are lucky, as I have been lucky, you might have a child, or spend a night beside a man who is about to die, and they might teach you how to recognize it. Those who are emerging from or returning to that other place know how to see where it has fallen into our lives. I was lucky enough to have my father. And I was lucky enough to have you and your brother, and now your sister.

Most of all, I was lucky to have your father, the master of the small gesture, who took care of the world, and watered the flowers, and carried your backpacks, and waited for all of us to come home. Who took the eternity he discovered in the desert and carried it down 350 stairs, so that all of us might share it, distilled into a cup of tea.

One day, it will be time for me to go. When this happens, you will have to keep your promise. You will be my father, and I will be your little girl.

I will ask for you to tell me one last story.

Tell me this story.

Of a man who climbed down a mountain for the woman he loved. Who won her hand in a game of chess.

Of a father who held his daughter's hand and walked her out of a nightmare.

Tell me the story of two little boys, looking at birds out the window. Of a broken city, sewn together by a narrow flight of stairs.

Of mermaids who appeared in a city at war.

I give you all of these details for you to keep, but one day I'll ask you to give them back to me.

Start with this story:

On the night before you were born, I looked out the window in Bethlehem. There was an orange tree and a lemon tree, and a pair of wounded hands, now healed. I took that image, and I sewed it into your heart.

Acknowledgments

I BEGAN THIS BOOK WHEN I WAS PREGNANT WITH MY first son, and it spans some of the most difficult and important years of my life. It would never have been possible without the love and support of a great many people.

I would like to thank my agent and dear friend Judy Heiblum, who encouraged me to be a writer when we met each other years ago, and has coaxed me through each book and worked hard to find a home for them. Many thanks also to Stephanie Bowen, who acquired *A Country Between*, to my editor Anna Michels, who saw it through to completion, and to my copy editor Michelle Lecuyer, who courageously fixed errors in so many languages.

To the community of Mar Musa: Father Paolo, Deema, Huda, Jens, Jihad, Jacques. To Father Eric Wyckoff, Father Peter DeBruel, Father Hans Puttman, Father Ivo Coelho, Father Giuseppe DiSario, Monsignor Boutros Melki, and in memory of Father Frans van der Lugt. Thank you for reminding me that hope is possible, even in the midst of war.

To my family: my mother, Steve, Rob, Lisa, Graham, Vanessa, Miranda, Henriette, Bernard, Elise, Nina, Toni, and my entire extended family of beloved aunts, uncles, and cousins—all equally dear but too numerous to mention here.

To my many friends in Jerusalem and abroad who sustained me during the long years of writing this book: Karen Brunwasser, Rebecca Granato, Molly Mayfield and Eric Barbee, Benjamin Balint, Matti Friedman, Wendell Steavenson, Charles Stang, Dustin Atlas, Jeffrey Champlin, Michael Fagenblat, Julia Meltzer, George Tsouros, David and Anna Dintaman Landis, Celia Bland, Jessica Marglin, Nada Sarkis, and many others.

Thank you to Al-Quds Bard College, which gave me time off and support to work on this manuscript, and to my students, who have reminded me daily that how we interpret stories will always be bound up in how we interpret the world: Sondos Shehedeh, Deena al-Halabieh, Ahmed Hmeedat, Noor Hamayel, Lana Ramadan, Abdullah Erikat, Adel Hroub, Muntaha Abed, Yara al-Efendi, and hundreds of others.

For the historical sections of this book, I often sought help from Jerome Murphy-O'Conner's marvelous Oxford archaeological guide to the Holy Land. The author lived just at the end of Nablus Road within the walls of the Ecole Biblique, and so I knew that he was approaching the city from the same vantage point that I was. His insights were invaluable. The writings of Naomi Shihab Nye were also never far from me, as her father went to school just around the corner from where I wrote this book. *The Princeton Field Guide to the Birds of the Middle East* was also invaluable, as was the Jerusalem Bird Observatory, where staff patiently answered my questions about the birds passing through my neighborhood.

To my teachers: Huda al-Habash, Barbara Ganley, Harvey Cox, Larry Yarbrough, and Helmut Koester, among so many others—I will forever be in your debt.

To my beautiful children: Joseph, Sebastian, Carmel. I cannot begin to tell you how much happiness you bring to my life. And to Frédéric: you will always be a miracle, for all of us. Thank you for holding the world in place.

Finally, to those who gave me their stories on Nablus Road: Abu Hossam, Umm Hossam, Sheikh Mazen, Omar Mazen, the Freij family, the Baramkeh family, Abu Salaam, the convent of the White Sisters, and all of the other neighbors, bread vendors, parrots, snakes, nuns, and priests. Thank you for welcoming us into your country. I promise that I will never forget.

Reading Group Guide

1. At the beginning of the memoir, Stephanie describes the Syrian monastery where she meets Frédéric as "a kind of anchor in world in which so much seemed in movement." Have you ever felt anchored to a specific place in that way? Where was it, and what made you feel grounded there?

2. Stephanie describes having a strong connection to Father Paolo and to her own father. Compare and contrast Stephanie's biological father with her spiritual father. Have you ever had a deep familial connection with someone who was not biologically related to you?

3. Nablus Road is a complicated street with an even more complicated history, dividing Jerusalem into East and West, Palestinian and Israeli. Explain the significance of the new couple settling on this fractured street. How does it affect them? Their new marriage?

4. Frédéric and Stephanie have strong ties to the Catholic Church. How does the church act as a support system for the newlyweds? How does this connection shape their lives?

5. Stephanie describes the different languages that make up Nablus Road, and the different languages that are a part of her own life (Arabic, French, Spanish, and English). How does Stephanie use language to maneuver through the delicate Middle Eastern world? Have you ever been in a situation where you've had to adapt to a new language? What was it like?

6. Describe Stephanie and Frédéric. How are they similar? How are they different? Do you find them to be a compatible couple?

7. How do the different religions, nationalities, languages, and politics all come together to make up the fabric of Nablus Road? Based on Stephanie's descriptions, do you think it is constantly tense or overall peaceful? Do you think a place like this sounds difficult to manage or exciting?

8. How does Stephanie react when she finds out she is pregnant? If you were in her situation, do you think you would return to Jerusalem to have your child, or remain in France? Why?

9. Why do you think Stephanie writes letters to her unborn child? If you were about to have a child, what would you write to him/her?

10. Describe how Nablus Road changes after Stephanie has Joseph. How does the community evolve to include the new family?

11. Do you think living in a war zone influences Joseph's otherwise happy childhood? Imagine if war broke out in your own hometown. Would you stay? Why or why not?

A COUNTRY BETWEEN   345

12. After Sebastian is born, how does the language spoken change in their home? Do you think it's beneficial for Stephanie's children to learn all of these different languages? If you could speak any language, which would it be?

13. How do Stephanie and her family define the word "home"? How would you define the word "home"? How is your home different than the one Stephanie and Frédéric built in Jerusalem?

14. What do you think Stephanie ultimately learns from her time on Nablus Road? Do you think her children benefitted from living there? Would you live there?

A Conversation
with the Author

What inspired you to write *A Country Between*?

When I found out that I was pregnant with Joseph, I began writing letters to him, even before I knew if he was a boy or a girl. I had no idea what these letters would lead to—I only knew that I needed to express something of the love I felt for my child and something of my uncertainty about bringing him into such a troubled world. Those letters formed the seed of what would eventually become *A Country Between*.

Describe your process when writing a memoir. Do you keep notes? A diary?

This memoir was very different than my first memoir. I wrote it over a seven-year period, and in the process of writing it, the stories contained within it were still happening. I had no idea at what point the story would end. My drafts of this book—of which there are many dozens—are in a sense a diary of a very tumultuous period of my life and of the modern Middle East. Contained within it are letters, notes I wrote down on scraps of paper and later turned into scenes, and chapters written in full. There is also a component of journalism, as I had to interview my neighbors to learn some of the details of their histories. I actually wrote many of the scenes about Nablus Road when I was in the Alps because I found that distance and solitude allowed me to see the street and the characters more clearly.

A Country Between ends with your family moving out of the house on Nablus Road and relocating. How has your family grown or changed since then? Have you continued to live in Jerusalem?

I had my third child—my daughter Carmel—just as I was finishing the very last edits of *A Country Between*. As I write this, we are still living in the Old City of Jerusalem, in our small, Crusader-era house in the Christian Quarter. Frédéric is just finishing his studies for the priesthood, and Joseph and Sebastian are growing up and teaching their little sister how to speak English and French. Frédéric and I just celebrated our ten-year anniversary, and in what seemed impossible at the onset of this book, I am actually about to officially become French.

Do you ever find it difficult to reconcile your home and the safety of your family with the war that divides your country?

Of course I do. This past year in particular saw a wave of violence around the Old City of Jerusalem, and I narrowly missed shootings on two occasions—once while taking my son to the doctor, and another while on the way to pick up my daughter from day care. Yet, unfortunately, this is the drama of mothers around the world. My friends in America also live with anxiety about school shootings and random violence, and there are many neighborhoods in America that are at least as dangerous as Jerusalem. Paris—another city where we might have presumably raised our children—was rocked by terrible terrorist attacks this year. We have friends from Syria who have fled terrible violence—and others who have decided to stay in Syria despite the war. I try to teach my children that love is stronger than violence—and that the single most important thing we are meant to do in our lives is to love others, especially when there is violence around us.

Do you find solace in writing?

I started writing when I was about seven years old. Since then, writing has always been a part of how I live in the world. I would not say that writing brings me solace—sometimes, especially when I am trying to sort out the structure of a book—writing is a source of anxiety. But ultimately, it is my way of interpreting the moment in which I live. It does not give me solace so much as it gives me purpose.

We know from the story that you teach literature at a local college. Who are your favorite authors to teach?

There are texts that I can teach over and over again and discover them anew each time: *Epic of Gilgamesh*, *The Odyssey*, the book of Genesis, the Gospel according to Luke, *The Conference of the Birds*. Yet the real gift of teaching comes when students connect texts to their own lives in unexpected ways. In the past few years, my students have been blown away by such diverse texts as *The Dead* by James Joyce, *The Narrative of the Life of Frederick Douglass*, *The Diving Bell and the Butterfly* by Jean Dominique Baubel, *The Trojan Women* by Euripides, and *If This Is a Man* by Primo Levi. These are all very different stories, but what they have in common is that they are about characters or real people trying to navigate their ways through seemingly impossibly situations. My students—who have lived their entire lives in the midst of conflict—read these books and feel less alone.

Who are your favorite authors to read?

What a question! As someone who moves so often between cultures, languages, and disciplines, I am always working my way through very different books. I try to read the poet Czeslaw Milosz at least once a year, as well as Rainer Maria Rilke and Simone Weil—and I keep them all near my writing desk. I've just started studying Greek, so I enjoy trying to fumble my way through the Gospels in the original. When I have time to read for pleasure instead of work, I will read anything written by Geraldine Brooks, Kathleen Norris, Rabih Alameddine, or Orhan Pamuk. As for journalism—Anthony Shadid was my hero. Travel writing? The descriptions in *Out of Africa* by Karen Blixen astonish. Give me a cookbook written by Claudia Roden any day: the food is poetry. With my children, I have recently rediscovered the brilliance of Dr. Seuss.

Language plays a huge part in your family's life, especially Joseph's—he grows up speaking multiple languages. What languages do you speak? What about your children?

I grew up speaking English, but Spanish was my mother's native language, and she was a Spanish teacher by profession. Even if I didn't grow up speaking Spanish, the language and cadence of it had an enormous influence on the way in which I live in the world and my own approach to language. I speak English, and with my husband and children, I have learned to speak decent French. I also speak Arabic, notably in the Syrian dialect, even though I have been away from Syria for more than a decade. This year, I decided to learn Koine Greek and Syriac, both in immersion programs that teach ancient languages as spoken languages, and this has been a frustrating and immensely beautiful experience, sort of like learning a difficult instrument in adult life.

My children are native French and English speakers. Sebastian, who has a passion for languages, speaks Arabic fluently. It is fascinating to hear them move from one language to the next. The Old City of Jerusalem is full of languages, and for a child this is magical: Sebastian can say "hello" in ten languages.

How would you describe your family in one word?
Miracle.

Your country?
Jerusalem.

What would you like readers to take away from your memoir?
This book was a way of passing on to my son the wisdom that my father and Paolo taught me: hope exists even in the darkest places, and there is always beauty to be found, even in the midst of war.

And I have known no greater hope in my lifetime than the hope that comes in the form of a child.

About the Author

Stephanie Saldaña received her BA from Middlebury College and her MTS from Harvard Divinity School. She was a Watson and Fulbright scholar and has won several awards for her poetry. She lives in Jerusalem with her husband and children and teaches at Al-Quds Bard College, a partnership between Al-Quds University and Bard College in New York. She is the author of *The Bread of Angels*.

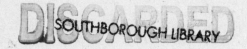